Pro iOS Apps Performance Optimization

Khang Vo

Apress®

Pro iOS Apps Performance Optimization

ISBN-13 (pbk): 978-1-4302-3717-4

ISBN-13 (electronic): 978-1-4302-3718-1

Trademarked names, logos, and images may appear in this book. Rather than use a trademark symbol with every occurrence of a trademarked name, logo, or image we use the names, logos, and images only in an editorial fashion and to the benefit of the trademark owner, with no intention of infringement of the trademark.

The use in this publication of trade names, trademarks, service marks, and similar terms, even if they are not identified as such, is not to be taken as an expression of opinion as to whether or not they are subject to proprietary rights.

President and Publisher: Paul Manning
Lead Editor: Tom Welsh
Technical Reviewer: Evan Coyne Maloney
Editorial Board: Steve Anglin, Mark Beckner, Ewan Buckingham, Gary Cornell, Morgan Ertel, Jonathan Gennick, Jonathan Hassell, Robert Hutchinson, Michelle Lowman, James Markham, Matthew Moodie, Jeff Olson, Jeffrey Pepper, Douglas Pundick, Ben Renow-Clarke, Dominic Shakeshaft, Gwenan Spearing, Matt Wade, Tom Welsh
Coordinating Editor: Corbin Collins
Copy Editor: Mary Behr
Compositor: MacPS, LLC
Indexer: SPi Global
Artist: SPi Global
Cover Designer: Anna Ishchenko

Distributed to the book trade worldwide by Springer Science+Business Media, LLC., 233 Spring Street, 6th Floor, New York, NY 10013. Phone 1-800-SPRINGER, fax (201) 348-4505, e-mail orders-ny@springer-sbm.com, or visit www.springeronline.com.

For information on translations, please e-mail rights@apress.com, or visit www.apress.com.

Apress and friends of ED books may be purchased in bulk for academic, corporate, or promotional use. eBook versions and licenses are also available for most titles. For more information, reference our Special Bulk Sales–eBook Licensing web page at www.apress.com/bulk-sales.

The information in this book is distributed on an "as is" basis, without warranty. Although every precaution has been taken in the preparation of this work, neither the author(s) nor Apress shall have any liability to any person or entity with respect to any loss or damage caused or alleged to be caused directly or indirectly by the information contained in this work.

Any source code or other supplementary materials referenced by the author in this text is available to readers at www.apress.com. For detailed information about how to locate your book's source code, go to http://www.apress.com/source-code/.

To my girlfriend, Ngan Huynh,
for the love and great encouragement and support.

Contents at a Glance

Contents v

About the Author ix

About the Technical Reviewer x

Acknowledgments xi

Preface xii

Chapter 1: Introduction to iOS Performance Optimization 1

Chapter 2: Benchmark Your Apps with Tools: Simulators
and Real Device Test 7

Chapter 3: Increase and Optimize UITableView Performance 39

Chapter 4: Increase App Performance Using Image
and Data Caching Techniques 59

Chapter 5: Tune Your App Using Algorithms and Data Structures 87

Chapter 6: Improve Parallel Data Access using
Multithreading Techniques 137

Chapter 7: Optimize Memory Usage for Better Performance 177

Chapter 8: Integrate Multithreading and Efficient Memory Usage for
Multitasking Apps Performance 197

Chapter 9: Improve Performance with Native C/C++ 219

Chapter 10: Comparing Android and Windows Phone
Performance Problems 241

Index 265

Contents

Contents at a Glance iv

About the Author ix

About the Technical Reviewer x

Acknowledgments xi

Preface xii

■ **Chapter 1: Introduction to iOS Performance Optimization** 1

A New Era of Smartphone 1

Why Performance Matters 1

Who Should Use This Book? 2

My Teaching Style 2

What Do You Need? 3

How to Use This Book 3

An Overview of the Book 3

Source Code 5

Contact the Author 5

■ **Chapter 2: Benchmark Your Apps with Tools: Simulators and Real Device Test** 7

Simulator and Device 8

Memory and Performance 8

Tools 9

    Basic Tools 9

    Memory Allocation 11

    Legacy Code 13

    Performance Tools 18

Summary 37

■ **Chapter 3: Increase and Optimize UITableView Performance** 39

Introduction to the Examples 39

    Reviewing the Instrument Tool 40

    First Example 41

    Second Example 50

    What Can You Learn from These Examples? 54

Other Techniques 54
   Caching the Height 54
   Opaque 55
   Avoid Graphical Effects 55
Performance for Editing/Reordering 56
Summary 57

Chapter 4: Increase App Performance Using Image and Data Caching Techniques 59

Differences in Performance Between Network, File, and Memory Processing 60
Introduction to Caching 62
   What is Caching? 62
   Cache Hit 62
   Cache Miss 62
   Retrieval Cost 63
   Storage Cost 63
   Cache Invalidation 64
   Caching Algorithms 65
   Measuring Cache 71
What You Should Cache 72
   Where Should You Store Your Images? 72
   Data Caching 77
Summary 85

Chapter 5: Tune Your App Using Algorithms and Data Structures 87

First Example 88
Theoretical Issues of Measuring Algorithmic Performance 89
   How to Measure Big-O 90
   Implementation Details 92
   Big-O of Famous Algorithms 92
Practical Measurement 93
Data Structure and Algorithms 95
   Cocoa Touch Data Structures 95
   Other Data Structures 106
   Binary Tree 119
   Graph 123
Other Algorithms and Problem-Solving Approaches 130
   Recursion 131
   SAX/DOM Parser for XML Parsing 132
Summary 133

Chapter 6: Improve Parallel Data Access using Multithreading Techniques 137

What Are Threads and Multithreading? 138
Threading Terminology 139
First Example 140
Benefits of Multithreading 142
How to Write Multithreaded Applications 143
   Create a Thread 143
   Configuring a Thread 150

Your Thread Entry 151

Risks of Threads 154

Thread Synchronization 169

Alternatives to Threads 171

Thread Instrument for iPhone 174

Summary 174

Chapter 7: Optimize Memory Usage for Better Performance 177

A Little Review 178

Old Object Ownership Policy 178

Autorelease 178

Autorelease Pool 179

Automatic Reference Counting 180

ARC Policy 182

New Qualifier for ARC 182

Object Property 183

Advanced Memory Issues 184

Retain/Relationship Cycles 184

Weak References 185

UIViewController 185

Load View Process 185

Unload View Process 186

Displaying and Hiding Views in the User Interface 187

Object Copy 188

Shallow vs. Deep Copy 188

Implementing a Deep Copy 189

Integrating a Copy Method into an Object 190

Advanced Autorelease Pool 191

Instruments 192

Static Analyzer 193

Leak Instrument 193

Zombie 194

Object Allocation 194

Memory Warning Levels 195

Summary 196

Chapter 8: Integrate Multithreading and Efficient Memory Usage for Multitasking Apps Performance 197

What is Multitasking in iPhone? 198

Multitasking Handler Methods 202

Multitasking Benefits and Costs 204

Background Services 205

Audio Service 206

Show Splash Screen 207

Location Service 207

Local Notification 211

Voice Over IP (VOIP) 211

Background Execution 211

What to Notice when Running in Background 213

System Changes Notification 215

Dealing with iOS Versions 216

Summary 216

Chapter 9: Improve Performance with Native C/C++ 219

Benefits and Costs 220

Basic C and C++ programming 221

    C Programming 221

    C++ Programming 231

A Practical Example 236

    SQLite 236

    Integrate C++ into Your Application 238

Summary 238

Chapter 10: Comparing Android and Windows Phone Performance Problems 241

Benchmarking on Emulator and Devices 242

    Emulator and Devices 242

    Benchmarking 244

    Android 246

    Windows Phone 248

Data Caching 249

    Android 250

    Windows Phone 251

Data Structure and Algorithms 253

Multithreading 255

    Android 255

    Windows Phone 257

Memory Management 258

    Android 259

    Windows Phone 260

Multitasking 261

    Android 261

Support of C/C++ Programming 262

Summary 263

Index 265

About the Author

Khang Vo is a software engineer and entrepreneur who loves working on the latest technologies and products. He has been developing on the iOS platform since 2009. He loves sharing and discussing different aspects of technology and business that help to create new value for consumers. Making and selling different applications in the Apple App Store and Android Market have been his main business. He is a Master's student at Carnegie Mellon University.

About the Technical Reviewer

 **Evan Coyne Maloney** taught himself how to program after inheriting an Apple IIe computer. As a young teen in the mid-1980s, he published an operating system for the Apple II line called FoscilDOS that was highlighted by both *Byte* and *A+* magazines. Evan began writing Internet software in 1994, creating the KeepTalking chat system, the first purely browser-based live-updating chat system. In 1996, Evan wrote the web-based political campaign simulation game DarkHorse for MSNBC.com. During the presidential campaign that year, the game logged many millions of hours of play and was even used in political science classes at various high schools and colleges. Since 2001, Evan has put his development efforts towards mobile content delivery and commerce. He conceived of and built the first several versions of the award-winning News Pro line of iPhone and iPad applications from the Reuters news agency. Evan joined online retailer Gilt Groupe in 2010, where he is now the principal engineer for the company's critically acclaimed and highly ranked iOS applications.

Acknowledgments

I would like to thank Steve Anglin, who approached me with the idea of creating this book and guided me through the initial process. I also want to thank Evan Maloney for providing many helpful suggestions over the technical part of the book. I learned many things from Evan while writing this book.

Thanks also to Tom Welsh, who helped me make the writing clear and easy for readers to understand. He has made lots of great suggestions to guide the book into its final form. I also want to thank Corbin Collins for his quick and helpful instruction when I asked questions.

I also thank developers and people who shared and helped me with technical difficulties in writing the book. It helped me to figure out what developers lack and how to help them get the necessary knowledge and skills.

Preface

The book is meant to help you to sharpen your iOS development skills in a specific area: performance optimization. The book is intended for people who already have basic skills in iOS development and want to make the best application for users.

Inspired by the art of application performance, I spend time practicing, learning, and sharing a lot about performance optimization in different platforms such as the web and smartphones. I love discussing this topic with people. While spending lots of time in forums and iOS communities like Stack Overflow and the Apple Developer Forum, I soon recognized that the majority of iOS developers have the same questions on how to improve the performance of their applications. I thought it would be useful to put all common issues together in a well-written and well-structured book so people can easily get the whole picture of the iOS performance optimization problem. That motivated me to write this book, and I tried my best to cover the most common problems and mistakes met by developers.

Moreover, I observed and record in my own notes many similar problems between iOS, Android, and Windows phones. The final chapter is written based on these notes, and I think this chapter will be really useful for anybody who wants to work in these three platforms or shift from one platform to another.

When approaching a performance bottleneck, it is good to see it in different ways and strike a balance between the performance of the application and the difficulty of implementing the solution. There are subtle problems that cause people to make mistakes unless they know about the solutions beforehand. My hope is that this text will help you to avoid those mistakes, spend your time improving your application, and create a better experience for your users.

## Chapter 1

Introduction to iOS Performance Optimization

This chapter will introduce general information about the book, including the following:

- Who this book will best serve
- The topics this book will cover
- The general structure and style of the book

A New Era of Smartphone

There are currently hundreds of thousands of iOS applications on the market and hundreds of millions of iOS users, making this a big market for any company or developer to explore. This market has been growing for many years and will keep growing in the next few years, as will the need for interesting and powerful applications. If you have a good idea for a new app, you need to make sure that the idea is implemented well; this includes creating a good user experience. Because of the unique technical limits of the Smartphone environment, good performance is a must for your application. People want an app that responds quickly to their interactions, one that can compute data and visualize it immediately.

Why Performance Matters

Performance is not just about algorithms, data structure, and memory. It's about making people feel that the application responds to any interaction as fast as possible. Therefore, performance optimization in your iPhone application is important. Users have to feel that they are interacting with real agents that receive their command and execute it almost immediately. What if you tap a button and two long seconds later, you see the effect. Are you happy with this performance? If you're not happy, your users are probably even more frustrated.

Of course, you can shift much of your storage and processing into the cloud where there are thousands of servers that can compute and return the result quickly. However, it's not enough to just put all your data and every computation into the cloud. Network data transfers are tricky and your users will still probably need to wait for couple of seconds before their data arrives.

Whether you are a game developer or a general application developer, you are likely to experience difficulties in improving the performance of your applications.

Who Should Use This Book?

This book is written mainly for beginner and intermediate iPhone developers who already know basic iPhone programming. If you're a performance lover and want to create an application on this new platform that is responsive and market-ready as well as innovative, this book is for you. Even advanced iOS developers can benefit from this book.

If you intend to go deeply into the Smartphone application programming world, this book teaches you enough so that you can apply what you know with iOS to Android and Windows Phone environment.

My Teaching Style

I believe that the learn-by-doing principle is the best way for a programmer to develop skills. This book is based on that idea. I discuss general and deep practices that stem directly from around two years of iPhone development experience and many years of Java development experience and training. The problems that I put before you will help you to avoid or fix many of your performance mistakes in iPhone development. I have chosen these problems based on experience and research into the issues popular on forums and social networks (such as Stack Overflow). I've identified common pitfalls and provide the information you need to avoid these errors.

The book is a combination of three things: basic concepts, story illustrations, and sample source code. Instead of just supplying an ad hoc tool for your specific problem, I hope to provide you with strong skills to use in your daily iPhone programming life. I employ different approaches to communicating concepts: sometimes an image is worth a thousand of words, some concepts are best explained by sample code, and some require those thousand words.

One of the best ways to start learning about performance is to develop a cool application that you love. This practical experience will teach you more than some non-realistic and very forgettable examples.

You don't need to know a lot about Cocoa Touch Framework because I explain the basic syntax and classes that you'll need to improve your application's performance. Each chapter consists of a separate topic, some of which may already be familiar to you.

You can also use this book as a general reference; whenever you have a specific problem, you can look it up and read about the solution.

Every chapter follows a simple format: a short overview about what that chapter delivers followed by the main sections and subsections. Each chapter concludes with a summary that helps consolidate your knowledge and reminds you of the important lessons, followed by some basic and realistic exercises so that you can have fun practicing what you just learned.

What Do You Need?

As an iOS developer, you need a Mac OS with Xcode installed. There is a free Xcode version from the iOS Developer Account, or you can download it directly from Apple Mac AppStore. You also need a copy of this book plus all of the sample code, which you can download from the Apress website. The sample projects were well tested on Xcode 4.2, with ARC turned on, so you can run my sample projects in that environment without any concern.

You can and should run every example to understand more about the illustrated concepts. There are some short blocks of code that aren't associated with any project; you should run that code, too.

How to Use This Book

Although the chapters are not closely related, reading the book from beginning to end will ensure that you have a solid knowledge of iPhone performance, optimization skills, and techniques. There may be some dependencies and references between chapters. The later chapters were written with the assumption that you have read or know about some previous chapters.

I also recommend reading each chapter from beginning to end. Each chapter opens with a quick conceptual introduction to the topic; then theory and practical iPhone samples are combined to help you to understand the topic thoroughly.

You should read the summary section carefully because it reminds you of the key knowledge that you should retain. I also recommend finishing all of the exercises as these will help cement your new knowledge.

An Overview of the Book

This book contains a good mix of basic concepts plus practical knowledge, techniques, and tips that will help you to be successful in the competitive iOS development world. The book's nine chapters cover nine different approaches to solving performance problems in iOS development.

▨ *Chapter 2:* The introduction to a range of tools and instruments so that you know how and when to use them. Many developers don't use these tools correctly because they simply don't know that they exist.

▨ *Chapter 3:* As an iOS developer, you will definitely use TableView in almost all of your projects, from trivial ones to complex ones, to display a list of data or options. The problem with the architecture of UITableView is that when you start customizing it, the scrolling performance suffers. You will definitely have this issue, even if in a subtle way. This chapter gives you a list of tools and techniques to improve your TableView scrolling.

▨ *Chapter 4:* You may believe that most performance issues can be solved using cloud computing and by simply adding more servers to your system. Even if that's true, network data transfer will always be an issue. Data transfer will remain a bottleneck for years. You should understand how to cache data locally and in memory with a limited environment like iOS.

▨ *Chapter 5:* Data structures and algorithms in the iOS development environment are similar and different than in other environments. You have a high level of support from the framework with many basic data structures like arrays, sets, and dictionaries. For some tasks, you can simply put it to the cloud, but for other tasks, especially gathering and processing data to make a good visualization, you still need to depend on the iOS environment.

▨ *Chapter 6:* Improving the performance of the application also means making the application respond to users' interaction faster. This means not blocking the main UI thread. Multithreading can help—not just to improve the user responsiveness but also to improve the general performance of your application. Multithreading is a difficult topic for any platform, and you will learn it here through a range of illustrations, examples, and clear explanation.

▨ *Chapter 7:* With the release of a new tool to make memory management automatic, developers now can take advantage of it to avoid common memory problems like memory leaks and crash. This chapter focuses on how you can best use your memory, and when you should load data in and unload data out of your memory. It also covers the new Automatic Reference Counting (ARC) mechanism of the new SDK to make sure you can understand and use it correctly.

▨ *Chapter 8:* With iOS 4 and above, all applications can take advantage of multitasking to improve the user experience. In fact, it's not actually multitasking but rather a fast app-switching mechanism (applications can't run in background) with some special background processing. This chapter will help you understand what features the iOS will support and what tasks you can process and run in background.

■ *Chapter 9:* In many iPhone applications, you don't need to use any C/C++ code to implement features. However, when you actually need it, especially for library integration, you will be in serious trouble. You may not need to write your whole application in C/C++ but you do need to understand how these languages work for any necessary troubleshooting.

■ *Chapter 10:* By now you should have a complete picture of all the different aspects of iPhone performance. You will definitely consider porting your application to Android and Windows Phone soon, so in this final chapter, I give you the whole picture on similarities between performance problems in iOS, Android, and Windows Phone. This will help to smooth your learning experience for new platforms.

Source Code

You should download the sample source code from the book's page on the Apress web site (www.apress.com) and try it on your own.

Contact the Author

If you have any questions, please email me at vodkhang@gmail.com or visit my web site at http://vodkhang.com. I shall be happy to have a chat about iPhone performance problems.

## Chapter 2

Benchmark Your Apps with Tools: Simulators and Real Device Test

In this chapter, you will learn about the following:

- The differences between a simulator and real device test environment.

- How memory management affects the performance of an app.

- Tools and techniques to benchmark your app's performance including the following:

  - Basic tools to measure the memory and performance.

  - Complicated tools to measure different aspects of memory management such as memory leaks and bad access.

  - Complicated tools to measure different aspects of performance in computer processing such as battery, file loading, and display information.

  - How to divide your program into smaller parts to easily identify the location of the performance bottleneck.

To improve performance, you need to carefully run benchmark tests to see where the problems lie. To carry out a useful benchmark test, you have to understand the different reasons that a program or a segment of code might run slowly.

Right at the outset, you should be aware of two fundamental choices: simulator versus real device environment, and the trade-offs between memory optimization and performance optimization.

First, you need to know the difference between the simulator and device environment.

Simulator and Device

The main problem with the performance of iPhone applications is that they are running in a restricted, slow-processing environment. The iPhone development environment simulator runs much faster than the real environment; in fact, the simulator's environment can be as fast as the machine running it.

As a result, you can get a big and unpleasant surprise when the program runs really fast in the simulator environment but runs much slower in the real environment. I have observed many people blaming slow application performance on the phone's network. This is certainly true in some cases. However, in many cases the app's performance can drop down a lot because of the code implementation itself, not because of a network problem. Therefore, careful testing and benchmarking your app against basic tools and standard environments will make you more confident about your app's performance and the user experience.

To demonstrate the significant differences between the simulator and real device, I tested a program in the iPhone simulator environment and the real iPhone environment. The results are surprising.

- It takes 0.5 seconds to finish the main calculation in the iPhone simulator.
- It takes 7 seconds to finish the same calculation on the iPhone device.

The program was simple: I did a simple test with two arrays, each with 1000 elements. Then, the code loops over both arrays to find the same number and print "hello." In the real world, you may not need to process 1000 items in an array or you may not choose to loop over arrays to find same number. However, this is not the point. I picked these actions to demonstrate that real iPhone environment is much slower than in the iPhone simulator.

This brings me to a point that I will mention many times in this book: you always need to test the app on both simulator and the real device. Well, why not just test on the device? Because simulator has the following significant benefits:

- It is faster to run the test in the simulator, which means less delay time for developers.
- It is good enough to test for memory leaks and memory allocation problems.

Memory and Performance

Memory and performance are different. Memory usually means the RAM storage, and it refers to how much storage you use and how much you have left. Performance is about how fast your app runs a specific feature.

Memory can have a significant effect on performance. When the device has more RAM and more storage space, you can preload and cache more data on it. RAM is fast access storage compared to file storage and the network. By preloading and caching more data on RAM, you can significantly speed up your program in many cases. For example, if your app is a game that needs to load many images, more memory is important to because you can preload the images and display them when necessary. Loading from RAM is 10 times faster than loading from the file system.

However, better use of memory does not always mean better performance. Some apps don't need to use much memory; therefore, you can optimize the memory only so far and the performance will not go up anymore. The inverse is not much better: an app can use up all the memory in order to achieve good performance, but then the app runs out of memory.

Therefore, you should always carefully benchmark both the memory and runtime performance to make sure that you strike a good balance between memory usage and runtime performance.

Tools

The tools fall into the following three main categories:

- Basic tools, without XCode instruments.

- Memory tools, which verify the correctness and measure the efficiency of your memory usage.

- Performance tools, which measure how fast each part of your program runs and pinpoint any bottlenecks.

Basic Tools

In this part, I discuss about logging as a basic tool to measure the running time between blocks of code.

Logging the Running Time

One of the most basic tools is logging the time difference between the start and end of a block of code. Usually, logging is implemented with NSLog. With this basic tool, developers can measure every line of code or block of code to see how fast that block of code runs.

For example, running this block of code

```
NSDate *date1 = [NSDate date];
for (int i = 0; i < 1000; i++) {
  // Do calculation here
}
NSDate *date2 = [NSDate date];
NSLog (@"time: %f", [date2 timeIntervalSinceDate:date1]);
```

returns this result

time: 0.0123 (measured in seconds)

Advantages:

- A straightforward and easy way to measure the performance.

- You can measure the performance of lines of code or blocks of code.

Disadvantages:

- You can't measure the UI performance (i.e. the rendering time of the UI thread).

- You can over-optimize (spend too much time on a very specific block of code just to optimize it a little bit).

- Running the application in simulator is usually fast, and at this fast level, NSLog can't help you distinguish between a difference in runtime performance. Otherwise, although NSLog is slow in the device, it can help you to detect the differences in runtime performance.

Usage:

- When you need an immediate tool to measure without much planning.

- When you need a tool that can return a result quickly.

- When you need to isolate a small block of code to verify a performance assumption.

Memory Tools

With memory problems, you have only one main concern: high memory usage. There are minor concerns with legacy code: memory leak and memory garbage. For the new projects, you should go straight with the new Automatic Reference Counting (ARC in short) support. For some old projects, you can try to convert them using the convert tool of Xcode.

However, not every project can be converted, there are many issues and memory management policy that prevents you from conversion. Trying to comply with the new management policy may cause you more troubles. So, I discuss mainly with you about the memory tools for object allocation and briefly about tools for memory leaks and memory garbage.

> **NOTE:** All the memory tools that I introduce here (and I introduce all Apple's tools for memory) can be run with simulator. The good thing about the simulator is that it runs really fast and installs apps quickly. However, be careful! I strongly recommend that you also test your apps on the device because the simulator and device are not always the same. They are built differently and have different architectures.

Memory Allocation

Memory Allocation helps you to understand how much object allocations you use. This may mean that you allocate and keep in memory so many objects. These objects are not released yet because it is still in use.

Allocation

Choose Product ➤ Profile and then choose Allocations in the open window (as shown in Figure 2–1)

Figure 2–1. *Choose Allocation in Profile Window*

After choosing Allocations instrument, you will be shown with a main Allocation panel, which gives you all the necessary information, as you can see in Figure 2–2.

The Allocations panel (Figure 2–2) shows you "created and still living" jobs so that you can see what objects are still in memory and what objects consume the most memory. You should use this tool if you start receiving many warnings from the iOS environment like "Received memory warning. Level =1".

The details will show you at which time which lines of code and which class is responsible for creating and handling the objects. With this information, you can easily figure out how to deal with memory. This is a good tool for tracking caching algorithms and methods (see Chapter 4 for more details).

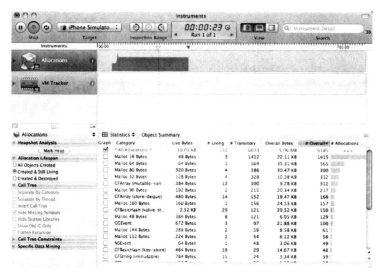

Figure 2–2. The main allocations panel

Figure 2–3 and 2–4 shows you more details about what objects are living and consuming the most memory for your application. In Figure 2–3, you see the list of details about objects are created and lived inside your application.

Graph	Category	Live Bytes▼	# Living	# Transitory	Overall Bytes	# Overall	# Allocations (Net / Overall)
☑	* All Allocations *	27.77 KB	565	55386	17.06 MB	55951	
☐	CFRunLoopTimer ○	11.72 KB	125	250	35.16 KB	375	
☐	CFBasicHash (value-st...	4.50 KB	135	1146	109.23 KB	1281	
☐	CFSet (mutable)	3.91 KB	125	266	12.22 KB	391	
☐	CFBasicHash (count-s...	2.36 KB	8	57	16.86 KB	65	
☐	__NSCFDate	1.94 KB	124	247	5.80 KB	371	
☐	CGEvent	672 Bytes	3	291	64.31 KB	294	
☐	Malloc 144 Bytes	576 Bytes	4	924	130.50 KB	928	
☐	Malloc 48 Bytes	480 Bytes	10	1353	63.89 KB	1363	
☐	Malloc 80 Bytes	320 Bytes	4	4787	374.30 KB	4791	

Figure 2–3. The allocation results

In Figure 2–4, you can see which methods are calling to create these objects.

Category	Timestamp	Live	Size	Responsible Library	Responsible Caller
Malloc 80 Bytes	00:22.186.397	•	80	CoreGraphics	CGClipStackCreateMutable
Malloc 80 Bytes	00:25.680.592	•	80	CoreGraphics	CGClipStackCreateMutable
Malloc 80 Bytes	00:26.680.849	•	80	AppKit	-[NSViewHierarchyLock lock...
Malloc 80 Bytes	00:26.680.980	•	80	CoreGraphics	CGClipStackCreateMutable

Figure 2–4. The allocation details

Advantages:

- It is accurate and provides many details on the time and situation in which the application consumes the most memory.

- It can also give you a good overview of the object's lifecycle over the application lifetime.

Disadvantages:

- The results depend on how developers run the app. It requires a good test suite preparation to cover as many cases as possible.

- It can take time and effort to create a good test case that helps developers to figure out the place and time the application consume the most memory.

- You need to test on the real device so that you can receive memory warning message. The simulator will almost never give the memory warning message. The problem with using the simulator is that your computer will have 2–4GB of RAM and your device probably has much less.

Usages:

- If you test your app and receive a memory warning, this is the one of the first tools you should reach for.

Legacy Code

At this release, the tool to automatically convert from a manual memory management project to new ARC project may fail. The tool may ask you to fix lots of places in your current code to make sure the project can be converted into an ARC project. It may be your open source library fails to convert into a new ARC style and you would not want to touch it. So, I think it is good for you to understand some background about manual memory management.

Memory Leaks

Memory leaks happen when you create a new object in memory and you don't release it properly. That object will stay in memory for the whole application life. The result is your application doesn't have enough memory to run fast, or even worse, the iOS will force your application to close.

Static Analyzer

This is a simple and straightforward tool to measure the memory leaks. As shown in the Figures 2–5 and 2–6, the tool will show you which line or block of code may **possibly** be causing the memory leak.

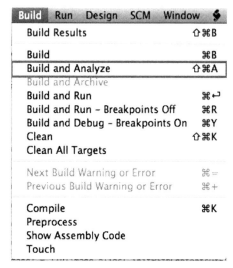

Figure 2–5. *Choose Product ➤ Analyze*

As shown in Figure 2–5, you need to choose Product ➤ Analyze or Command + Shift + B

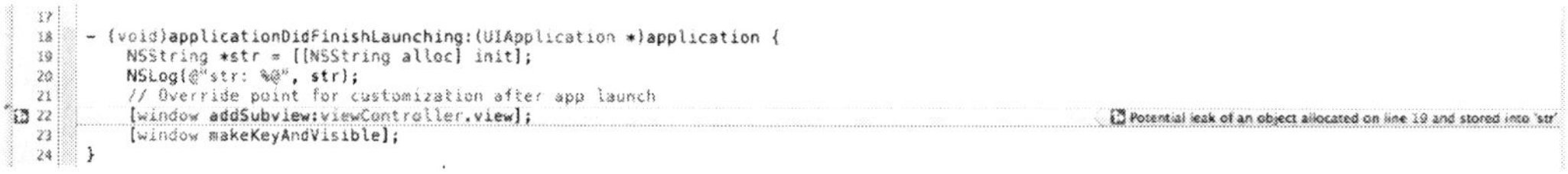

```
17
18    - (void)applicationDidFinishLaunching:(UIApplication *)application {
19          NSString *str = [[NSString alloc] init];
20          NSLog(@"str: %@", str);
21          // Override point for customization after app launch
22          [window addSubview:viewController.view];          Potential leak of an object allocated on line 19 and stored into 'str'
23          [window makeKeyAndVisible];
24    }
```

Figure 2–6. *Static Analyzer reports a potential leak of an object allocation on line 19 and stored in str.*

As you can see in Figure 2–6, the str object in line 19 is never released; in this case, Static Analyzer provides a correct warning.

Advantages:

- It gives you a quick and general look at possible places where memory leaks can happen.

- It has a really fast process: it only builds and looks at the source code. Static Analyzer doesn't need to run the program.

- This tool requires no effort from the developer; you just click on Build and Analyze.

Disadvantages:

- Sometimes it's not accurate. It can give an incorrect warning or doesn't indicate places where there is a memory leak.

Usage:

- Developers should use this tool first to measure the memory leak because it's fast and requires almost no effort.

Leaks Instrument

This is a better instrument that measures the memory leak in runtime (when the app is running). This makes sure that the object is really leaked out; if an object is leaked out, it will have to be reported to the user. You keep trying different features of the app, and the Leaks Instrument will report memory leak places.

You will need to look for places where the Leaks horizontal bar shows a vertical column. The height of the column will show how much memory the app has leaked at that time (see Figure 2–7).

Figure 2–7. Shows how many leaks you have had from running the code

Then, when you go inside the details of the leaks, you may see a list of leaks happening in your code. By sorting by responsible library and looking for your app name (in this case, LeaksViewController), you will see two leaked objects. A quick look tells you that you leaked two images inside the class RootViewController.

Leaked Object	#	Address	Size	Responsible Library ▼	Responsible Frame
UIImage		0x8026020	16 Bytes	LeaksViewController	-[RootViewController
UIImage		0x4b2a250	16 Bytes	LeaksViewController	-[RootViewController
Malloc 9.00 KB		0x5026a00	9.00 KB	ImageIO	initImageJPEG

Figure 2–8. A list of leaks inside your program

As shown in Figure 2–8, next to the address is a small arrow; by clicking on it, the Leaks Instrument will guide you to the correct place in the app that caused that leak (see Figure 2–9).

```
- (void)tableView:(UITableView *)tableView didSelectRowAtIndexPath:(NSIndexPath *)indexPath {
    NSString *avatarFile = [NSString stringWithFormat:@"a0"];
    NSString *avatarName = [[NSBundle mainBundle] pathForResource:avatarFile ofType:@"jpeg"];
    UIImage *image1 = [[UIImage alloc] initWithContentsOfFile:avatarName];
    NSLog(@"image: %@", image1);
    image1 = [[UIImage alloc] initWithContentsOfFile:avatarName];
    NSLog(@"image: %@", image1);
```

Figure 2–9. Lines of code that created the leaks

At this point, you can observe the line of code that created the memory leak. Usually, Leaks Instrument will give you exact details about where the memory leak happened so that you can easily fix it.

Advantages:

■ Leaks Instrument is very accurate and detailed.

Disadvantages:

■ The results depend on how developers run the app. It requires a good test suite preparation to cover as many cases as possible.

■ It can be slow because developers need to run it a few times to see how the app performs in many different cases.

Usages:

  ▨ This tool should be used after the Static Analyzer is used. It will cover all other small and niche cases that the Static Analyzer missed.

I recommend that you run Static Analyzer first. If you still have some concerns over memory usage or receive memory warning from the iOS runtime environment, you should use Leaks Instrument.

Memory Garbage

At the first look, memory garbage may not seem to be related to performance issues. However, having your application crash is even worse than slow performance as it stops performance cold and kills the whole user experience that you want to create. Therefore, you should know how make the best use of memory.

Zombie

You choose Product ➤ Profile ➤ Allocations.

You will be shown a running instrument. The problem is that this instrument does not measure anything or help you with the Zombie issue, so you need to stop it. Then, you need to configure the Allocations to work with the Zombie. In other words, when a crash happens, the Instrument will report where the crash happens.

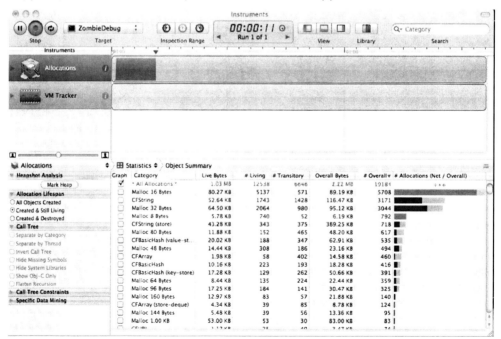

Figure 2-10. The screen for Allocations Instrument

For now, you do not need to care about the data in the lower part of Figure 2–10; you only need to care about how to configure the Allocations Instrument to check for Zombie crash. Figure 2–11 shows you how.

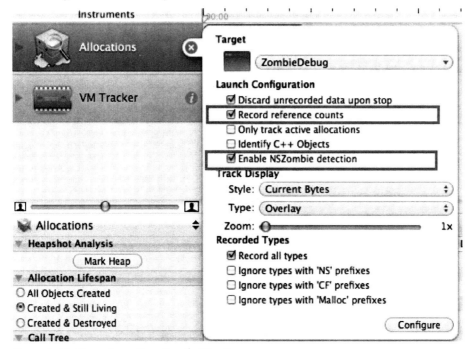

Figure 2–11. The main configuration for Allocations

After configuring Allocations, you need to run the record action again; this will run the iPhone Simulator or device.

Then, you just keep running and trying different features of the app until it crashes. The Allocations Instrument should give you a message like that in Figure 2–10.

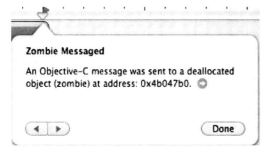

Figure 2–12. The Zombie crash message

If you click the arrow to go into the details, the lower part will show you a list of memory action on the specific object, like malloc, autorelease, retain, release (as shown in the

Figure 2–13). Your sample project is called ZombieDebug, so you only need to look at the second, third, and fourth lines.

#	Category	Event Type	RefCt	Timestamp	Address	Size	Responsible Li...	Responsible Caller
0	CFNumber	Malloc	1	00:14.433	0x4b047b0	16	Foundation	-[NSPlaceholderNumber ...
1	CFNumber	Autorelease		00:14.433	0x4b047b0	0	ZombieDebug	-[ZombieDebugViewCon...
2	CFNumber	CFRetain	2	00:14.433	0x4b047b0	0	ZombieDebug	-[ZombieDebugViewCon...
3	CFNumber	CFRelease	1	00:14.433	0x4b047b0	0	ZombieDebug	-[ZombieDebugViewCon...
4	CFNumber	CFRelease	0	00:14.433	0x4b047b0	0	Foundation	-[NSAutoreleasePool rel...
5	CFNumber	Zombie	-1	00:14.977	0x4b047b0	0	Foundation	-[NSCFString appendFor...

Statistics ⇕ Object Summary History: 0x4b047b0

Figure 2–13. The list of memory actions, like malloc, autorelease, retain and release

Figure 2–14 shows the corresponding block of code for the chosen statement in Figure 2–13.

```
-(IBAction) tapButton:(id)button {
    NSNumber* n = [NSNumber numberWithLong:random()];
    [objArray addObject:n];
    [self rewriteText];       +[NSNumber numberWithLong:]
}
```

Figure 2–14. The code block that corresponds to the malloc/autorelease/retain/release statement in the instrument.

Advantages:

■ It provides exact details about where the memory crash happened.

■ It can be tested on simulator.

Disadvantages:

■ The result depends on how you run the app. Bad access may sometimes happen under specific conditions.

Usages:

■ This tool should only be used when you receive a EXEC_BAD_ACCESS error.

Performance Tools

Memory is not the only source of performance problems. There are other techniques to improve application performance: better handling of reading and writing data from the file system and network, improving user interface responsiveness, and utilizing multithreading. To measure how good the performance of the application is, you can measure CPU usage, time usage, and battery energy usage. Moreover, these are all interrelated and I shall explain their relationships.

CPU problems are related to how much your CPU has to process at one time in the worst scenario. The worst scenario is when CPU has too many tasks or it runs continuously. Generally, when there is no task, the CPU should not run, and it may only run in an event-oriented way when users interact with the app. However, when there are lots of tasks coming at the same time, such as processing user input, reading from file, and networking, the CPU should not have idle time. When there are lots of tasks and CPU has idle time, it means that CPU is not being used efficiently. To utilize the CPU when it comes to an intensive processing, you may need to use multithreading, and I will highlight some tools to keep track of thread usage.

File I/O and network access is a time-consuming task when you need to read from a file to the memory. Therefore, for a good performance balance, you always need to have a good strategy for accessing files and the network. If you often read from a file and the network or read from it too late, users will have to wait a long time until data is displayed. However, if you read from them too early and store too much in memory, you will soon run out of memory or lack enough memory for other tasks. Therefore, measuring the file and network activity is an important task for developers.

There is a huge difference between how well the app runs and how users perceive the performance of the app. The app can run with perfect memory usage or really fast data processing algorithms but users still feel that the app does not work or respond to their interactivity well. The reason is that the UI thread is too busy to respond or receive any user interactivity. You can measure how well the UI thread works in different cases.

There is one unique thing about iOS. Generally, the Smartphone system is based on battery power. Energy is really important for these systems because users can't keep charging them all day. Also, the system doesn't have room for a big battery, like you find in a laptop. Desktops and servers are really different because they are always plugged in, which provides unlimited power, so developers don't need to care much about energy. Laptops are more stable and have bigger battery life than mobile and handheld devices. Therefore, you will have to measure the energy usage of your app carefully.

Instrument Applications

You can choose Run ➤ Profile or you should open the Instrument Application by typing Command + Space and then typing "Instrument." The MacOS should give you the options shown in Figure 2–15.

Figure 2–15. The Instrument Panel

They are two main categories of instruments: instruments for iOS Simulator and ones for iOS Devices. Some of them can run in both environments but you have to be careful because the results can be sometimes different. As I already explained, the iOS Simulator is really different than the iOS device.

CPU Measurement

One of the most important instruments is the CPU Measurement Instruments. The CPU Measurement Instruments will tell you how different CPU activities run when your application is executing. They can show you how intensive and how long a CPU activity is running for a specific task in your application.

CPU Sampler

The tool samples the target application at fixed intervals; the default interval is 10ms but you can change it to something else. Each time the CPU is sampled, the tool also records a stack trace. The sample and stack trace is usually enough for you to recognize the bottlenecks that need fixing inside your app.

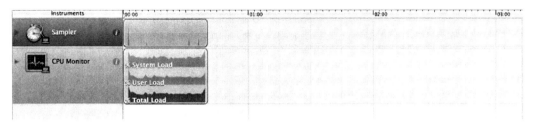

Figure 2–16. *The main CPU sampler panel*

As shown in Figure 2–16, the CPU Sampler gives you the data about System Load and User Load. System Load is the loading time by system such as file, networking, and logic processing while user load relates to the UI and the interaction between the user and the app.

Figure 2–16 shows that the general usage and loading for system and user is stable over time but goes up a little bit at some points and significantly at the end of the sample time. This information is normally not enough to figure out any problems, though. So you will need to look further into the main area.

Before I continue, you should configure your Sampler to show only areas directly related to your code by checking the box named Hide System Libraries, as shown in Figure 2–17.

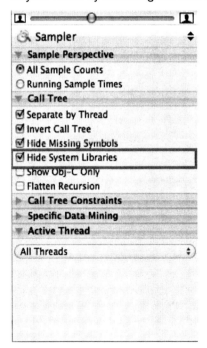

Figure 2–17. The main CPU sampler panel

Then, in the main list result, you will see something like Figure 2–18—a list of main functions called, how many times they are called inside the sample time, and the percentage of number of times compared to the general process.

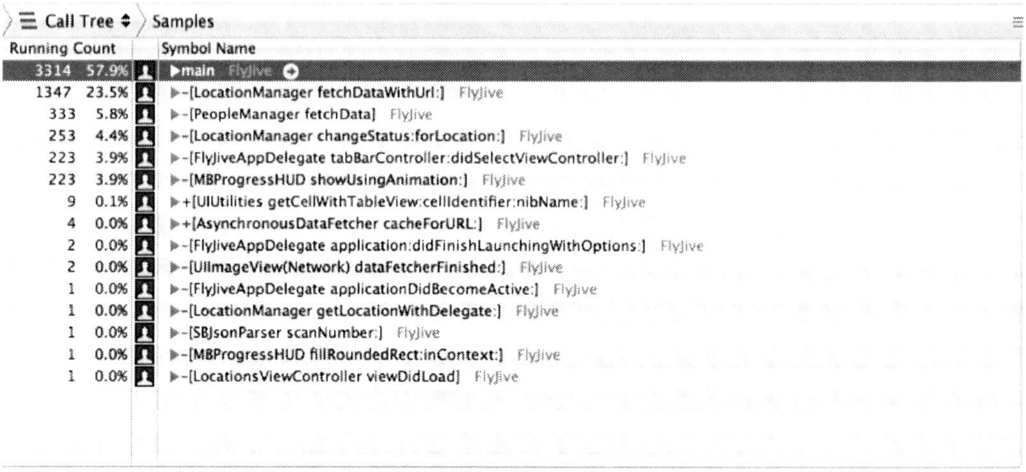

Figure 2–18. *The running count and percentage of each function call*

You can also switch the running count to be the running time to show how much time each function takes to finish, as shown in Figure 2–19.

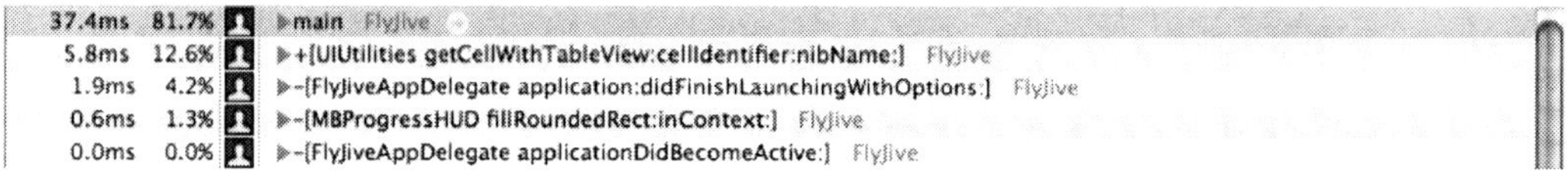

Figure 2–19. *The running time and percentage of each function call*

You can actually view more details of each function call inside its own stack trace by opening the small arrows in the left, as shown in Figure 2–20.

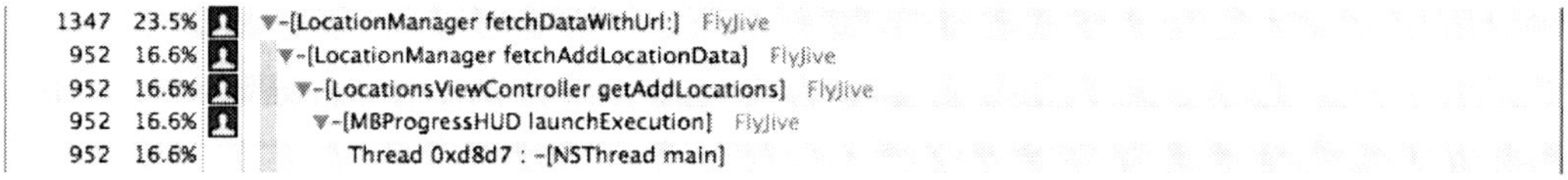

Figure 2–20. The detailed running time of functions inside the stack trace

Advantages:

■ The tool is accurate and gives you details on which time and which case the application consumes the most processing time.

Disadvantages:

■ The results depend on how developers run the app. It may depend on the priority and which function is called first.

▓ It can take time and effort to create a good test case to cover all the functions.

▓ You need to test on the real device if you want to see the exact running time of each function in iOS runtime environment.

Usages:

▓ If developers already know which area will have the bottleneck and want to test to verify or know more details about the bottleneck or which exact function or a group of functions caused the bottleneck.

Activity Monitor

This is the tool to show the CPU time, physical memory, virtual memory, and number of threads when running on the iOS device. It gives a good overview on the whole app when the app is running on the operating system. Therefore, you can know when it requires the most CPU time, real memory, and virtual memory (see Figure 2–21). This number should be compared to other background-running apps as well as the general specification of the iOS. The latest iPhone 4 only has 500 MB of RAM so you can't exceed that number. It's good to combine this test with CPU Sampler and Allocations Instrument to get the whole picture about your app's performance.

Process ID ▼	Process Name	User Name	% CPU	Threads	Real Mem	Virtual Mem	Architecture	CPU Time	Sudden Terr
1426	TestLoopPerforma	mobile	0	3	3.29 MB	71.93 MB	ARM	04.75	N/A
1423	DTMobileIS	root	3.9	8	1.77 MB	17.54 MB	ARM	03.81	N/A
1422	notification_pro	mobile	0	3	576.00 KB	13.25 MB	ARM	00.01	N/A

Figure 2–21. The detailed running time of functions inside the stack trace

Advantages:

▓ Provides a general view of the app's runtime performance, including comparing your app to others as well as to the standard iOS environment.

Disadvantages:

▓ Lacks details on how each function inside the app is running.

▓ Developers can't know for certain where the bottleneck is, but they can guess when playing with the app to see if the memory or %CPU goes up or not.

Usages:

▓ The tool should be used in combination with other detailed tools like CPU Sampler or Allocations Instrument.

Time Measurement

Now let's discuss another important topic regarding performance: time. Generally, when users complain about your application, they will only tell you that the application runs slowly here and there. Therefore, you need to measure how long it takes for your application to perform a specific task.

Time Profiler

Similar to the way CPU Sampler runs, Time Profiler gives you a general overview of how your app is running in regards to time, specifically the longest duration that your app is running and which functions inside your app take the most time to run (see Figure 2–22). The only difference between Time Profiler and CPU Sampler is that the former is about the time it takes the functions to run, not the CPU usage it takes to run a function.

Figure 2–22. The Time Profiler Interface

Running Time		Symbol Name
392.0ms	68.7%	▶ main JoinMe
23.0ms	4.0%	▶ –[RootViewController showImagePicker] JoinMe
16.0ms	2.8%	▶ +[CKImageCacher saveImage:withPath:uniqueUrl:imageFormat:] JoinMe
14.0ms	2.4%	▶ –[CKEventCreatingViewController sendSMSOrEmail] JoinMe
13.0ms	2.2%	▶ +[ViewControllerHelper loadViewWithNibName:owner:class:] JoinMe
11.0ms	1.9%	▶ –[FBDialog init] JoinMe
10.0ms	1.7%	▶ –[CKCommentsViewController viewDidLoad] JoinMe

Figure 2–23. The running time of each function

As you can see in Figure 2–23, the Time Profiler looks like the CPU Sampler in that it shows each function and you can actually go into each function to examine the running time for that function on the stack trace.

Advantages:

- Time Profiler gives you accurate and detailed information on how much time each task takes to execute.

Disadvantages:

- The results depend on how developers run the app. It may depend on the priority and which function is called first.

- It can take time and effort to create a good test case to cover all the functions.

- You need to test on the real device if you want to see the exact running time of each function in iOS runtime environment.

Usages:

- If the developer already knows which area has bottlenecks and she wants to test to verify or know more details about the bottleneck or what exact function or a group of functions caused the bottleneck.

User Interface Response Time Measurement

Imagine that your application is running with perfect efficiency, yet the users still think that it runs slowly or it doesn't respond to the users' interaction, or even worse, it does not change the UI in the correct time. According to CPU Sampler or Time Profiler, your functions are running perfectly. However, when you run the app, it still does not respond well to your event. If this is the case, there is a big chance that the UI thread does not render your UI well. Therefore, you may need to use another UI-related tool to check if the rendering time in the UI is acceptable. Core Animation and OpenGL ES Driver Instruments are two good tools in iPhone to measure and test your application.

Core Animation

Core Animation mainly measures how many frames per second the UI thread can render (in other words, draw) your UI to the user. UI thread is also the main thread to take care of the interaction of your users.

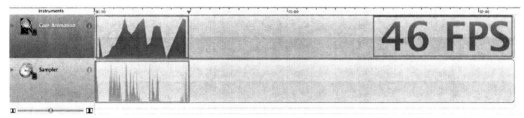

Figure 2–24. Three main panels in Core Animation results

As you can see from Figure 2–24, there are three main panels that you may need to look at to figure out the UI rendering performance. The first one is the graph in the first horizontal cell. This graph shows the changes in number of frames per second. The biggest number in the right shows the current number of frames per second; this absolute value should be as high as possible, and the highest value is 60 frames per second (60 FPS).

The second graph is the sampler of the frames per second over a specific time; 10 seconds is the default value of Core Animation.

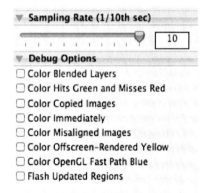

▲	Frames Per Second
0	0
1	27
2	0
3	0
4	4
5	13
6	15
7	24
8	32
9	49
10	33

Figure 2–25. The list of number of frames per second

Figure 2–25 actually gives you the list of number of frames per second over the last 10 running times. Generally, if inside the test you still interact with your application and expect it to run smoothly, the number should be around 55-60. If the number is small, it could mean one of two things. Either your UI thread has nothing to draw or it can't get any CPU time to draw. In the later case, you have a serious performance problem that is keeping the UI thread so busy that it can't draw anything.

▼ **Sampling Rate (1/10th sec)**

▼ **Debug Options**
- ☐ Color Blended Layers
- ☐ Color Hits Green and Misses Red
- ☐ Color Copied Images
- ☐ Color Immediately
- ☐ Color Misaligned Images
- ☐ Color Offscreen-Rendered Yellow
- ☐ Color OpenGL Fast Path Blue
- ☐ Flash Updated Regions

Figure 2–26. The list of options to configure the Core Animation

The list of options in Figure 2–26 will give you more information when you run the instruments.

■ *Color Blended Layers* adds a green layer for views that are opaque and red for those that are not opaque. This is important for the scrolling performance that you will see in Chapter 3. Making your view all opaque will make the rendering performance faster because the GPU does not need to draw twice in the same point. The colors will be displayed as shown in Figure 2–27.

Figure 2–27. Core Animation instrument with color blended

Advantages:

- Core Animation provides a general overview about the UI thread renders/draws the UI of your app and how fast the process is.

- You can gain more details by configuring the option inside the Core Animation Instrument.

Disadvantages:

- You definitely need to run this tool on the device.

- It does not offer details about specific code-related problems.

Usages:

- When the application runs slowly, developers should always check for UI rendering because the problem may lie inside rendering code, not in the logic processing code.

OpenGL ES Driver

The OpenGL ES Driver Instrument will give you almost the same information as the Core Animation instrument so I won't show the example to you again. However, there is one significant difference between OpenGL and Core Animation. Core Animation is a higher level framework than OpenGL so Core Animation actually uses OpenGL. However, if your code does not use any direct OpenGL code, you don't need to use the OpenGL ES Driver Instrument. It's good only for applications or games that use OpenGL framework.

Advantages:

◼ Same as Core Animation.

Disadvantages:

◼ Same as Core Animation.

Usages:

◼ For applications that use OpenGL code.

File and Network Access Measurement

For performance, there is one main important issue that all developers need to remember. That is file and network I/O. This process is slow because in I/O, you need to handle or wait for events that happen far slower than the processor instructions. So, unless it is done efficiently, it is possible that your application will waste a huge amount of time. You will learn more about file and network caching to save time when performing file and network I/O processing in Chapter 4. To measure the performance of the file and network I/O, you have two main tools: System Usage and File Activity.

System Usage

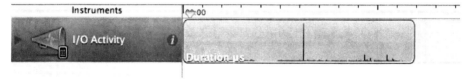

Figure 2–28. System I/O Performance

System Usage is used to test the file and network I/O in the iOS runtime environment. As you can see in Figure 2–28, there is some point that the I/O activity spikes. This can be a potential problem for performance if this file processing takes a long time, thus requiring users to wait for it to finish.

#	Function	Duration µs	In File	In Bytes ▾	Out File	Out Bytes	Thread ID	Stack Depth	Error	Path	Parameters
2701	read	36	6	1.68 KB	0	1.68 KB	775	33		...6EA/JoinMe.app/TableCellViewController.nib	buf=0xabfc00
2709	read	41	6	1.68 KB	0	1.68 KB	775	33		...6EA/JoinMe.app/TableCellViewController.nib	buf=0xa2c600
2717	read	39	6	1.68 KB	0	1.68 KB	775	33		...6EA/JoinMe.app/TableCellViewController.nib	buf=0xa40600
40	read	36	6	1.49 KB	0	1.49 KB	775	24		...FC80C45576EA/JoinMe.app/MainWindow.nib	buf=0xa1e400
43	read	33	6	979 Bytes	0	979 Bytes	775	37		...45576EA/JoinMe.app/RootViewController.nib	buf=0xa1e000
16	read	29	6	891 Bytes	0	891 Bytes	775	13		...~8B19–FC80C45576EA/JoinMe.app/Info.plist	buf=0xa07800
101	read	24	6	722 Bytes	0	722 Bytes	6147	17		...vateFrameworks/WebKit.framework/Info.plist	buf=0xa4be00
98	read	25	6	648 Bytes	0	648 Bytes	6147	16		...Frameworks/Foundation.framework/Info.plist	buf=0xa4b200
11	read	25	4	608 Bytes	0	608 Bytes	775	21		...brary/Frameworks/UIKit.framework/Info.plist	buf=0xa07400
19	read	30	6	512 Bytes	0	512 Bytes	775	10		...76EA/JoinMe.app/SlowPerformanceTableView	buf=0x2fdff5b8
20	read	22	6	32 Bytes	0	32 Bytes	775	12		...76EA/JoinMe.app/SlowPerformanceTableView	buf=0x2fdff098

Figure 2–29. Detail List for System Activity

Figure 2–29 shows a detailed list of the file and network I/O processing. If you observe the list carefully, you will see that the file `TableCellViewController.nib` keeps loading from the file system. This can be a potential problem. So, a small optimization would be to cache the file or keep the object in the memory so that you don't need to load it too many times.

The information collected from System Activity and Object Allocations should be combined together to make sure that you have a good balance between performance and memory. You can't simply cache any file you need when you have a really limited memory.

Advantages:

■ It provides detailed information about which file is loaded, how big the file is, and how often the file is loaded.

Disadvantages:

■ You need to run the test on the device.

Usages:

■ It helps developers make the right decision about caching files or reducing the file loading until they need the file. It can help with decisions about early-loading files to make sure that when the application needs the file, it's already there, which will significantly reduce the waiting time for users.

File Activity

The File Activity Instrument works like the System Usage Instrument, but it gives more details about the file as well as the library reading. As Figure 2–30 shows, the Instrument gives really good details about file activity, reads/writes, file attributes, and directory I/O.

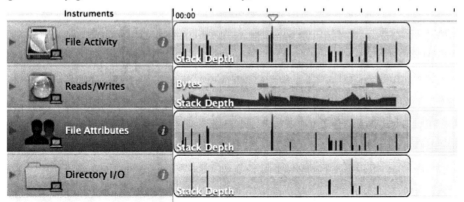

Figure 2–30. Main list of the File Activity instrument

You will usually be more concerned about file activity and reads/writes than other parts because these attributes relate to the performance issues we are discussing.

#	Caller	Function	FD	Path
584	_NS...	close	15	...loper/SDKs/iPhoneSimulator4.0.sdk/System/Library/CoreServices/SystemVersion.plist
585	CPFi...	stat64		/Users/vodkhang/Library/Application Support/iPhone Simulator/4.0.2/Library/AddressBook
586	unix...	stat64		...plication Support/iPhone Simulator/4.0.2/Library/AddressBook/AddressBook.sqlitedb
587	sqlit...	open	15	...plication Support/iPhone Simulator/4.0.2/Library/AddressBook/AddressBook.sqlitedb
588	fillIn...	fstat64	15	...plication Support/iPhone Simulator/4.0.2/Library/AddressBook/AddressBook.sqlitedb
589	sqlit...	fstat64	15	...plication Support/iPhone Simulator/4.0.2/Library/AddressBook/AddressBook.sqlitedb
590	sqlit...	fstat64	15	...plication Support/iPhone Simulator/4.0.2/Library/AddressBook/AddressBook.sqlitedb
591	sqlit...	fstat64	15	...plication Support/iPhone Simulator/4.0.2/Library/AddressBook/AddressBook.sqlitedb

Figure 2–31. Detailed list of file activities

From Figure 2–31, you can see that File Activity provides information about the AddressBook reading. This is not offered by the System Usage Instrument.

Advantages:

■ It provides detailed information about which file is loaded, the size of the file, and how often the file is loaded.

■ It has more information about directory, file attributes, and how much read and write are executed.

Disadvantages:

■ The data on simulator may not be accurate.

Usages:

■ The tool should be combined with System Usage.

Measure Thread Performance

The Thread Measurement in iPhone is not really useful in measuring performance. However, it delivers very good information the state of each thread running in your application. For example, it will tell you if some threads are blocked for too long or if you have already created too many threads (see Figure 2–32). Blocked threads are a significant sign that something is wrong in your code. Usually, when you want to utilize the operating system's capability, you will create many threads to handle the processing in parallel. This is when the problems happen and when you need to use Threads Instrument to measure the threads.

Figure 2–32. List of threads and their states when the application is running

Advantages:

- It gives you a general view about threads and their states.

- You can run the instrument on the simulator. Although there are some differences between iOS and simulator architecture, many problems still happen in a similar way on both architectures.

Disadvantages:

- It does not give much detail about each thread.

Usages:

- It helps you figure out any problems with threads, especially when you do a lot of optimization to boost the performance by applying multithreading techniques.

Battery Power Measurement

One of the last important measurements regarding performance in iOS devices is the battery. Battery is a huge issue in mobile devices because you can't keep charging it when you are out with your friends. This problem is even more pronounced with mobile devices than with laptops. People with mobile devices always want to have a high mobile and agile capability for the device.

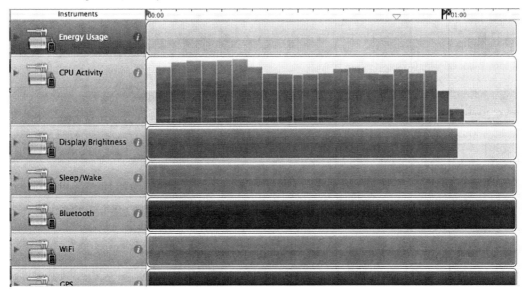

Figure 2–33. List of main concerns about the battery in iOS devices

There are some important measurements in this Energy instrument. It includes energy usage, CPU activity, display brightness, sleep/wake, Bluetooth, Wi-Fi, and GPS. These are energy-consuming tasks. Figure 2–33 does not clearly show the changes inside each measurement. However, if you keep testing the device for the long time, you will see changes inside each of them; for example, Wi-Fi will consume some memory and GPS may be the most energy-consuming task.

⊞ CPU Activity ⬍				
Time	Total Activity	Foreground App Activity	Audio Processing	Graphics
00:02.028 – 00:05.042	76.1%	55.1%	6.6%	9.6%
00:05.035 – 00:08.038	82.7%	52.3%	7%	17.7%
00:08.048 – 00:11.053	85%	60.9%	7.7%	12.6%
00:11.051 – 00:14.066	84.4%	56.4%	6.3%	15.6%
00:14.063 – 00:17.074	85.4%	57.1%	6.3%	17.6%
00:17.068 – 00:20.070	87%	51.6%	7.3%	17.3%
00:20.080 – 00:23.097	76.2%	55%	6.3%	10.3%
00:23.097 – 00:26.100	67%	56.6%	7.3%	1.3%
00:26.096 – 00:29.107	66.1%	55.5%	7.7%	1.7%
00:29.062 – 00:30.985	65.1%	52.5%	6.2%	1.6%

Figure 2–34. CPU activities that consume the most battery power

Figure 2–34 shows the features that consume the most battery—foreground app activity, audio processing, and graphics. Based on this information, you can make decision about how much energy your application is consuming.

⊞ Brightness ⬍	
Time	Brightness Level
00:00	34%
01:01.827	0%

Figure 2–35. Brightness Measurement

Figure 2–35 shows another important aspect of energy consumption: the brightness level of the device.

Advantages:

▨ It gives you a general view about all energy-consuming tasks.

Disadvantages:

▨ You need to run the test on the device for a specific time to gather information.

Usages:

▨ If the application depends much on Wi-Fi, Bluetooth, GPS, graphics, and audio, you should pay attention to energy measurements to make sure that the app does not consume too much battery.

Combination of Tools

So far, you have seen how each of the instruments works and contributes to your performance benchmarking process. But you may be wondering how to measure them all together or combine groups of them to measure. This will save you a ton of time. So I will show how you can do that within Instruments.

As Figure 2–36 shows, you first need to open the Instruments Application and choose the Blank Template.

Figure 2–36. Choose the Blank Template

You will see that there is nothing here but the small box tells you to open the Library List. When you select that small arrow, a list of all possible instruments appears on the right hand side to help you to add the necessary instruments into the template for testing (see Figure 2–37).

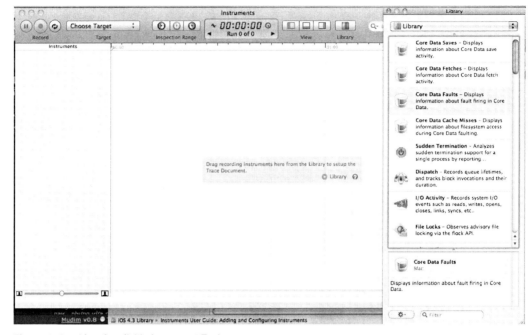

Figure 2–37. *List of available Instrument Tools*

After dragging all the necessary instruments into your template, you can start testing them normally with any instrument that you have been working on until now.

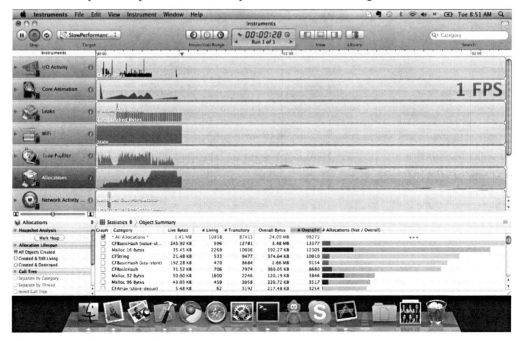

Figure 2–38. All instrument results

As Figure 2–38 shows, you now can see a list of results at the same time. With this advantage, you can know if an increase in performance (measured by CPU Sampler or Time Profiler) means an increase in memory usage (measured by Object Allocations) as well. Keep them in a balance mode to make sure your application runs perfectly.

Advantages:

- You can observe all the instrument results at the same time.

Disadvantages:

- This approach can lead to a really slow app if you add too many instruments. If you test with ten instruments, the app will run terribly. So, be careful about the number of instruments you add.

Usages:

- It helps you get a general overview. It is good to test with several instruments simultaneously after you have identified all the bottlenecks and fixed them.

All Instruments

Table 2–1 summarizes all instruments.

Table 2–1. Summary of All Instrument Tools

Instrument	iPhone / Simulator	Usages	Advantages	Disadvantages
NSLog	Both	Basic, fast, adhoc	Measures to lines of code	Can't measure UI over-optimization
Static Analyzer	Both	First tool to measure leaks	Fast, easy	Not always accurate
Leaks	Both	Use after Static Analyzer	Accurate, detailed	Need effort to use properly, can be slow
Zombie	Both	When you get a EXEC_BAD_ACCESS error	Accurate, detailed	Crash doesn't happen all the time
Allocation	Both	When you get a memory warning	Accurate, detailed, good overview	Takes time and effort
CPU Sampler	iPhone	Test/verify the bottleneck	Accurate, detailed	Needs to be run on real device, takes time and effort

Instrument	iPhone / Simulator	Usages	Advantages	Disadvantages
Activity Monitor	iPhone	Combined with CPU Sampler	General view	Sparse details, doesn't indicated the location of bottlenecks
Time Profiler	iPhone	Provides details about a specific bottleneck	Accurate, very detailed (method level)	Depends on the test case, takes time and effort, needs to be run on real device
Core Animation	iPhone	Should always be used to check if app is slow because of UI	General view, more details are available by using the options	Must be run on real device, doesn't offer details about specific code problem
OpenGL ES Driver	iPhone	Same as Core Animation	Same as Core Animation	Same as Core Animation
System Usage	iPhone	When doing lots of file/network processing	Information about I/O processing	Must be run on real device
File Activity	Simulator	Same as above	Can be run on simulator, provides more information about file and directory	Data on simulator may not be accurate
Threading	Both	When program is used with multithreading	General view about threads and states	Not detailed about each thread
Energy	iPhone	When using Wi-Fi, Bluetooth, GPS, graphics	General view about energy-consuming aspects of app	Must be run on real device
Combination	Both	Combines multiple instruments	Can observe many results at the same time	Can make the app run slowly if testing too many instruments at once

Summary

This chapter walks you through the list of possible instruments and gives you the details and the summary of the advantages and disadvantages of each instrument.

The tools were divided into three main categories with subcategories inside: basic tools, memory tools, and performance tools.

Memory and performance are highly related to each other; you have to measure each carefully to see if the problem you have belongs to a memory or a performance problem.

Within performance problems, I divided the tools into subcategories like CPU, File Processing, User Interface Rendering, Threading, and Energy. Each of them can affect to other properties of application; in other words, a bottleneck in one area can hide a bottleneck in another area. Therefore, you need to measure each aspect carefully to make sure that you fix the right problem. For example, if the problem is the slow rendering process of iPhone, there is not much thing you can do with CPU, logic, and data processing. In that case, you need to jump right into the displaying code and possibly change from Interface Builder to custom code to draw the UI.

EXERCISE

1. Use memory tools discussed in this chapter to test the memory usage of your existing applications and figure out what you can do to improve them.

2. Choose a game inside your current iPod/iPhone/iPad and test to see how much energy, Bluetooth, Wi-Fi, or 3G it uses with an appropriate instrument tool.

3. Choose an app with some complicated `UITableView` and use the appropriate tool to test the scrolling performance of that `UITableView`.

## Chapter 3

Increase and Optimize UITableView Performance

In this chapter, you will do the following:

- Use the benchmark tools you saw in Chapter 2 in a real example.

- Work step by step with an example of scrolling performance optimization.

- Use techniques to optimize UITableView performance.

  - Basic techniques to optimize simple and basic cells in UITableView.

  - Hardcore techniques using code to actually draw the view inside the cell.

  - Basic optimization techniques for cells need animation like editing and reordering.

  - Other basic techniques that developers need to know.

iPhone apps usually display data in the list format. Apple provides excellent tools for basic developers: UITableView and UITableViewCell. If developers only want to use basic features to display a small image on the left and text in the center, the default Apple control should work well. However, when you have to do lots of customization to the listing order to have two or three images and text in different places, you'll run into problems. Sooner or later, you'll run into performance problems with jerky scrolling of the UITableView, especially on old devices like iPhone 3G.

Introduction to the Examples

For this exercise, I will measure the performance based on two main factors: the speed the tableView dequeues, creates a new cell, or returns the cell back for the operating system (OS); and how fast the OS can render your cell to display it to the machine. The first one can be measured by NSLog easily enough; the second one is more complicated and can only be measured by CoreAnimation.

To demonstrate, I will walk you through two different examples. One just contains an avatar and a textblock; the other one has complicated views with many subviews inside. By going through these two examples, you will see many different ways to optimize the scrolling performance of a UITableView.

At the end of this chapter, I will also list other important points that I don't have time to cover in detail in this chapter. These are not usual mistakes, but if a developer is careless enough to make one of these mistakes, it will cost him a whole day of benchmarking and testing to figure out the problem. I want to make sure that you have enough skills and knowledge under your belt to handle any situation.

Sometimes, optimization is so simple that it only requires a few changes here and there inside the code. However, in other cases, like in the second example, optimization will require rewriting the whole code base to fit into a better, more optimized model. I hope that after I go over the examples, you will have a clear idea of the program's structure so you can make the right decisions at the beginning and will not need to rewrite the whole code base.

Reviewing the Instrument Tool

For this chapter, you will use the CoreAnimation tool to benchmark the render performance of iPhone OS. This will help you to know if the problem is within the computing process or in the displaying process. Chapter 2 covered this tool, so this chapter only provides a brief review.

Figure 3–1 shows the main view of the CoreAnimation tool with the three parts that you need to look at when running the tool and Figure 3–2 shows the performance readings.

Figure 3–1. *Main parts in the CoreAnimation tool*

⊞ Table ⬍	
▲	Frames Per Second
0	0
1	27
2	0
3	0
4	4
5	13
6	15
7	24
8	32
9	49
10	33

Figure 3–2. *Recent display performance*

First Example

The first example will show you the step-by-step process to optimize the scrolling performance of the UITableView. The initial version of the source code contains many performance errors that I gathered from many developers. In the process, you can see that the performance goes up after every step you implement to optimize the performance.

Introduction to the First Example

As Figure 3–3 shows, your problem is a general and practical one where you need to develop a UITableView with one image and one textblock in each cell. I will walk you through the source code of this example. Let's look at general apps like Facebook; the app would need one image for the avatar and one image for the content of the link that users share there. The app can also have other small images to represent icons in the cell. For this first benchmark, please refer to the project called SlowPerformanceTableView.

Figure 3–3. *The application for the first example*

Standard Benchmark

Before you start any project, you must know your final goal; in this case, it's what performance you want to achieve so that you can give your users a good user experience when scrolling and using your app. So, by running a normal, non-custom UITableViewCell with simple image loading needs and reusing images, Table 3–1 shows the running time from my log.

Table 3–1. *Results from Running the Test on the Example*

Test Number	Preparation Time (Seconds)	General Time (Frames per second)
1	0.000200	55
2	0.000209	56
3	0.000200	55
4	0.000226	54
5	0.000217	60
6	0.000376	59

The best performance for frames per second (fps) by CoreAnimation is 60 fps (the higher number, the better the performance). For a standard UITableViewCell, the usual speed will be around 55-60 fps; this should be one of your goals. The other goal is to make sure the preparation time is small enough. When the general time is reduced, the cell preparation time is also reduced. However, reducing the cell preparation time is easier, so I will focus on reducing it first in this example.

Initial Benchmark

For the first example, I run an initial benchmark test and get a random result of six cells scrolling. Table 3–2 shows the results of benchmarking the performance using tools like NSLog and CoreAnimation.

Table 3–2. *Results from Initial Benchmark on the First Example*

Test Number	Preparation Time (Seconds)	General Time (Frames per second)
1	0.013282	38
2	0.012456	31
3	0.013496	43
4	0.013560	37
5	0.013815	50
6	0.013090	20

So, from the result, you can see that generally it takes 10 milliseconds to return a cell for drawing. Due to this huge delay, the general measurement (fps) also drops down significantly. Therefore, my first goal is to reduce the cell preparation time process.

There is one note in the source code about the difference between [UIImage imageNamed:name] and [[UIImage alloc] initWithContentsOfFile:name]. I will explain this difference later and why you will use imageNamed instead of initWithContentsOfFile.

Reusing UITableViewCell

Optimizing the UITableView is often easy; what you need to do is double check that you reuse the UITableViewCell in the correct manner. Creating a UITableViewCell for iOS is a CPU-intensive process. So, if the CPU needs to create a new cell every time user scrolls up and down to a new cell, the whole performance will decrease. Apple's standard (and default) way to improve this process is to reuse the cell whenever the cell is out of the screen.

Standard TableView Cell

For the standard `UITableViewCell`, the generated code should work really well and give you a fast, high scrolling performance.

```
- (UITableViewCell *)tableView:(UITableView *)tableView
cellForRowAtIndexPath:(NSIndexPath *)indexPath {

    static NSString *CellIdentifier = @"Cell";
    UITableViewCell *cell = [tableView dequeueReusableCellWithIdentifier:CellIdentifier];
    if (cell == nil) {
        cell = [[UITableViewCell alloc]
    initWithStyle:UITableViewCellStyleDefault
reuseIdentifier:CellIdentifier];
    }
```

Note the use of `reuseIdentifier:CellIdentifier` and `dequeueReusableCellWithIdentifier:CellIdentifier`. These two parts will help you reuse the `UITableViewCell` correctly.

There are two main ways to create a new custom cell, either by using `InterfaceBuilder` or by writing the custom code directly by calling the `addSubview:` method

Custom TableView Cell by Interface Builder

While using the `InterfaceBuilder`, developers usually forget to set the identifier, which is really easy to do. The identifier can be modified by open the xib file, going to the first tab, and changing the first row, as shown in Figure 3–4.

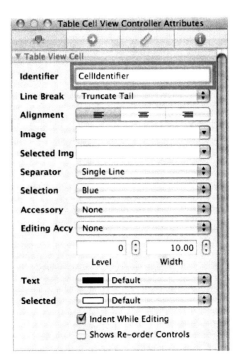

Figure 3–4. *Setting the Reuse Identifier for the Cell*

Now, inside the initialization code for cell, you need to use exactly the same identifier.

```
- (UITableViewCell *)tableView:(UITableView *)tableView
cellForRowAtIndexPath:(NSIndexPath *)indexPath {
   static NSString *CellIdentifier = @"CellIdentifier"; // must match the one in
InterfaceBuilder

   UITableViewCell *cell = [tableView dequeueReusableCellWithIdentifier:CellIdentifier];
   if (cell == nil) {
       cell = [[UITableViewCell alloc] initWithStyle:UITableViewCellStyleDefault
                                    reuseIdentifier:CellIdentifier];
   }
```

Custom TableView Cell by Code

If you build your own custom cell by coding without any interface builder, you can return it inside your custom class ReuseTableViewCell.

```
        TableCellViewController.h
@interface TableCellViewController : UITableViewCell {
}
@end

        TableCellViewController.m
#import "TableCellViewController.h"

@implementation TableCellViewController
```

```
- (NSString *)reuseIdentifier {
        return @"CellIdentifier";
}

@end
```

> **NOTE:** The main difference between these two approaches is the way you load and initialize your
> `UITableViewCell`. To make sure that you can understand and differentiate between these
> two examples, I'll show you some main code.

Loading Cell from Nib File

First, you need the code to load the nib file from file system to memory and then parse
to get the `UITableView` object out.

```
- (UITableViewCell *)cellWithTableView:(UITableView *)tableView cellIdentifier:(NSString
*)cellIdentifier nibName:(NSString *)nibName {
  UITableViewCell *textCell = [tableView
dequeueReusableCellWithIdentifier:cellIdentifier];
    if (textCell == nil) {
        NSArray *topLevelObjects = [[NSBundle mainBundle] loadNibNamed:nibName
                                                    owner:nil
                                                    options:nil];

        for (id currentObject in topLevelObjects) {
            if ([currentObject isKindOfClass:[UITableViewCell class]]) {
                textCell = (UITableViewCell *)currentObject;
                break;
            }
        }
    }
    return textCell;
}
```

You can call the method `cellWithTableView:cellIdentifier:nibName:` to load the table
view from the nib `TableViewController` with the following code:

```
ReuseTableViewCell *cell = (ReuseTableViewCell *) [self
                        getCellWithTableView:tableView
                            cellIdentifier:CellIdentifier
                                    nibName:@"ReuseTableViewCell"];
```

This code is not perfect; you need to change the nib file yourself to make sure that
everything runs well. However, my purpose is to make sure that you can differentiate
between two approaches, so I won't go into the details.

Loading Cell from Custom Code

```
- (id)initWithStyle:(UITableViewCellStyle)style reuseIdentifier:(NSString
*)reuseIdentifier {
    self = [super initWithStyle:style reuseIdentifier:reuseIdentifier];
    if (self != nil) {
```

```
        UIImageView *imageView = [[UIImageView alloc] initWithFrame:CGRectMake(20, 20,
30, 30)];
        [self.contentView addSubview:imageView];
    }
    return self;
}
```

A small exercise for you is to create a new project and try to make a custom cell; then you should check everything to make sure that you reuse the cell correctly.

Running Benchmarks Again

After reusing the cell, you can benchmark the scrolling performance again. As you can see in Table 3–3, the performance doubles after you reuse the cell correctly.

Table 3–3. *Results from Benchmark After Reusing the Cell*

Test Number	Preparation Time (Seconds)	General Time (Frames per second)
1	0.007310	40
2	0.006888	35
3	0.006996	48
4	0.006934	42
5	0.006902	55
6	0.006863	25

This shows you that you are going in the right way; however, the current performance is still not good enough. You always want the performance to go up to around 0.0006-0.0001; this is a normal performance for a standard UITableViewCell, as I showed in the first section. So you will go to the next section to learn how to reuse images instead of creating new image every time it's called.

Here is the reason why you should always reuse the cell. It takes time and memory for the OS to create and load a new cell into the memory. This is why the tableView will always queue the cell for reuse whenever the cell is out of the screen. If you reuse that cell, the OS doesn't need to create a new cell to display; it just needs to get the old cell, change some attributes, and then redisplay that cell. This process is much faster than when the OS needs to create a new cell.

Reusing Images

The general problem with displaying images is that the loading time, either by file I/O from the File System or by networking I/O, takes so long. This loading process may also affect users' scrolling experience when the iOS cannot return the cell to render the UI.

For this section, please refer to the project named ReuseImageViewController. Let me explain first why I choose not to use [UIImage imageNamed:@""] for these samples. The imageNamed does an important job: it will cache the image for you in memory and it will reuse it when you ask for it again. The problem with this method is that it can only get the image from your bundle—in other words, just images that come with the source code of the app. You can't get images from the Internet and load them to memory this way. Usually, what you have to do is call the method [[UIImage alloc] initWithContentsOfFile:@""]; or [UIImage alloc [initWithData:Data]]. With these methods, the OS will not automatically cache the image in the memory for the app.

So, I want you to cache the images yourself by using a small dictionary to store the image in memory (see Chapter 4). Another important part of dealing with images is multithreading (see Chapter 6). Using this technique, you can put the heavy processing jobs out of the current processing thread. In my current example, I will not use multithreading because it would be asking you to assimilate too many new ideas at once. You should try it yourself as an exercise at the end of the chapter.

Here is the main code to store images in an NSDictionary (please do not use this way to store images in your app because it will cause memory warning issue).

```
// Code to store the image in the dictionary
- (UIImage *)imageWithName:(NSString *)name {

    if ([self.imageDictionary objectForKey:name]) {
        return [self.imageDictionary objectForKey:name];
    }

    UIImage *image = [[UIImage alloc] initWithContentsOfFile:name];
    [self.imageDictionary setObject:image forKey:name];
    return image;
}
```

Here is the main code to extract the latest image out.

```
// Customize the appearance of table view cells.
- (UITableViewCell *)tableView:(UITableView *)tableView
cellForRowAtIndexPath:(NSIndexPath *)indexPath {
    static NSString *CellIdentifier = @"CellIdentifier";
    ReuseTableViewCell *cell = (ReuseTableViewCell *) [self
                    getCellWithTableView:tableView cellIdentifier:CellIdentifier
                            nibName:@"ReuseTableViewCell"];

    NSString *avatarFile = [NSString stringWithFormat:@"a0"];
    NSString *avatarName = [[NSBundle mainBundle] pathForResource:avatarFile
ofType:@"jpeg"];
    cell.avatar.image = [self imageWithName:avatarName];
    cell.userName.text = [NSString stringWithFormat:@"hi here: %d", indexPath.row];
```

```
        // Configure the cell.
    return cell;
}
```

With the updated code, you can run the benchmark again. As you can see from Table 3–4, you get a much better result. The average running time is now 0.002 and the general performance fps is now nearer 60. You're getting a much faster performance than previously with ReuseTableViewCell.

Table 3–4. *Results from Benchmark After Reusing Images*

Test Number	Preparation Time (Seconds)	General Time (Frames per second)
1	0.002314	54
2	0.002233	59
3	0.002313	55
4	0.002307	49
5	0.002323	60
6	0.002307	55

Perfect! The fps rate now is almost 60, and the preparation time is decent. If your apps can reach to this level, you don't have to worry about scrolling performance anymore; it should be smooth. Generally, this is good performance for a normal, simple UITableViewCell with many subviews inside. It is a good thing because you don't have to do much work from the beginning. If the scrolling performance is still jerky, however, you may need to use a much better but also much more complicated way to get the same performance.

As already stated in Chapter 1 and Chapter 2, you should always be careful to avoid over-optimization. It's not worth the effort to spend too much time optimizing for a small improvement of performance. So, at this point, only if you're still suffering from poor scrolling performance should you move forward to the second example, which is using the UITableViewCell for drawing techniques.

Reducing Preparation Time

Generally, I want to reuse the images by caching them and I want to reduce the initialization process. When the OS needs to render a new cell for the TableView, it will ask for a new cell by calling the following method:

```
- (UITableViewCell *)tableView:(UITableView *)tableView
cellForRowAtIndexPath:(NSIndexPath *)indexPath {
        // Initialize and return the Cell here

}
```

So, if you block it for a long period of time, the UserInterface rendering process will be blocked; it can't do anything or display anything new. This is part of the reason why users will see that the scrolling just stops at one place forever.

To make this process as fast as possible, you can remove logic, delay calculation, and cache data and images that you can reuse them. Another approach is to reuse a cell with default image and data first. You can also use multithreading so when you get the image/data, you can fill in the cell later. From the users' perspective, this approach results in smoother scrolling and images that load quickly.

Second Example

Drawing a custom cell can improve your application's performance when you have many subviews or are using an old device. For iPhone 4 and above, there is a significant performance improvement, so you'll see a big difference with the drawing custom cell technique.

In this example, I will increase the complexity of the cells by adding up to 10 subviews with images and text from a real application. Thus, you can see that in some real applications (like Facebook, the one we are trying to emulate), scrolling performance can be significantly affected by the complicated subviews structure. The app that I benchmark will have a user interface like the one you see in Figure 3–5.

Figure 3–5. *The second example application*

Every cell inside the app will have an avatar, a username, and a post with image, title, and content. It also shows which application made the post at what time. The results for the benchmarks are in Table 3–5.

Table 3–5. *Benchmarks Results After Reusing Images*

Test Number	Preparation Time (Seconds)	General Time (Frames per second)
1	0.004199	44
2	0.004388	52
3	0.004237	47
4	0.004245	54
5	0.004197	51
6	0.004232	43

Table 3–6 shows the benchmark results from running the code again with the custom drawing code.

Table 3–6. *Benchmark Results with Custom Drawing Code*

Test Number	Preparation Time (Seconds)	General Time (Frames per second)
1	0.004652	53
2	0.004764	53
3	0.004568	43
4	0.005015	54
5	0.004743	56
6	0.004743	60

From Tables 3–5 and 3–6, you can see that the use of custom drawing code increases rendering time quite markedly. At this point, with a complicated subview, this performance is good enough so you don't need any more optimization.

For the cell that is not optimized yet, it will be made up by a number of components and subviews. Look at Figure 3–5 to make sure you understand the problem.

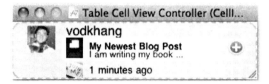

Figure 3–6. *The cell*

The TableViewCell in Figure 3-6 has four images and one subview in a different color. The subview is a general approach that developers use if you want to have a different background color or to a manage view component inside easier. This approach causes performance issue for table view scrolling, so you want to avoid it.

Now, let's go into the source code for the new approach, where I will draw the view myself and there will be no subview anymore. You will see what you need to do to implement this behavior, then I will sum up the advantages and disadvantage of the different techniques. The sample source code comes from the project DrawingCellViewController. Here is the main source code.

For UITableViewController:

```
- (UITableViewCell *)tableView:(UITableView *)tableView
cellForRowAtIndexPath:(NSIndexPath *)indexPath {
    static NSString *CellIdentifier = @"CellIdentifier";
    CustomDrawingTableViewCell *cell = (CustomDrawingTableViewCell *) [self.tableView
dequeueReusableCellWithIdentifier:CellIdentifier];

    if (cell == nil) {
        cell = [[CustomDrawingTableViewCell alloc]
initWithStyle:UITableViewCellStyleDefault reuseIdentifier:CellIdentifier];
    }

    [cell updateMyCell];
    return cell;
}
```

So, as you can see, the main code in the UITableViewController does not change much. The only difference between this and the standard UITableViewCell is how you initialize your cell. For example,

```
[[CustomDrawingTableViewCell alloc] initWithStyle:UITableViewCellStyleDefault
reuseIdentifier:CellIdentifier];
```

compared to

```
[[UITableViewCell alloc] initWithStyle:UITableViewCellStyleDefault
reuseIdentifier:CellIdentifier];
```

within the custom UITableViewCell (i.e. CustomDrawingTableViewCell)

```
- (id)initWithStyle:(UITableViewCellStyle)style reuseIdentifier:(NSString
*)reuseIdentifier {

        if (self = [super initWithStyle:UITableViewCellStyleDefault
reuseIdentifier:reuseIdentifier]) {
```

```
                CGRect subFrame = CGRectMake(0.0, 0.0,
self.contentView.bounds.size.width, self.contentView.bounds.size.height);

                drawingView = [[CustomDrawingView alloc] initWithFrame: subFrame];
                drawingView.autoresizingMask = UIViewAutoresizingFlexibleWidth |
UIViewAutoresizingFlexibleHeight;
                [self.contentView addSubview:drawingView];
        }
        return self;
}
```

And now you get to the most important part: how to draw text, image and control into the view.

```
CustomDrawingView.m
- (void)drawRect:(CGRect)rect {
   self.backgroundColor = [UIColor whiteColor];
   // Drawing code.
   [self.userName drawInRect:CGRectMake(70,0, 95, 21) withFont:userNameFont
lineBreakMode:UILineBreakModeTailTruncation
                   alignment:UIBaselineAdjustmentAlignBaselines];


   // Drawing Image
   [self.avatarImage drawInRect:CGRectMake(20, 5, 36, 34)];

   // Drawing button
   [self.button drawInRect:CGRectMake(50, 5, 36, 34)];
}
```

In short, constructing a custom UITableViewCell in the UITableViewController is the same as before; you just need to dequeue it if it is nil, and then initialize a new object for it. Inside the initialize method, you have to add a subview into the cell content. For the subview, you need to override the drawRect method and then draw the text or image by method drawInRect.

The reason why the drawing code will run much faster than loading from nib files or from creating and adding subview directly is the GPU (Graphic Processing Unit) will run the drawing code. The GPU is quite fast at rendering and displaying the UI; therefore, the drawing code is the fastest way to deal with complicated subviews.

> **NOTE:** One important thing ito remember is to set the background color of CustomDrawingView to white. The default color is black.

What Can You Learn from These Examples?

From the two preceding examples, there are some basic lessons you should always remember.

- Use ReuseIdentifier. It will help speed up performance.

- Try to reduce the work inside the cell preparation process, especially the time and effort to load an image from file IO/network IO. This will display the image in the shortest amount of time.

- If the app has too many subviews and/or a complicated structure, consider drawing it by code. This will allow the GPU to speed up the process.

> **WARNING:** As you can see from the benchmark results, the fps result becomes much better and even closer to the perfect number of 60. However, by using this method, you don't get the advantage of InterfaceBuilder to construct the UI. You always need to calculate the position and the size yourselves and put that information into drawRect. This will quickly cause a headache in terms of maintenance and feature bloat (adding more features into your application). So, be careful with drawRect and with over-optimization.

Other Techniques

I've discussed the important techniques to improve the performance for table view scrolling. There are other small techniques that you usually don't need to use, but I include them here anyway. If you can understand the concept, you can apply the same technique to other cases.

Caching the Height

You need to cache the height of the rows because TableView requests this information whenever it needs to create a new cell. If your cell's height is fixed, you don't need to worry. However, if it's not fixed, you need to make sure your cell calculation is fast enough.

Try something like this:

```
- (CGFloat)tableView:(UITableView *)tableView heightForRowAtIndexPath:(NSIndexPath
*)indexPath {
   return 80;
}
```

And try to avoid something like this:

```
- (CGFloat)tableView:(UITableView *)tableView heightForRowAtIndexPath:(NSIndexPath
*)indexPath {
  for (int i = 0; i < 100; i++) {
```

```
  // find the smallest possible height for the row
}

  return smallestHeight;
}
```

The OS will run the first code snippet a couple of times when it needs to render the cell or when it needs to edit/reorder the cell in the animation process. With a loop inside like this, the OS will need to run a loop that repeats 100 times whenever it needs to know the height of the cell.

Opaque

If possible, make all layers and subviews of the UITableViewCell opaque. When a view is transparent, the iOS will need to render one pixel twice or more because that one pixel belongs to many subviews at the same time. This can be a time-consuming process.

This part can be done easily through code or through InterfaceBuilder. Developers should double-check to see that all the subviews are opaque. Figure 3–7 shows how to set the opaque checkbox for the subview inside the cell.

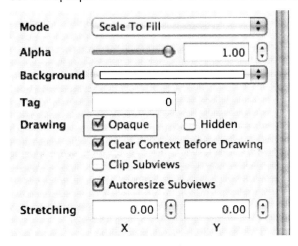

Figure 3–7. *Set opaque for the subviews*

For the custom code, you can also set it by code, as follows:

```
view.opaque = YES;
```

Avoid Graphical Effects

Avoid complicated graphical effects (such as gradients) that are not already in the UIImage. You should check for graphical effects and problems by using the CoreAnimation with some small configuration, as shown in Figures 3–8 and 3–9.

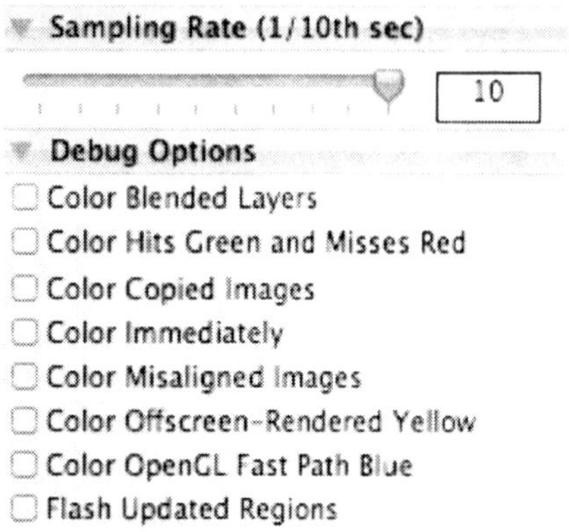

Sampling Rate (1/10th sec)
10
Debug Options
Color Blended Layers
Color Hits Green and Misses Red
Color Copied Images
Color Immediately
Color Misaligned Images
Color Offscreen-Rendered Yellow
Color OpenGL Fast Path Blue
Flash Updated Regions

Figure 3–8. *CoreAnimation options to set up debug options*

iPod
11:06 PM
Hi There
Hi There
Hi There
Hi There
Hi There

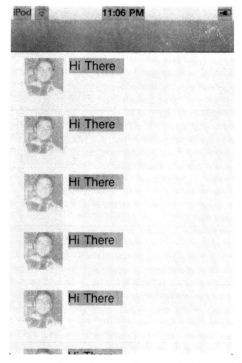

Figure 3–9. CoreAnimation Instrument with color blended

Performance for Editing/Reordering

In the previous sections, I showed you that by drawing directly, you can optimize the performance of your apps significantly. However, the drawing approach also has some serious problems in animation and reordering performance.

When you use subviews, the animation will become faster and UIKit does not have to redraw or change anything during the animation. Therefore, it is usually faster for UIKit if you use subviews and don't draw the view by code. If you draw the view by code in the animation edit or reordering, you then have to draw the view again to fit into the new view. This makes for more work, both in creating and maintaining the code.

This is a tradeoff that you always have to think about when you have performance issue with UITableViewController. My recommendation is to always start with a subview if you are sure that you will not have too many subviews, or you will have to allow users to do some editing/reordering of the cell. This can make the app run slower but still well enough.

Summary

By going through examples with source code, you learned a number of important techniques to improve application performance.

- **Benchmark carefully with NSLog and CoreAnimation**: I let you see a real example of using the Instrument and benchmark tools efficiently to understand the nature of the problem and how much improvement you make after every optimization step.

- **Reuse the Cell properly**: This is the first and most important step. It is easy to implement cell reuse but many applications lack this step. So, if you have any performance problems, make sure to double check this.

- **Cache/reuse the images/data correctly**: Another important step is to reduce the time to load data and do logic processing while returning a cell for displaying.

- **Reduce the total loading and calculating time**: It's not just the I/O process that will slow down and block the UI thread; any kind of data processing can slow this process. Therefore, you should always try to reduce this processing as much as possible.

- **Custom drawing the cell**: To utilize the full computing capacity of the CPU while rendering the table view, you may need to consider using drawing methods directly. This will boost the rendering process a lot and increase the performance measurements; the fps rate becomes almost maximal. You can draw your custom cell by overriding the drawRect method and drawing every UI element yourself with different drawing methods inside each element.

- **Opaque**: This small problem is encountered when developers position their user interface elements into the view. If they don't set each of the views to opaque (i.e. not transparent), the rendering process will need to run through each point twice to redraw the same point.

▓ **Caching the height**: This is another small mistake that developers often make. There are two main methods called every time a cell is requested.

▓ **Avoid graphical effects**: The more graphical effects you have on a cell, the slower the rendering process. Therefore, you should test for this as well. You can definitely use the CoreAnimation to see the rendering effect of each UI element.

▓ **Edit/reordering performance**: Optimizing the performance for scrolling can cause performance problems for editing and reordering because the UIKit and animation framework is optimized to work well with subviews. If you draw the cell yourself, those framework optimizations will become ineffective.

EXERCISES

A. Theory

1. Create a checklist to make sure you follow all the necessary and basic steps to have a good, high performance UITableViewCell.

B. Practice

1. Write a small app using drawRect to see how it behaves under the editing/reordering control.

2. Do the exercise from the "Reusing Images" section. Try it with multithreading technique to load images from file to display.

3. Practice creating a custom UITableViewCell yourself using the following:

InterfaceBuilder

Adding subview code

Using drawing code

## Chapter 4

Increase App Performance Using Image and Data Caching Techniques

In this chapter, you will learn about:

- How network and file IO processing affect app performance.
- Common problems and techniques related to caching algorithms.
- Specific problems in iPhone Caching techniques.
    - What you should cache.
    - When you should cache.
    - How to implement caching.
    - Where you should cache data and images.
- The tradeoff between memory consumption and performance.

For most iPhone apps today, developers usually either load data from their own servers or consume data from third-party services. A minority of apps have data stored in the file system and load it to display to users when necessary. Very few apps do not use any kind of network or file IO processing. Therefore, understanding the impact of these types of processing helps you to figure out problems and solve them easier.

Differences in Performance Between Network, File, and Memory Processing

Let's see how long it takes to load an image from file system to memory and from a given server to memory. Of course, the results will vary depending on how quickly the server processes the request, the speed of the network, and how far the server is from the testing machine. However, I want to demonstrate the important idea that loading an image across the network is much slower than loading it from a file and that loading it from a file is much slower than having the image already in memory. I tested the performance based on loading a 50kb image. Here are the results:

```
File Loading Time:  0.001147
Network Loading Time:  4.160634
```

Loading the image from the file system took 1 millisecond, while loading from network took 4 seconds—a huge difference! The 1 millisecond doesn't seem like much in terms of performance; however, imagine if you needed to load 10-20 images at a time and some of the images were large in size—up to few hundred kbs. The total time for loading all those images would be more than couple of seconds.

How to Identify the Bottleneck

There are two main problems with loading from a file or the network.

- Users have to wait a long time before the app shows the image. This time may increase proportionally with the number of images. If the user interface (UI) needs to load many images while running something like `UITableView`, users will have to wait every time they scroll down to see more information.

- It can block the UI, thus user can't interact with the UI properly. This is also covered in Chapter 6.

Thus, because loading from file/network takes much more time than loading and processing data/images in memory, this loading process is usually your performance bottleneck. If your app has to wait for the data from the network, all other processes must wait as well. So testing for file/network loading should always be the first thing you do when you run into performance issues. As you saw in Chapter 2, you can observe the data loading process with System Activity and File Activity. Figure 4–1 shows the UI of those instruments.

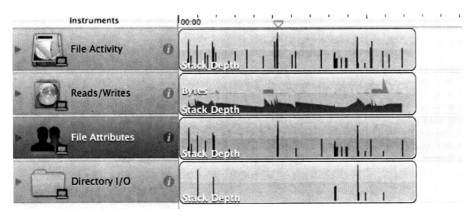

Figure 4–1. File Activity instrument

#	Caller	Function	FD	Path
584	_NS...	close	15	...loper/SDKs/iPhoneSimulator4.0.sdk/System/Library/CoreServices/SystemVersion.plist
585	CPFi...	stat64		/Users/vodkhang/Library/Application Support/iPhone Simulator/4.0.2/Library/AddressBook
586	unix...	stat64		...plication Support/iPhone Simulator/4.0.2/Library/AddressBook/AddressBook.sqlitedb
587	sqlit...	open	15	...plication Support/iPhone Simulator/4.0.2/Library/AddressBook/AddressBook.sqlitedb
588	filln...	fstat64	15	...plication Support/iPhone Simulator/4.0.2/Library/AddressBook/AddressBook.sqlitedb
589	sqlit...	fstat64	15	...plication Support/iPhone Simulator/4.0.2/Library/AddressBook/AddressBook.sqlitedb
590	sqlit...	fstat64	15	...plication Support/iPhone Simulator/4.0.2/Library/AddressBook/AddressBook.sqlitedb
591	sqlit...	fstat64	15	...plication Support/iPhone Simulator/4.0.2/Library/AddressBook/AddressBook.sqlitedb

Figure 4–2. List of results from File Activity

Figure 4–1 shows the file activities including loading and writing file/directory and reading the file attributes. Figure 4–2 shows more details about each activity, which helps you to see what kinds of file activities are running most often.

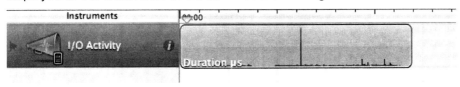

Figure 4–3. *System Usage instrument*

#	Function	Duration µs	In File	In Bytes	Out File	Out Bytes	Thread ID	Stack Depth	Error	Path	Parameters
2701	read	36	6	1.68 KB	0	1.68 KB	775	33		...6EA/JoinMe.app/TableCellViewController.nib	buf=0xabfc00
2709	read	41	6	1.68 KB	0	1.68 KB	775	33		...6EA/JoinMe.app/TableCellViewController.nib	buf=0xa2c600
2717	read	39	6	1.68 KB	0	1.68 KB	775	33		...6EA/JoinMe.app/TableCellViewController.nib	buf=0xa40600
40	read	36	6	1.49 KB	0	1.49 KB	775	24		...FC80C45576EA/JoinMe.app/MainWindow.nib	buf=0xa1e400
43	read	33	6	979 Bytes	0	979 Bytes	775	37		...45576EA/JoinMe.app/RootViewController.nib	buf=0xa1e000
16	read	29	6	891 Bytes	0	891 Bytes	775	13		...-8B19-FC80C45576EA/JoinMe.app/Info.plist	buf=0xa07800
101	read	24	6	722 Bytes	0	722 Bytes	6147	17		...vateFrameworks/WebKit.framework/Info.plist	buf=0xa4be00
98	read	25	6	648 Bytes	0	648 Bytes	6147	16		...Frameworks/Foundation.framework/Info.plist	buf=0xa4b200
11	read	25	4	608 Bytes	0	608 Bytes	775	21		...brary/Frameworks/UIKit.framework/Info.plist	buf=0xa07400
19	read	30	6	512 Bytes	0	512 Bytes	775	10		...76EA/JoinMe.app/SlowPerformanceTableView	buf=0x2fdff5b8
20	read	22	6	32 Bytes	0	32 Bytes	775	12		...76EA/JoinMe.app/SlowPerformanceTableView	buf=0x2fdff098

Figure 4–4. *List of results from System Usage*

Figure 4–3 and 4–4 shows more about System Usage, which is more general and covers more data types. As you can see in Figure 4–4, there are activities with the plist and nib files.

Introduction to Caching

This section will explain many important terms and concepts in caching and will introduce some basic algorithms for caching in general environments such as web and desktop applications. Many of these algorithms can be applied to the iPhone environment; these will be explained in subsequent sections of this chapter.

I will explain the following concepts: cache hit, cache miss, storage cost, retrieval cost, invalidation, replacement policy, and measuring cache. Then I will explain some of the most used caching algorithms: Belady's algorithms, random replacement, first in first out (FIFO), least frequently used (LFU), simple time-based, least recently used (LRU), and adaptive replacement cache (ACR).

What is Caching?

Caching is when you store part of a set of data/images in a nearer level. For example, if the original images come from the network, you would store data/images in your file system so that next time your app won't need to go through the network to get the data/images again. Likewise, if the data/images are already on the file system, you would store it in memory so that your app can calculate or display these data/images immediately when necessary.

Cache Hit

Cache hit happens when your app looks for a specific data/image and it finds it in the cache and loads it directly from there. This is a good thing because it doesn't require loading it from the original source. In other words, it saves time.

The cache hit ratio is usually used to determine if your algorithm is a good or bad one. It is usually combined with how much size you save whenever a cache hit happens. For example, if you decide to store small images with 4kb per image and you have a cache hit around 90%, then you already save 3.6kb. This savings helps you to improve the loading time from both network and file activities. However, if you save big images (200kb per image) and you have a cache hit around 10%, you already save the cost of loading 20kb. Another perspective to consider is how your users feel about the performance: if users know that they will be receiving a big image and are willing to wait for the network, then it's fine to not cache that image often.

Cache Miss

Cache miss happens when your app looks for a specific image/data and it can't find it in the cache and so needs to retrieve it from the original place. This can be a bad thing for your app, for example, when the app is not connected to the Internet. When the app is not connected to the Internet and many cache misses happen, the app may show blank image/data to users. To avoid this, you usually need to cache many images and data when the app is online to show them offline.

Retrieval Cost

Retrieval cost is the cost to load image/data from network/file to the next data level. This can be separated into two cases.

- *Loading from network to file*: As shown in the previous example, this consumes the highest amount of time compared to loading from file and memory. The retrieval cost for the network data is high.

- *Loading from file to memory*: This consumes less time to load from a file to memory so the retrieval cost in this case is low.

Storage Cost

Storage cost is also divided into two cases: storing in file and storing in memory.

- The file system is usually bigger than the memory system; therefore you can store more data/images inside the file system. The iPhone file system can contain up to 8, 16, or 32GB, depending on the device itself. If you use an rss reader to read news and this reader keeps storing all the images from the news, you will get to 8GB quickly. You have to remember that within that 8GB, the user is storing their music, videos, and all other apps' caching. Your app should only use up to few hundred megabytes; otherwise, the user may delete your app soon.

- The memory system in the iPhone 4 device is really limited to storing up to 512MB, and most of that memory is consumed by other background-running apps and the operating system. The maximum memory that an app can use to store its own internal data to process is around 256MB. Old iPhone devices like iPhone 3gs or iPhone 3g can only use up to 64 or 128 MB. Also, don't forget all the nibs and view controllers that you need to display and store when displaying the app. Finally, for the latest iPhone, you can store around 50 1MB images. This is actually not much compared to many of the memory-consuming apps and games in the iPhone App Store.

Cache Invalidation

"There are only two hard problems in Computer Science: cache invalidation and naming things."

— Phil Karlton

As this statement suggests, cache invalidation is a hard problem. When developers cache images/data, it can become out of date quickly. The problem is how to know if images/data are out of date and when to check for the latest data.

For images, if every image is uniquely named by a URL/name, then when that URL/name changes (e.g. user changes his avatar), your application will immediately know that the image is out of date and the application can get the new image.

However, if the URL/name of image doesn't change, you can set a specific period of time after which you get a new image, such as 3-7 days. Happily, most web services will take care of this and will change the URL when the image is actually changed.

For data, it's harder. If you cache the data in your file system (by using a database or plain text; I will explain more about this later in this chapter), then you may never know if your data is out of date. If every time you use the data you have to go to the network to check if there is new data in the server, you lose all the benefits of caching data within your file system.

There are a couple of ways to solve this cache invalidation problem.

- Accept that your data will sometimes be out of date and that you have to use that data to calculate and display to the user. After some specific period of time, the app will check for latest data and replace the whole data with new data.

- Do your best to get data from network as fast as possible.

- Invalidate the cache based on users' requests.

Usually developers use a combination of the first and third approach because it makes more sense. You can only reduce the size of data so much; after that, you can't reduce it any more. The third approach can be done easily with a refresh button, and the app can reload for new data when the app is open or is closed, which can also be done easily.

Replacement Policy

Replacement policy is a strategy (usually implemented by a specific algorithm) to determine which piece of data/image will get deleted if necessary. It can also tell you at what time you should check to delete cache to keep a fresh cache base. There are four main things you should always consider when you pick one replacement policy over other policies.

▓ *Cache hit ratio*: As already explained, this tells you how often your app can find a specific data/image in the cache compared to the number of times the app requests data from cache. The higher this number, the better.

▓ *Latency*: Usually refers to two different types of latency. The first meaning is the time it takes to load data from the cache in case you have a cache hit. The second meaning is the time it takes to load data from the original source in case you have a cache miss. You will have to consider if you want to cache the heaviest items (such as 1MB and above) or if you want to cache smaller items (less than 10KB). The smaller item will give you a higher cache hit ratio, but it may not save bandwidth and time like the heavier item.

▓ *Storage constraint*: This is usually a trade-off with cache hit ratio because you only have limited available space (both memory and file space) in an iPhone, so you have to consider it carefully. Otherwise, you can store as much as you want in order to increase the cache hit ratio.

▓ *Algorithm complexity*: How hard will it be to implement the algorithm to match your favorite policy? In many algorithms, you may need to keep track of a specific file or database to track the usage of each of piece of data/image you use to optimize your cache. This is a big trade-off; you will use more memory, and the app needs to spend CPU and time to execute the algorithm to determine if it should delete a piece of cache. Note that the more complex the algorithm, the more you will need to spend to build, maintain, and fix any bugs inside your own algorithm.

Caching Algorithms

I will cover some very basic and easy-to-implement algorithms like random replacement, first in first out and simple time-based plus more complex algorithms like least recently used and least frequently used.

Belady's Algorithm

This is a theoretical algorithm that states that if a piece of information is not necessary in the future, the app should go ahead and delete it. Why do I say that this is a theoretical algorithm? Because in many real-world cases, you never know if that piece of information will be necessary in the future or not. For example, say the web site changes the image to some new image and the app figures out that it doesn't need to use the old image anymore. Bing! The image gets deleted. Then the web designer changes his mind and replaces back the old image. Now the app needs to reload the old image. Therefore, most of time (but not always), Belady's algorithm is not practical and actually impossible to implement with real code. However, this algorithm is used as a benchmark to compare other algorithms.

Random Replacement

There is not much to tell about this algorithm. You delete cache based on some random access.

Advantage:

▪ It requires almost no effort to implement the algorithm.

Disadvantage:

▪ It may not offer much benefit in terms of cache hit and cache invalidation. The algorithm may mistakenly delete some files that are still necessary while keeping an unused file for a long time.

Implementation:

File:

```
// File Random Replacement

NSFileManager *fileManager = [NSFileManager defaultManager];
NSString *filePath = NSTemporaryDirectory();
NSDirectoryEnumerator *fileNames = [fileManager enumeratorAtPath:filePath];
NSString *firstFileName = @"";
for (NSString *fileName in fileNames) {
    firstFileName = fileName;
    break;
}
[fileManager removeItemAtPath:firstFileName error:nil];
```

Memory: For memory caching, you will usually use a dictionary that binds a unique URL/name to the object. This helps you retrieve the data easily by passing the unique URL/name to the dictionary. In this sample, I use `cacheDictionary` to store the memory data.

```
// cacheDictionary is a dictionary to store a map between a name of image and the
// image itself
NSObject *firstObj = nil;
for (NSObject *obj in [cacheDictionary allKeys]) {
    firstObj = obj;
    break;
}
[cacheDictionary removeObjectForKey:firstObj];
```

First In First Out (FIFO)

In short, this algorithm tells you that the first one come into the cache will be the first one gets deleted.

Advantages:

▪ It's really simple and requires almost no effort to calculate and compare.

■ It can provide a slight benefit if you assume that the older the cached item, the more likely it should be deleted.

Disadvantage:

■ It doesn't take into account which piece of cache get requested most often or has a higher chance to be requested in the future.

Implementation:

File: You need to base it on the creation date of the files. You will need to find the creation date of all files and get the oldest creation date to delete.

```
NSFileManager *fileManager = [NSFileManager defaultManager];
NSString *filePath = NSTemporaryDirectory();
NSDirectoryEnumerator *fileNames = [fileManager enumeratorAtPath:filePath];
NSString *smallestDateFilePath = @"";
for (NSString *fileName in fileNames) {
    NSString *uniquePath = [filePath stringByAppendingPathComponent:fileName];
    NSDictionary* attributes = [fileManager attributesOfItemAtPath:uniquePath
error:nil;
    NSDate *createdDate = [attributes objectForKey:NSFileCreationDate];

    // I will let you find the smallest createdDate yourself as a small exercise
    //  if (createdDate is smallest) {
    //      smallestDateFilePath = uniquePath;
    //  }
}
[fileManager removeItemAtPath:smallestDateFilePath error:nil];
```

Memory: It can be built with a dictionary to keep track of all data/images and an array to keep track the order of the data/image. I use an array cacheOrders to store the list of unique names of images. This array stores data in an ordered manner: the oldest item is at index 0 and the newest item is at the end of the array.

```
// cacheDictionary is a dictionary to store a map between a name of image and the
// image itself
    NSString *firstName = [cacheOrders objectAtIndex:0];
    [cacheDictionary removeObjectForKey:firstName];
    [cacheOrders removeObjectAtIndex:0];
```

Simple Time-Based

This algorithm is based mainly on time. You specify a basic period of time for a cache. After that specific period of time, the app checks how long a cache exists (the age of the cache). If the cache is older than a specific age (for example, 14 days), the cache is automatically deleted.

Advantages:

■ It is really simple—even simpler than FIFO.

■ It doesn't take much time and CPU to calculate the age of every cache.

▪ You don't need to keep track of more information (like the order of cache in FIFO).

Disadvantages:

▪ It usually leads to either deleting too much or too little, which means you may delete more caches than you need to delete. For example, if you only need to delete 10MB of images in file system to have more space, and 20MB of the images are older than a specific data, you may over-delete.

Implementation: Usually used with file system cache rather than memory cache.

File: You need to base it on the creation date of the files. You will need to find the creation date of all files and extract the files that have creation date older than your specified date. Then you delete those files.

```
NSFileManager *fileManager = [NSFileManager defaultManager];
NSString *filePath = NSTemporaryDirectory();
NSDirectoryEnumerator *fileNames = [fileManager enumeratorAtPath:filePath];
NSTimeInterval maximumTimeInterval = 7 * 24 * 3600;  // 7 days caching
for (NSString *fileName in fileNames) {
    NSString *uniquePath = [filePath stringByAppendingPathComponent:fileName];
    NSDictionary* attributes = [fileManager attributesOfItemAtPath:uniquePath
error:nil;
    NSDate *createdDate = [attributes objectForKey:NSFileCreationDate];

    if ([createdDate timeIntervalSinceDate:[NSDate date]] > maximumTimeInterval) {
        [fileManager removeItemAtPath:uniquePath error:nil];
    }
}
```

Next are the more difficult caching algorithms that you probably won't ever need to use. From my own experience, because the file storage can be really big, and you may only need to delete it once per several months, you can just use the simple time-based algorithm. For memory, because the memory is really limited in terms of storage but fast in terms of retrieval, you may need to use FIFO or LFU.

Least Recently Used (LRU)

This algorithm is more complex than the algorithms covered up to this point. Imagine that you have a list of items. Whenever the same item is requested, you put that item at the head of the list. When you need to delete an item, you delete an item from the tail of the list. Table 4–1 displays an example array of four items.

Table 4–1. *The Current State of the List After Every Request*

Step	Current List	New Request Item
1	1, 2, 3, 4	1
2	1, 2, 3, 4	1
3	1, 2, 3, 4	2
4	2, 1, 3, 4	4
5	4, 2, 1, 3	5
6	5, 4, 2, 1	3
7	3, 5, 4, 2	

As you can see in step 5, because a new item comes in (called 5) and I can only store four items inside the list, I have to delete item 3. But in a later step, item 3 is requested, and I don't have enough space to cache it, so I delete item 1.

Advantage:

■ It deletes the cache based on a better policy. The policy is based on the assumption that if a cache hasn't had a request in a long time, it should be deleted.

Disadvantage:

■ It doesn't care much about how often a cache is requested. In this example, if item 1 is requested three or four times in a row and then isn't requested in the next three steps, should you delete it or keep it? I will cover another algorithm that will try to approach this issue later in this chapter

Implementation: It can be implemented both with file and memory. But as mentioned, unless you need to store lots of data (especially images/videos) in file system and frequently need to access/delete them, you will not need to use this algorithm.

Memory: I'm only showing you one way to implement this algorithm so that, but it might not be the best way to do it. However, I hope that you get the main idea.

```
// cacheArrays is an array that stores cached items in an attempt to make the least
//   recently used object to be at the end of the array.
NSString *requestedItem = @"5";
if ([cacheArrays containsObject:requestedItem]) {
    // If the caller requests an existing item, I add that item to the top of the
    //   array
    [cacheArrays removeObject:requestedItem];
    [cacheArrays insertObject:requestedItem atIndex:0];
} else {
    // If the code requests a new item that does not exist, I remove the last item
    // (if  the cacheArrays is full) and add that new item into the top of the array.
    [cacheArrays removeLastObject];
    [cacheArrays insertObject:requestedItem atIndex:0];
}
```

Least Frequently Used (LFU)

This algorithm is a little bit different than the least recently used algorithm. It focuses on how often an item is requested. If an item is requested more often than other items, it should be kept on the cache. Table 4–2 demonstrates the least frequently used algorithm.

Table 4–2. *The Current State of the List After Every Request*

Step	Current List	New Request Item
1	1 (0), 2(0), 3(0), 4(0)	1
2	1 (1), 2, 3, 4	1
3	1 (2), 2, 3, 4	2
4	1 (2), 2 (1), 3, 4	4
5	1 (2), 2 (1), 4 (1), 3	5 (item 5 comes and item 3 will be deleted because it has 0 request)
6	1 (2), 2 (1), 4 (1), 5	3
7	1 (2), 2 (1), 4 (1), 3	

As you can see, with the same initial list and the same list of item requests, these two algorithms generate different results at the end.

Advantage:

- It actually involves the cache hit ratio into the policy to determine if an item should be kept or deleted from cache.

Disadvantage:

- Think about the following scenario: Item 1 is accessed 100 times right at the beginning. However, in the long term, it's no longer accessed. The problem is that the item 1 will still be kept in the cache because no other item has been accessed more than 100 times.

Implementation: It can be implemented both with file and memory. But, as mentioned, unless you need to store lots of data (especially images/videos) in file system and frequently need to access/delete them, you won't need to use this algorithm.

Memory: As a quick exercise, write a small objective-C code to implement the algorithm. Don't look at the hints below and finish the algorithm yourself.

Again, try to do it yourself as an exercise before moving to the next page to see the hints.

> **HINTS**: You should use two dictionaries, one to keep track of the name → object of the cache and the other of the name → count of access. Whenever a new request comes in, you increase the count and check if you need to delete the old cache. If you need to delete the old cache, then you should choose the cache name with the smallest count of access.

Measuring Cache

Let's try some sample exercises to demonstrate some important points. As stated in the replacement policy, you will have to face four main issues when deciding your caching policy: cache hit ratio, latency, storage constraint, and algorithm complexity. The algorithm complexity depends on your capability; if you are a good developer, it may not have much effect on the decision over other factors.

Imagine that you have two file-caching scenarios related to cache hit ratio and retrieval constraint.

- One strategy is that you try to cache 1,000 small items (less than 30KB/item). Your cache hit ratio is 70%.

- Another strategy is that you cache 60 big items (about 500KB/item). Your cache hit ratio is 10%.

As you can see, the storage cost for both strategies is the same: 30MB. The cache hit ratio of the first strategy gives you 21KB while the other strategy gives you 50KB. In terms of retrieval cost, you already saved more bandwidth and loading time with the second strategy.

Table 4–3 offers a quick summary of the terms you just learned.

Table 4–3. *Common Terms and Techniques Used in Caching*

Term	Definition
Cache hit	When a new request comes and a cache is found for that request.
Cache miss	When a new request comes and no cache is found for that request.
Storage cost	How much cache you can store before deleting old cache.
Retrieval cost	How much time or CPU is wasted if a cache is not found (in other words, a cache miss happens).
Invalidation	How you know if a cache is out of date or not synchronized correctly with that piece of data on the server.
Replacement policy	The general policy you apply to store and invalidate cache, based on a number of factors: cache hit ratio, latency, storage constraint, and algorithm complexity.
Measuring cache	How to measure cache in real-world situations.

What You Should Cache

Developers should only care about caching few things: images, videos, data, or sometimes HTML files so they can be loaded quickly in UIWebView. I separate them out into two main types: either you cache the whole file or you cache data and the relationship between that data. For each kind, I will show you some important features that you need to remember when you store those files.

Where Should You Store Your Images?

For files that you don't store inside your bundle, you have to think about where you should store your files. In other words, where should you cache your files so that you can retrieve them and not worry about its lifetime? There are some classic locations where you can store your files: tmp directory, cache directory, documents directory, photo albums (for images/videos only), and application bundle. Each of them has a unique characteristic that you need to know and remember.

Temporary Directory

You can access and store data inside this directory by calling NSTemporaryDirectory();

Advantages:

- It won't get backed up. In fact, it will be deleted by the OS at some indeterminate time. The temporary directory will also be deleted when the user restarts their iOS device.

- You don't need to worry about when to delete these files because it's the responsibility of the OS.

Disadvantages:

- The application may not run when this directory get deleted; therefore, you can't do anything or have any control over the deleting process.

- If you decide later that you want to retrieve files/images from this directory, they most likely won't be there.

Usage:

- If you want to store something quickly and temporarily. For example, you want to store some screenshots of the app to show to users while they are waiting. Because the screenshots are specific to the application state, you don't care too much about storing them for long time.

Cache Directory

You can access and store data inside this directory by using the following code snippet:

```
+ (NSString *)userCacheDirectory {
  NSArray *paths = NSSearchPathForDirectoriesInDomains(NSCachesDirectory,
NSUserDomainMask, YES);
  return [paths objectAtIndex:0];
}
```

Advantages:

- It won't be backed up. This will help the backup process faster when your user syncs the app with his iTunes.

- It won't be deleted automatically by the iOS. You have control over what and when you store your files.

Disadvantages:

- You need to make sure that this directory doesn't grow too much. In other words, you need to make sure it doesn't consume too much of your users' hard drive.

Usage:

- The main directory for you to store your caching files. It's a perfect place to store images/videos/files that you can later display to users.

Documents Directory

You can access and store data inside this directory by using the following code snippet:

```
+ (NSString *)userCacheDirectory {
    NSArray *paths = NSSearchPathForDirectoriesInDomains(NSDocumentDirectory,
NSUserDomainMask, YES);
    return [paths objectAtIndex:0];
}
```

Advantages:

■ It will be backed up. Therefore, you may never lose the files/images you store inside this folder.

■ It won't be deleted by the OS.

Disadvantages:

■ You have to take care of the folder and make sure that it doesn't grow too much. I have seen many apps store data in this folder and it takes hours to back up my whole device. The main time is spent storing images inside the documents directory.

■ If your app allows file sharing through iTunes, any file that you stored here will be shown in iTunes (see Figure 4–5). Therefore, be careful that you don't store files with stupid names that confuse users.

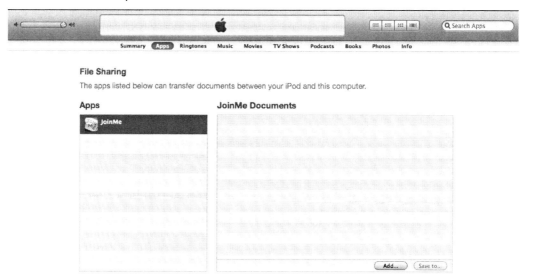

Figure 4–5. *List of documents inside the document folder*

Usage:

- If you want your files to be backed up and not to be lost later, then you should consider using this Document directory. It's a good place to download documents or photos from a web service that users always want to keep with them.

Photo Album

This directory belongs to the OS and will be shared between many applications. You are allowed to store photos and videos inside these albums. The main application for users to see all photos and videos in an iOS device is the Photos app, as shown in Figure 4–6.

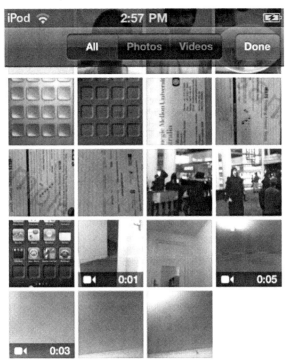

Figure 4–6. *Images and videos inside the Photos app*

To store photos and videos inside the Photos app, use the appropriate code snippet.

For images:

```
UIImageWriteToSavedPhotosAlbum (imageToSave, nil, nil, nil).
```

Note that the imageToSave is an UIImage variable.

For videos:

```
// I assume that this video will be downloaded from the Internet
NSData *videoData = [self getVideoDataFromNetwork];
NSString *moviePath = [NSTemporaryDirectory() stringByAppendingPathComponent:
@"video.mp4"];
UISaveVideoAtPathToSavedPhotosAlbum (moviePath, nil, nil, nil)
```

Advantages:

- It will be backed up.

- It can be shared with other apps.

Disadvantages:

- You have no way to delete these photos and videos after you save them into the photos album.

- After you save the images and videos, they are absolutely out of your application's control.

Usage:

- This is good if you want to share images and videos that your app generates or gets from a web service to other apps so user can view them.

Application Bundle

Images and videos will be bundled to your app when you develop the app and will be installed with the app, as shown in Figure 4–7.

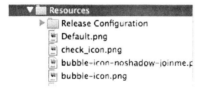

Figure 4–7. *Images bundled with the application*

To get files, you can use the following code snippets:

Images:

```
UIImage *image = [UIImage imageNamed:@"check_icon.png"];
```

Other Files:

```
NSString *path = [[NSBundle mainBundle] bundlePath];
NSString *questionsPath = [path stringByAppendingPathComponent:@"Questions.plist"];
NSArray *questionData = [NSArray arrayWithContentsOfFile:questionsPath];
```

Advantages:

- It goes with your application.

Disadvantages:

- These images/videos are static so you can't change, add, or delete any.

- If you put too many files into the application bundle, it will become too heavy. Users will have to wait too long for it to download and install.

- The only way to change the image or video is to release a new update.

Usage:

- For static images and videos that you know for sure you will use often in your app. These are generally icons or videos that you will show again and again inside your app.

Data Caching

For data caching, you may have to handle structured data; it's up to you to decide how and where to store that data. Here are the main ways to store your data.

Storing in plist/xml/json

You can store your structured data in a simple form with the plist or XML format; this can be visualized easily, as shown in Figure 4–8.

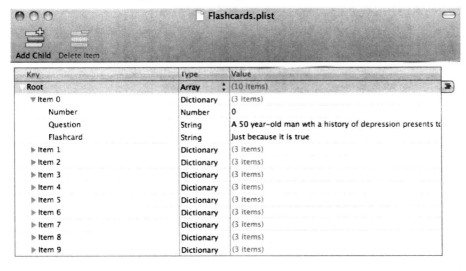

Figure 4–8. *Data can be stored easily and visualized*

You can also see the data in XML format, as shown in Figure 4–9.

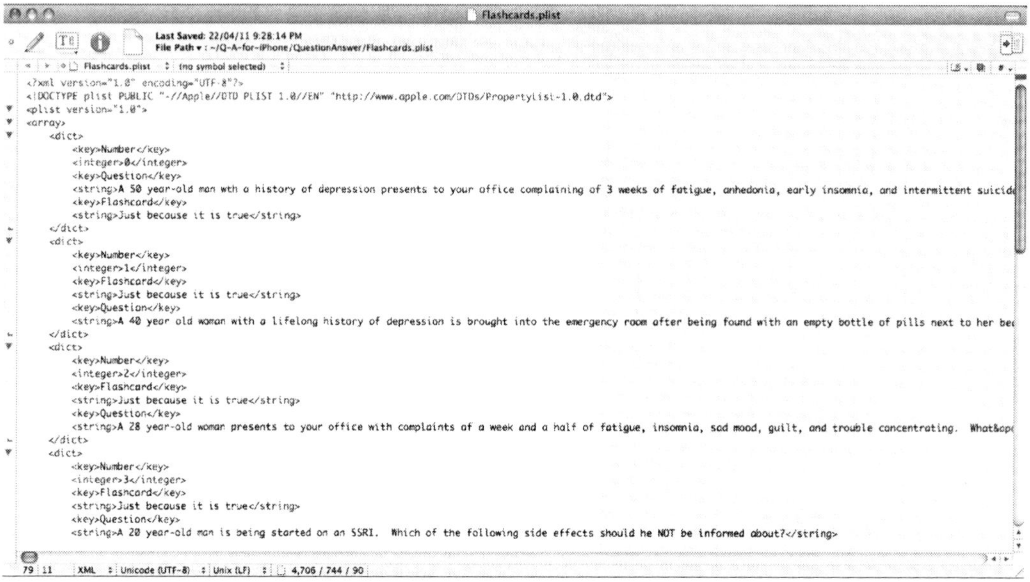

Figure 4–9. *DPlist Data can be viewed and edited in XML format*

You can load and parse the plist file by using the following code:

```
NSString *path = [[NSBundle mainBundle] bundlePath];
NSString *questionsPath = [path stringByAppendingPathComponent:@"Questions.plist"];
NSArray *questionsData = [NSArray arrayWithContentOfFile:questionsPath];
```

Advantages:

- It's easy to visualize and add/edit/change your data.
- It is easy to parse data because all data will be translated to NSArray, NSDictionary, NSString, NSNumber, etc.

Disadvantages:

- When you need to load the plist file, you need to load the whole file, which is very time- and CPU-consuming.
- You can't create a complicated object model with plist.

Usage:

- To create an initial and static data for your application to use.

Storing in CoreData

CoreData is a strong and powerful built-in framework provided by Apple to help developers manage and control their data easily. It creates a layer of object-oriented abstraction over the relational relationship problem between data. You can create your object relational model using drag and drop. Figure 4–10 shows an example of a CoreData model between questions, answers, and their categories.

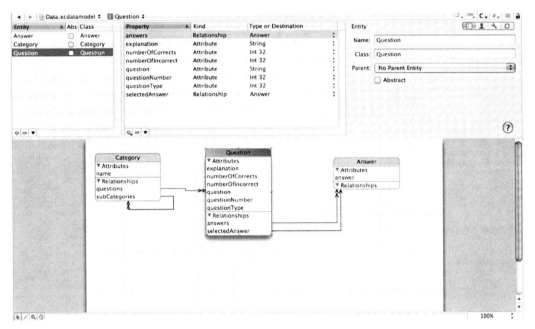

Figure 4–10. *CoreData object relational model*

CoreData will also generate code automatically. Figures 4–11 and 4–12 show you the code that is generated for the object question in Figure 4–10. CoreData will take care of all actions from storing, retrieving, and managing relationship between objects. There are great books on CoreData if you're interested in more information on using it to store data.

```
#import <CoreData/CoreData.h>

@class Answer;

@interface Question :   NSManagedObject
{
}

@property (nonatomic, retain) NSNumber * numberOfIncorrect;
@property (nonatomic, retain) NSNumber * questionNumber;
@property (nonatomic, retain) NSString * question;
@property (nonatomic, retain) NSString * explanation;
@property (nonatomic, retain) NSNumber * questionType;
@property (nonatomic, retain) NSNumber * numberOfCorrects;
@property (nonatomic, retain) NSSet* answers;
@property (nonatomic, retain) Answer * selectedAnswer;

@end


@interface Question (CoreDataGeneratedAccessors)
- (void)addAnswersObject:(Answer *)value;
- (void)removeAnswersObject:(Answer *)value;
- (void)addAnswers:(NSSet *)value;
- (void)removeAnswers:(NSSet *)value;

@end
```

Figure 4–11. *Code generated for the header file of the object*

```
#import "Question.h"

#import "Answer.h"

@implementation Question

@dynamic numberOfIncorrect;
@dynamic questionNumber;
@dynamic question;
@dynamic explanation;
@dynamic questionType;
@dynamic numberOfCorrects;
@dynamic answers;
@dynamic selectedAnswer;

@end
```

Figure 4–12. *Code generated for the implementation file of the object*

Advantages:

- It can help you to create an object-oriented model.

- You don't need to worry about storing, managing, or updating your data with code. CoreData will take care of it.

- It offers better performance than SQLite, actually. From my own experience and testing, CoreData runs faster than SQLite in many cases.

Disadvantages:

- It's not easy to visualize your data. You do not have a UI to manage the initial data.

- Sometimes you don't need to have a separate object model.

Usage:

- It's a powerful tool to manage your dynamic data. You should use this to cache your data in most cases.

Storing in SQLite

CoreData uses SQLite as its backend storage. However, CoreData can be implemented with other SQL database frameworks, so it's hard to say if CoreData is more powerful than SQLite. Using SQLite is just like using other SQL database frameworks, with a few minor changes here and there.

Advantages:

- It's a relational database. If you're familiar with relational databases, you should have no problem.

Disadvantages:

- It's hard to visualize all the data inside your SQLite database.

■ You may need to write more SQL to implement all features you need.

Usage:

■ You want to have a portable database between different platforms: iPhone, Blackberry, Android, and Windows Phone. Because SQLite is written purely in C. CoreData has a tight relationship with Cocoa and Cocoa Touch Framework.

When Should You Check and Delete Cache?

In general, I can't provide any techniques or offer any advice on when you should check the cache. This decision depends on the environment in which you are working; in other words, an iOS environment is different than a web environment. In a web server, you can run a check method in a loop to see if any cache is outdated and delete it. In an iOS environment, this is time- and CPU-consuming.

When you should check cache contents and delete them depends much on the selected algorithm that you use to cache them. For example, if you mainly use FIFO, LRU, or LFU, you may need to wait until a new request comes in. Or you can check if the cache is full; if it's full, you can delete the old cache based on your algorithm. This approach is usually used for memory caching where you need more precise algorithm and have a strict storage constraint.

For file caching, you will usually choose a simple time-based algorithm. File caching does not have a strict limited storage capacity like memory does. With a simple time-based algorithm, you don't need to worry too much about every single file because you may delete a set of files at the same time.

If you expect that you won't need much time to do calculations or when retrieving file information to check for the attributes of the cache, you may not to worry about when you check and delete them at all. Again, here is an important lesson: don't over-optimize. If you think your approach can cause a bottleneck, you can try to benchmark it. It the current approach runs well, it doesn't matter if your app checks and deletes cache right at the beginning, at the end, or the first time the app requests and stores some new cache.

Here are some main approaches:

■ *When the app starts*: It may slow down the start process a little bit, but if you use multithreading it won't be any problem.

■ *When the app closes*: Be careful if you use multithreading—the app may end before you finish the checking and deleting cache process. If you don't use multithreading, the time for the app to close takes longer.

■ *When you store a new piece of cache*: It may be slow the first time you request that piece of cache, but it will be faster on subsequent tries. I recommend not using multithreading in this case because you may delete a file that another thread is reading.

Memory Caching

Here are some specific details about how to do memory caching and the specific problems you may encounter when you do memory caching in iOS environment.

Because there is a strict storage constraint in memory, you can't and shouldn't cache too many images here. If you do, the iOS run-time environment will keep giving you memory warnings until your app is forced to close.

Some people are scared of storing in memory because of the limited memory environment. Not to worry: you do have memory to use; you just need to learn how to utilize and maximize your memory capability to improve your performance. If you're concerned, don't forget to double check if you are using too little or too much memory via the instruments you learned about in Chapter 2, as shown in Figure 4–13.

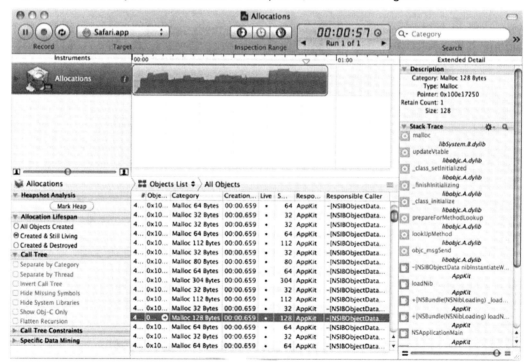

Figure 4–13. *Memory allocations and usage*

If you see that you are using too little memory compared to the capability of the memory environment, don't hesitate to use more. The more you can cache data and images in memory, the better performance your app will get. However, if you are using too much memory, be aware that your app may get memory warning or to be forced to close.

Global Access vs. Strict Access

For memory caching, you may need to think about whether you want this caching to be available to any class and methods within your application or only strictly to some classes and methods. If this is global access, anybody can change the cache whenever they want. However, if you keep the caching data so private and hard to access, the cache becomes useless because some classes or methods may need the data and will just request it from the server again. The actual software engineering term is *data encapsulation*, which means you should protect your data and only share it with the classes/methods that need it.

Global Access:

You may need to use static to define global object.

```
#import <UIKit/UIKit.h>

@interface MyObject {
}

static NSMutableDictionary *imagesCaching;

@end
```

Strict Access:

```
#import <UIKit/UIKit.h>

@interface RootViewController : UITableViewController {
 @private
    NSMutableDictionary *imageCaches;
}
- (void)cacheImage:(UIImage *)image withName:(NSString *)uniqueURL;
- (void)getCacheImageWithName:(NSString *)uniqueURL;
@end


#import "RootViewController.h"
@implementation RootViewController
- (void)cacheImage:(UIImage *)image withName:(NSString *)uniqueURL {
    // main code goes here
}
- (void)getCacheImageWithName:(NSString *)uniqueURL {
    // main code goes here
}
@end
```

Preload vs. Just In Time

Preloading is when you load the image before you actually need it. The good thing about this is that it saves time when you actually need to display the file/image. The difficult part is that you may need to guess if you need to preload the images. Here's a simple case where you may need to preload images for faster performance (Figure 4–14).

Figure 4-14. *Preloaded image for paging view*

As Figure 4-14 shows, for a view like PageView where user wants to have a smooth scrolling experience, preloading images into cache is the best way to keep the scrolling smooth. Otherwise, the user either has to wait after scrolling to the view (for multithreading or loading the image after stopping in the view) or they have a stuck scrolling experience

Another way to load the images into cache is called just in time. This saves the actual bandwidth or CPU-loading process until you are sure that you really need that data/images. The bad part about this is that it may slow down and keep your users waiting for the data. This approach is good if you need really big data/images that will consume a lot of memory and your users are willing to wait for a couple of seconds.

Figure 4-15. *Big image view*

Figure 4–15 is an example where the user knows that he may need to wait for a couple of seconds in order to get the big image view. If you load from file to memory to display, the loading time will be quite fast; therefore you may not need to worry about preloading the images into memory. Another problem is if the image is big, preloading it into memory will cost your app a huge amount of memory.

Summary

Based on my tests, you can see that the performance from network is much slower than performance from file and the performance from file is much slower than performance from memory. You should always try to identify the bottleneck with instrument tools before spending too much of your time to optimize some parts. In other words, please avoid over-optimization.

You learned about basic topics in caching such as cache hit, cache miss, storage cost, retrieval cost, replacement policy, and several well-known algorithms. Some of them are really basic but not efficient; some of them can be efficient but cost time and effort to implement. You will probably use the random replacement algorithm for simplicity and LRU or LFU for complex cases.

You also learned about all the possible ways to store cache and the sceanrios in which to use each approach. You can store your data in the temporary folder, the cache folder, or document folder based on the specific purpose of your requirement. You may also choose to use the photos album so you can easily share it with other applications. You also learned the techniques to store/cache data inside your app and the different results, advantages, and disadvantages.

Lastly, you learned about memory caching. Should you allow global access or strict access to your memory cache data? Should you preload data into memory or load them just in time? Both offer benefits and drawbacks that you will need to consider carefully before making your decision.

EXERCISES

1. Implement the LFU caching algorithm yourself. If you have any problems, you can look at my hints.

2. Benchmark two different algorithms (FIFO and LRU) by using appropriate instruments.

3. Write a simple program to get a plist file and parse it to a corresponding structured data.

4. Take the plist file (Questions.plist) attached inside the program and convert it into data inside CoreData.

## Chapter 5

Tune Your App Using Algorithms and Data Structures

In this chapter, you will learn about:

- How bad algorithms and data structure can affect your app's performance.

- Theoretical issues of measuring your algorithms.

- Practical measurement of your app's performance.

- Main data structures and algorithms:

    - iPhone data structures: NSSet, NSArray, and NSDictionary.

    - Other important data structures and their implementations.

    - Other algorithms and problem-solving approaches:

        - Recursion

        - SAX vs. DOM in XML parsing

You may hear that in mobile phone development you don't need to worry about algorithms and data structure due to the computing power of the server side. However, as mentioned with regards to caching issues in the previous chapter, especially when your phone is offline, you should store your data locally and compute it within the phone environment. Here is the issue: your phone environment is not as powerful as your server environment. In other words, you don't have the power of cloud computing or a data center.

First Example

This first example will show you how a bad algorithm can affect your program when it runs in the strict mobile phone environment.

My sample code is simple:

- In the first benchmark, the example contains two arrays, each of which contains 1,000 elements. The first and second arrays are the same in terms of the number of elements. I loop through two arrays to check how many common elements are contained between the two arrays.

- In the second benchmark, the example contains two sets, each of which contains 1,000 elements. I use a special method inside the NSSet API to get the set of common elements between the two original sets.

Then, I benchmark each of them based on a simulator, a new device (iPhone 4 with iOS4), and an old device (iPhone 3G with iOS3). The results are shown in Table 5–1.

Table 5–1. *Benchmark Test Results Between Different Data Structures and Algorithms*

Environment	First Benchmark with Arrays	Second Benchmark with Sets
Simulator	0.099	0.001
New Device	0.9	0.0084
Old Device	5.44	0.05

Table 5–1 shows that the second benchmark is 100 times faster than the first benchmark. Considering that 1,000 items is not practical when you deal with real applications, 5.44 seconds may not be much for new devices. However, remember that there are many old devices with less power out there, and their owners may not update these devices any time soon. In that light, 5.44 seconds is actually a significant delay when running in those old devices.

What follows is a look at the initial source code and few explanations before I move on to explain some concepts in-depth.

The purpose of Listings 5–1 and 5–2 is to count how many objects inside the first array/set also belong to the second array/set. Listing 5–1 solves the problem by using an array and loop while Listing 5–2 solves the problem by using a set.

Listing 5–1. *First Benchmark Using an Array and Loop*

```
// [self defaultData] returns an array with 1000 thousands different NSObjects
NSArray *myFirstArray = [NSArray arrayWithArray:[self defaultData]];
NSArray *mySecondArray = [NSArray arrayWithArray:[self defaulData]];

NSDate *date1 = [NSDate date];
```

```
    int i = 0;
    for (NSObject *obj in myFirstArray) {
        for (NSObject *secondObj in mySecondArray) {
            if ([secondObj isEqual:obj]) {
                i++;
                break;
            }
        }
    }

    NSDate *date2 = [NSDate date];
    NSLog(@"time: %f", [date2 timeIntervalSinceDate:date1]);
    NSLog(@"i: %d", i);
```

Listing 5–2. *Second Benchmark Using a Set*

```
- (void)secondBenchmark {
    NSArray *defaultArray = [self defaultData];
    NSMutableSet *myFirstSet = [NSMutableSet setWithArray:defaultArray];
    NSMutableSet *mySecondSet = [NSMutableSet setWithArray:defaultArray];

    NSDate *date1 = [NSDate date];

    [myFirstSet intersectSet:mySecondSet];

    NSDate *date2 = [NSDate date];
    NSLog(@"time: %f", [date2 timeIntervalSinceDate:date1]);
    NSLog(@"count: %d", [myFirstSet count]);
}
```

For the first benchmark, I put 1,000 elements into each array and then looped through the two arrays to find if any two items are the same. To avoid a duplicate count, after the program finds the item in the second array, the program stops looping over the second array.

The second approach is much simpler; with the use of NSSet, you only need to store all elements inside the NSSet and call the correct method to do the job for you. The intersect method will find same items inside two sets and put them into the variable myFirstSet.

As you can see, a wrong approach can be 100 times slower than a correct approach. Moreover, the correct approach may save you a few hours of coding when trying to reuse all the necessary data structures and algorithms. Therefore, it's a good idea to choose the correct approach the first time.

Theoretical Issues of Measuring Algorithmic Performance

I've shown you one way to measure the algorithm's performance using NSLog and NSDate in Listings 5–1 and 5–2. However, in computer science, people don't use NSLog or the instruments tool to talk about how fast an algorithm is compared to other algorithms. Computer science requires exact data and standards to make sure that some algorithms are actually better than others.

People usually use Big-O notation to describe how an algorithm scales (performs) in the worst case scenario. (There are other terms and definitions used in computer science that I will not cover here.) For example, if you have an algorithm with the performance O(N), then that algorithm when working on an array of 25 elements will take 25 steps, compared to 5 steps for an array with 5 elements. So, it takes 5 times longer for the 25-element array to finish the task.

How to Measure Big-O

To determine the Big-O of an algorithm, you need to look at how the size of the input affects the time it takes the algorithm to execute. Another way to accomplish this is to logically think through the algorithm execution. Listing 5–3 should help you understand this concept.

Listing 5–3. *How to Measure Big-O*

```
int myFirstCount = 0;
int mySecondCount = 0;
// Outer Loop
for (int i = 0; i < [myFirstArray count]; i++) {
    // Inner Loop
    for (int i = 0; i < [mySecondArray count]; i++) {
        myFirstCount++;
        mySecondCount++;
    }
    NSLog(@"my first Count: %d", myFirstCount++);
    NSLog(@"my second Count: %d", mySecondCount++);
}
```

For the purposes of illustration, Listing 5–3 contains duplicate code of two variables, myFirstCount and mySecondCount, which do exactly the same thing. I will explain them further later.

So, looking through each line of code, you can see that the two main computation logics is myFirstCount++; and mySecondCount++; . There are other computing logics like NSLog(@"my first Count: %d", myFirstCount); and NSLog(@"my second Count: %d", mySecondCount);.

In this part, m and n are the number of elements in myFirstArray and mySecondArray respectively. Programmatically, after the outer loop, myFirstCount and mySecondCount each has the value of (m * n + m). The sum of them will have the value of 2 * m * n + 2 * m.

The following explanation will give you the details of why the total result is 2 * m * n + 2 * m. This helps you do performance analysis yourself without using the actual counting code.

The outer loop (the loop that runs over myFirstArray) runs m times. Because the outer loop runs m times, every computation logic inside the outer loop runs m times as well.

So the number of computation of the outer loop is m * (the number of computation inside the outer loop).

To calculate the number of computation inside the outer loop, I consider the inner loop and the two NSLog lines. For each cycle of the loop, the inner loop and two NSLog lines run once. So, the number of computation of the outer loop is m * (the number of computation of the inner loop + 2). (*)

Then, I let n to be the number of elements in mySecondArray. Similarly to the previous situation, the inner loop runs n times, and every computation logic inside the inner loop runs n times. There are only two computation logics inside the inner loop, myFirstCount++ and mySecondCount++. Therefore, the number of computation logic inside the inner loop is 2*n. Place this result into the (*) equation and you have m * (2 * n + 2) = 2 * m * n + 2 * m.

Therefore, the total calculation is 2 * m * n + 2 * m.

To make the calculation simple, I will let m = n. It can be rewritten as 2 * n * n + 2 * n by replacing m with n. It can be further simplified as $2n^2 + 2n$. The next step is to keep the most significant term (or the fastest growing term) in the formula, so you have only $2n^2$ left. The last step is to remove all constants in the formula, so you have n^2 left, which you can write in the theoretical format as $O(n^2)$.

> **NOTE:** You can see why I put duplicate code into Listing 5–3; it demonstrates that the final result doesn't depend much on any constants. Using either n^2 or $2n^2$ doesn't make any difference.

Each of the operations has its own growth rate. Here's an example of the growth rate of operations: $\log(n)$, n, n^2.

For n – 1, you have $\log(1) = 0$, n = 1, and $n^2 = 1$.

For n = 10, you have $\log(10)=1$, n=10, and $n^2=100$. You can see that by increasing n by 9 units, the $\log(n)$ only increases 1 unit, n increases 9 units, and n^2 increases 99 units.

For n = 100, you have $\log(100)=2$, n=100 and $n^2=10,000$. You can see that by increasing n by 9 units, the $\log(n)$ only increases 1 unit, n increases 9 units, and n^2 increases 99 units.

Thus by increasing the same number of units, different operations grow differently. Figure 5–1 shows how fast each operation ($\log(n)$, n, n2 and n3) grows when you increase n.

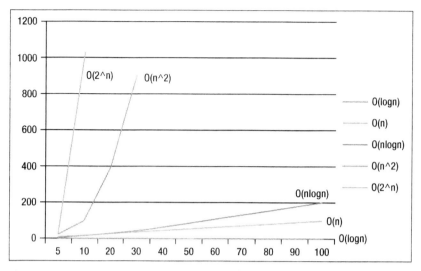

Figure 5–1. *Results of each Big-O notation when the input (variable n) increases*

Implementation Details

The Big-O notation doesn't mention anything about implementation details; it neither tells you how much memory you need to embody an algorithm nor how difficult it will be to implement such an algorithm into your system. It also doesn't tell you which algorithms may be better in a small scale input but repeated many times. For example, in a small scale, an insertion sort will be faster than a quick sort; when repeated 100 times, the total performance of insertion sort will beat the quick sort. Therefore, Big-O notation gives you a general understanding about algorithms, which you can use to quickly compare different algorithms and approaches.

> **NOTE:** There are other notations in the family of notations to describe average and best cases performance. These notations indicate how good each algorithm is when you take individual circumstances into consideration.

Big-O of Famous Algorithms

To give you a better understanding of Big-O, Table 5–2 lists famous algorithms and their corresponding Big-O notation so that you can see how these algorithms will behave theoretically.

Table 5–2. *General Performance Analysis for Different Algorithms*

Algorithms	Description	Big-O Notation
Bubble sort	A simple algorithm to loop over the array and exchange the items when they aren't in a correct order.	O(n)
Merge sort	An algorithm to separate the array into smaller parts and then sort those smaller parts.	O(n * log(n))
Quick sort	This is the quickest algorithm and it uses pivot and sorting techniques.	O(n * log(n))
Linear search	This loops over the whole array/collection to search for an item.	O(n)
Binary search	This searches by dividing the collections into subcollections and then searches inside the correct subcollections.	O(logn)

You may get confused about the order in which you should understand the Big-O notation. The order is like this: $O(\log(n)) < O(n) < O(n * \log(n)) < O(n^2)$.

If you take a look at Table 5–2, this means that:

- Bubble sort is slower than merge sort and quick sort.

- Linear search is slower than binary search.

Thus, because merge sort and quick sort run faster than bubble sort, you should choose these sorting algorithms over bubble sort in most cases.

Practical Measurement

In practical use, you will need to combine some theory about Big-O with the instruments and analysis tools covered in Chapter 2. Here's a quick review of the important tools for measuring the performance of your algorithms and data structure: CPU Sampler and Time Profiler.

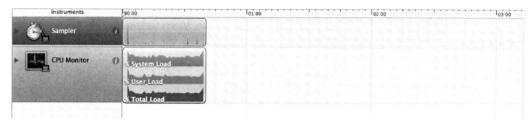

Figure 5–2. *Results of running CPU Sampler over the program*

Running Count		Symbol Name
3314	57.9%	▶main FlyJive
1347	23.5%	▶-[LocationManager fetchDataWithUrl:] FlyJive
333	5.8%	▶-[PeopleManager fetchData] FlyJive
253	4.4%	▶-[LocationManager changeStatus:forLocation:] FlyJive
223	3.9%	▶-[FlyJiveAppDelegate tabBarController:didSelectViewController:] FlyJive
223	3.9%	▶-[MBProgressHUD showUsingAnimation:] FlyJive
9	0.1%	▶+[UIUtilities getCellWithTableView:cellIdentifier:nibName:] FlyJive
4	0.0%	▶+[AsynchronousDataFetcher cacheForURL:] FlyJive
2	0.0%	▶-[FlyJiveAppDelegate application:didFinishLaunchingWithOptions:] FlyJive
2	0.0%	▶-[UIImageView(Network) dataFetcherFinished:] FlyJive
1	0.0%	▶-[FlyJiveAppDelegate applicationDidBecomeActive:] FlyJive
1	0.0%	▶-[LocationManager getLocationWithDelegate:] FlyJive
1	0.0%	▶-[SBJsonParser scanNumber:] FlyJive
1	0.0%	▶-[MBProgressHUD fillRoundedRect:inContext:] FlyJive
1	0.0%	▶-[LocationsViewController viewDidLoad] FlyJive

Figure 5–3. *Detailed results of each method and function inside the program*

Figure 5–2 shows the usage of CPU Sampler showing system load, user load, and total load when the program is running. Figure 5–3 provides more details about each method inside the program, such as how often each method is called and how long it takes for a method to finish.

Figure 5–4. *The Time Profiler instrument*

Running Time		Symbol Name
392.0ms	68.7%	▶main JoinMe
23.0ms	4.0%	▶-[RootViewController showImagePicker] JoinMe
16.0ms	2.8%	▶+[CKImageCacher saveImage:withPath:uniqueUrl:imageFormat:] JoinMe
14.0ms	2.4%	▶-[CKEventCreatingViewController sendSMSOrEmail] JoinMe
13.0ms	2.2%	▶+[ViewControllerHelper loadViewWithNibName:owner:class:] JoinMe
11.0ms	1.9%	▶-[FBDialog init] JoinMe
10.0ms	1.7%	▶-[CKCommentsViewController viewDidLoad] JoinMe

Figure 5–5. *Detailed results of the Time Profiler*

The Time Profiler (Figure 5–4) focuses more on the running time of your program. Figure 5–5 shows the detailed results of the time perspective.

You should use the instruments to figure out which method you actually need to optimize. All methods may run slowly or need optimizing but you should only focus on methods that run frequently through your program's life cycle. You have limited time and resources to optimize the algorithms and data structure for that method.

Data Structure and Algorithms

Cocoa Touch framework of iOS environment gives you three main data structures for most usages: NSSet, NSArray, and NSDictionary. Each of them has benefits and best usage scenarios. I will discuss each of these main data structures for iPhone, then I will walk you through some other important data structures via code and samples so you can build your own in case you need a better performance data structure: linked list, binary tree, stack, queue, and graph.

When discussing data structures, you can't separate the algorithms used inside the data structure out to a separate part. For example, there is no use in talking about NSDictionary and hash table without knowing what a hash function does. Similarly, it's hard to understand about a balanced binary tree without understanding binary search. Therefore, I will discuss them in parallel; I will talk about data structures and what algorithms they use to speed up their performance. In the last sections, I talk separately about common algorithms shared between data structures.

Cocoa Touch Data Structures

Actually, you will have NSMutableArray and NSArray, NSMutableSet and NSSet, NSMutableDictionary and NSDictionary. The difference between the NSMutable kind of classes and NS kind of classes is that you can change the content of NSMutable classes but you can't change the content of NS classes. The advantage of the latter is to protect the data and make sure that any code that can touch the data can't change its content. Because you can't modify NSArray, I will use cases of NSMutableArray in my examples.

When discussing data structures, I will talk about their performance in terms of these main issues: insert, delete, search, access, and sort. I use the Big-O notation to give you the idea of how fast each data structure performs under each insertion, deletion, search, or sort.

NSMutableArray

An array is the simplest form of data structure. So, understanding how an array works when you retrieve, insert, update, or delete data from it will help you improve your app's performance.

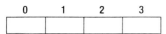

Figure 5–6. *Array illustration*

An array is a collection of individual items put into a block, like in Figure 5–6, where each block is numbered from 0 to the length of the array. NSArray stores data in an order and so won't let you insert data just anywhere. NSArray also allows you to store duplicate data in the array.

Insert/Delete:

 ■ If you insert/delete into the end of the array, it's quite fast: O(1).

 ■ If you insert into the middle or the beginning of the array, all data has to be shifted to the right, as in Figure 5–7: O(n).

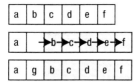

Figure 5–7. *Inserting an item into the second position of the array*

Search:

 ■ Every time you search for an element, you need to loop over the whole array: O(n). The process is shown in Figure 5–8. A similar problem with searching inside an array is determining if that array contains a particular element .

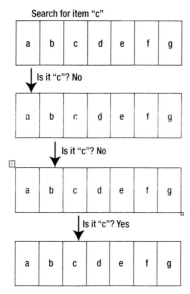

Figure 5–8. *Searching for a specific item inside the array*

Access:

   ■   You can access to any index inside the array really quickly: O(1).

Sort:

   ■   Generally, sorting in an array is implemented by merge sort or quick sort. The sort performance for NSMutableArray sort should be O(n * log(n)).

Table 5–3 covers common methods and APIs for NSMutableArray.

Table 5–3. *Common Methods and APIs of NSMutableArray*

Task	Common Methods/APIs
Insert	- (void)addObject:(id)anObject
	- (void)addObjectsFromArray:(NSArray *)otherArray
	- (void)insertObject:(id)anObject atIndex:(NSUInteger)index
Delete	- (void)removeObject:(id)anObject
	- (void)removeObjectAtIndex:(NSUInteger)index
	- (void)removeObjectsInArray:(NSArray *)otherArray
Replace	- (void)replaceObjectAtIndex:(NSUInteger)index withObject:(id)anObject
	- (void)replaceObjectsAtIndexes:(NSIndexSet *)indexes withObjects:(NSArray *)objects
Search	- (void)filterUsingPredicate:(NSPredicate *)predicate
	- (BOOL)containsObject:(id)anObject
	- (NSUInteger)indexOfObject:(id)anObject
Access	- (id)objectAtIndex:(NSUInteger)index
	- (id)lastObject
Sort	- (void)sortUsingComparator:(NSComparator)cmptr
	- (void)sortUsingFunction:(NSInteger (*)(id, id, void *)) compare context:(void *)context
	- (void)sortUsingSelector:(SEL)comparator

Hashing

Hashing is an important technique in computer science and software engineering. It's used to improve the performance of storage collections. In iPhone apps, hashing is implemented inside NSSet and NSDictionary. To fully understand why NSSet and NSDictionary run so fast when searching for items, you need to understand hashing first.

The general task of a hashing function is to make sure that it creates a unique hash value for each distinct item. And the same item should always return the same hash value.

For example, @"khang" and @"vo" (my names) are two different strings; therefore, the hash functions should try to create a different value for each string. A real hashing algorithm is complicated and requires lots of optimization, so I will use an easy hash calculation as an example. With a string, I can use the integer value of each character in the alphabet table and the position of the character to compute the hash value of the string (Figure 5–9).

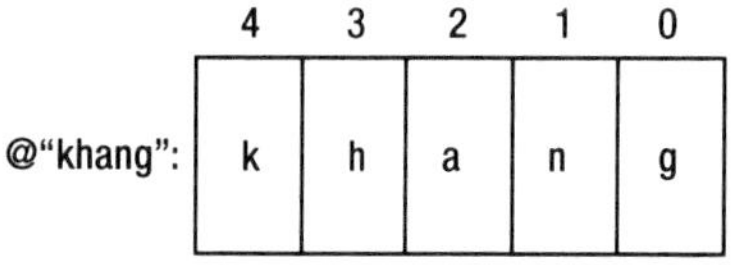

Figure 5–9. *Positions of all characters inside the string*

=> @"khang" = 11 * 10 ^ 4 + 8 * 10 ^ 3 + 0 * 10 ^ 2 + 14 * 10 ^ 1 + 7 = 110,000 + 8,000 + 0 + 140 + 7 = 118147

 Do a similar job for "vo" and you will get the hash value of 22 * 10^1 + 15 = 235.

Using this hash function, you can see that you created two unique hash values of two distinct items. The purpose of the hash function is to generate a unique value for a specific piece of data. Later, I will examine the benefits of having this unique representation of data.

isEqual and Hash Methods in Objective-C

In objective-C, as in other object-oriented programming languages, every object has two important methods: `isEqual:` and `hash`. Hash was just discussed so you should have a clear picture of what the `hash` function does. I will discuss how you should implement/override the `hash` method in objective-C after discussing the `isEqual` method.

isEqual

In most object-oriented programming languages, when people talk about the equality of two objects, they mean one of two things: the exact object in memory, and semantic equality (equality of meaning). By default for a single object, these two things are the same. The first equality is talking about if variables hold the same object in the memory, checked by obj1 == obj2. However, for the latter, the equality of two objects is checked by the method [object1 isEqual:object2]; so if the method returns YES, then the two objects are equal, which is different than checking the memory reference.

To make it clear, here is a class MyItem that overrides the isEqual: method, as follows:

```
MyItem.h
@interface MyItem : NSObject {
 @private
   NSString *identifier;
}

@property (nonatomic,  copy) NSString *identifier;

- (id)initWithIdentifier:(NSString *)anIdentifier;

@end

MyItem.m
@implementation MyItem
@synthesize identifier;

- (id)initWithIdentifier:(NSString *)anIdentifier {
   if (self = [super init]) {
       self.identifier = anIdentifier;
   }
   return self;
}

- (BOOL)isEqual:(id)object {

   // By default, if two variables point to the same object in memory, it should always be
   //  equal
   if (object == self) {
      return YES;
   }

   if (![object isKindOfClass:[MyItem class]]) {
       return NO;
   }

   MyItem *myItem = (MyItem *)object;
   return [myItem.identifier isEqual:self.identifier];
}

- (NSUInteger)hash {
   return [self.identifier hash];
}

@end
```

For this class, you can easily create a mock object that is equal to a specific object by giving them the same identifier. For example, if the first object is created by MyItem *item1 = [[MyItem alloc] initWithIdentifier:@"1"]; and another object is created by MyItem *item2= [[MyItem alloc] initWithIdentifier:@"1"]; then

[item1 isEqual:item2] returns YES while item1 == item2 returns NO;

Hash Method

As mentioned, two objects that are equal must have the same hash value. Therefore, people usually use the overridden method of the `isEqual` method to write the hash method. If your `isEqual` method is determined by a variable `identifier`, your hash should be something like that in Listing 5–4.

Listing 5–4. *Hash Method*

```
- (NSUInteger)hash {
    int hash = 0;
    hash = 37 * [self.identifier hash];
    return hash:[self.identifier1 hash];

}
```

The number 37 was picked randomly in this case, but whatever number you choose must be a prime integer. Therefore, if you don't have a big performance issue, you can pick the same number or any prime integer without any issue.

> **NOTE:** In Listing 5–4, I wanted to demonstrate how to write a hash algorithm yourself so I calculated a new hash value based on the string hash value. In a simple case like this, you can just return `[self.identifier hash];` directly.

NSMutableSet

NSSet is an Apple implementation for an abstract concept, set. A set is an unordered collection that contains no duplicate elements. In other words, NSSet contains no pair of elements e1 and e2 such that `[e1 isEqual:e2]; return YES.`

Based on the unique characteristics of a set, people usually implement a set based on a hashing algorithm. The hashing algorithm will make it really easy for a set to find any elements inside.

Now, imagine that you have a set like that in Figure 5–10. Your set has the capacity to contain seven elements.

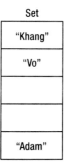

Figure 5–10. *Finding an item inside a set using the hash method*

A new item, called "vo" arrives and you want to add it into the set. Because your set can't contain duplicate elements, the first task is to see if your set contains the item "vo" already. As shown in Figure 5–8, if you want to do this with an array, you have to loop over that array to check for equality. However, with a set, it's simpler.

First step: Hashing

@"vo" → 118147 mod 13 = 1 (I get mod 13 because the capacity of a set should be a prime integer, and I choose 13 as an example for a capacity of a set here.)

Second step: You check the item into the index 1 spot, as in Figure 5–11.

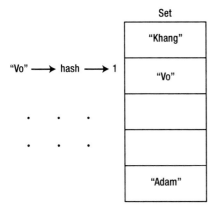

Figure 5–11. *Finding an item inside a set using the hash method*

So you've found it. If the set already contains the element @"vo", it shouldn't add a duplicate. If it doesn't contain anything in that index, then @"vo" should be added into that index position. (For simplicity, I won't discuss what happens if two distinct elements have the same hash, which can happen in reality.)

Insert/Delete:

- As shown in the previous example, insert/delete will perform instantly with the hash functions and add it into the correct index position. The performance is: O(1). However, you can't determine the position of insertion.

Search:

- If you want to search for an object, you probably have three purposes. The first purpose is to check if that object is contained inside the set. The second purpose is to find an object in the set that is equal to the object you have in hand. The last purpose is to see if the object inside the set has a specific property that satisfies a condition.

    - For the first purpose, you can just use the method [set containsObject:obj1]; and it will return your item really fast: O(1).

■ For the second purpose, you need to create a mock object that is equal to the object you are finding. As an example, in the **isEqual:** part, you can create the new object such that [newObj isEqual:oldObject] returns YES. The good thing is that the cost of creating the new object is either cheap or you don't need to know much information. After that, you can call MyItem *oldObject = [set member:newObject]; and you have your old object with full information. The performance for this case is: O(1).

■ The last purpose is to find a property, such as a name that starts with character "k." You will need to loop over all the elements as in the array. The performance for this case is: O(n).

Access:

■ You can't access any item directly by its index, like in array. One way to access the element discussed in the search section is by creating a mock object that isEqual: to the object you want to access. The performance is O(1).

Sort:

■ Cocoa Touch framework doesn't provide a good way to sort an NSMutableSet. It only provides you with a method to return a sorted array. Based on the sorting performance of an array, I can estimate that the performance for a sorting in set is: O(nlogn).

Table 5–4 shows the common methods and APIs for NSMutableSet.

Table 5–4. *Common methods and APIs of NSMutableSet*

Task	Common Methods/APIs
Insert	- (void)addObject:(id)object
	- (void)addObjectsFromArray:(NSArray *)array
Delete	- (void)removeObject:(id)object
	- (void)removeAllObjects
Search	- (BOOL)containsObject:(id)anObject
	- (id)member:(id)object
Access	- No API for random access. You'll need to construct a similar object that satisfies the isEqual and hash method and uses the member method.

Task	Common Methods/APIs
Sort	- (NSArray *)sortedArrayUsingDescriptors: (NSArray *)sortDescriptors - For simplicity, you can convert your NSSet to an NSArray and then sort the array.
Set Manipulation	
Union: If you have a set of {A, B, C} and a set of {C, D, E}, the union gives you all elements in either first set or second set or both: {A, B, C, D, E}	- (void)unionSet:(NSSet *)otherSet
Minus: If you have a set of {A, B, C} and a set of {C, D, E}, the minus gives you elements in first set and not in second set: {A, B}	- (void)minusSet:(NSSet *)otherSet
Intersect: If you have a set of {A, B, C} and a set of {C, D, E}, the minus gives you elements which belong to both set: {C}	- (void)intersectSet:(NSSet *)otherSet

> **NOTE:** One important factor for in using NSMutableSet and NSSet is their rich API for set manipulation. Like a set concept in mathematics, you may need to use a special calculation like union, intersect, and minus. If you need to manipulate collections with unique data a lot and are concerned with union, intersect, or minus, set is the best choice.

For example, you are given two lists: one of people who play tennis and the other of people who play football. Now, you need to find three lists:

- People who play both tennis and football.
- People who only play tennis.
- People who only play football.

I will leave this as an exercise for you to practice. You should try it with both approaches: an array approach and a set approach.

NSMutableDictionary

NSDictionary and NSMutableDictionary are specific implementations of the hash table concept in computer science. The specification for a hash table is you have a list of unique keys and that each key corresponds to a value, which does not need to be unique. The hash table utilizes the hash concept to make sure that it has a list of unique keys.

As Figure 5–12 shows, your NSMutableDictionary contains a list of key/value pairs. The key is associated with an object, and that object can be accessed through the key.

When you have a new pair of (key values) that you want to add into the NSMutableDictionary, you need to calculate the hash and add them in, like the way you did with NSMutableSet above. The key collection is like a set and can only contain unique items. After the hashing function, you can determine the index of the key in the key collection, and then you insert both the key and value into the correct position.

	Key (name)	Value (age)
"Khang"→ hash →0	"Khang"	20
"Vo" → hash →1	"Vo"	25
. . .		.
. . .		.
"Adam"→ hash →4	"Adam"	30

Figure 5–12. *Illustration for the Dictionary concept*

In the simplest case where the key is an integer, you can understand that the NSMutableDictionary works similarly to an array, with the index in the left and the value on the right. In the case of a dictionary, the main difference is that the key will be hashed to create an index.

Now, let's analyze the performance of NSMutableDictionary in each operation (insert/delete, search, access and sort).

Insert/Delete:

■ As in the set case, the insert/delete for dictionary will happen instantly by determining the correct key position. The performance is O(1).

Search:

■ The same as the set case, you need to create an object for which the call of [newObj isEqual:oldObj] returns YES, and use that object to look up the value. The performance is O(1).

Access:

- In dictionary, you only care about accessing the value of a pair. If you already know the key, then the performance for accessing the value is O(1).

Sort:

- You can't sort a dictionary, so you can choose to either sort the key collection or the value collection. Either way will make you create a new array from the dictionary and then sort it. The performance is the same as if you sort an array: O(nlogn).

Table 5–5 shows the common methods and APIs for NSMutableDictionary.

Table 5–5. *Common Methods and APIs of NSMutableDictionary*

Task	Common Methods/APIs
Insert	- (void)setObject:(id)anObject forKey:(id)aKey
Delete	- (void)removeObjectForKey:(id)aKey-
	- (void)removeAllObjects
	- (void)removeObjectsForKeys:(NSArray *) keyArray
Search	- (id)objectForKey:(id)aKey
Access	- (id)objectForKey:(id)aKey
Sort	- You have to get an array of keys or values and then sort them.

> **NOTE:** For an object to be put as a key into a NSMutableDictionary, the corresponding class has to conform to nscopying protocol, and implement the method `copyWithZone:`. For example, NSString conforms to NSCopying protocol but `UIView` does not. Therefore, you can't use a `UIView` as a key inside NSDictionary.

I have finished the three main important data structures and their APIs that Cocoa Touch framework provides free as built-in data structures. These classes and their methods will handle most of your problems in a reasonable amount of time. Next, I will introduce other important and useful data structures for specific cases. Remember to benchmark and test your app's performance before spending your time building a new data structure. Using these built-in and well-tested data structures should always be your first choice.

Other Data Structures

If you need to think beyond basic built-in classes, here are some other basic data structures:

- Linked list: Good when you need to do a lot of insert/delete and want to keep an ordered collection like array.

- Binary tree: Good when you need a collection that always sorted. This is different than whenever you insert a new item into an array and you need to sort the array again. Searching in NSArray, even a sorted array, will always require a linear search because there is no way to know that the array is already sorted. Binary tree is better when you need to do a binary search for the item. Binary search compared to linear search is O(logn) compare to O(n).

- Stack and queue: These are good when you need to build an API that only allows you to add at the end and get out from the end (stack), or add at the end and get out from the beginning (queue). You can easily implement them by a linked list or a normal array.

- Graph: This is an important concept in mathematics and computer science to demonstrate difficult problems. Although many problems will be solved in server side, knowing about the graph will help you with many problems on the iPhone side.

Linked List

The specification and supported public methods (API) of a linked list and an array are usually the same in many cases. You can add an object in anywhere into a linked list, retrieve object from any index inside the linked list, check for the existing object inside the linked list, and sort the linked list. However, the main difference between a linked list and an array is shown in Figure 5–13.

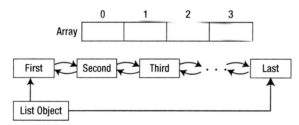

Figure 5–13. *Comparison between an array and a linked list*

As you can see, in an array, you store items in an indexed position and you can access any item inside the array using the index. However, in linked list, the main List object that holds the List will only hold the first and the last item. (For simplicity, I won't discuss the doubly linked list inside which you can go forward and backward). To access any object inside the linked list, you have to go from one of two sides: the first item or the last item. If you go by the first item, you move forward one by one item until you reach the index that you want. If you go by the last item, you move backwards one by one item until you reach the index that you want. Figures 5–14 and 5–15 illustrate the process.

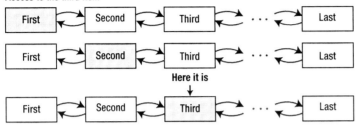

Figure 5–14. *Accessing the item at index 2 (third item) in the linked list*

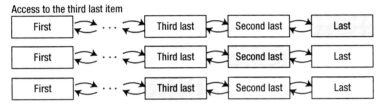

Figure 5–15. *Accessing the third last item in the linked list*

I will give you a sample implementation for linked list; it's not a perfect implementation but you can use it in most cases. You should download the source code project LinkedList for a full version of the sample. I shall briefly explain the most important parts to make sure you fully understand the linked list concepts.

There are two main objects in the implementation, Node and List. The List object holds the first and the last node, as shown in Figure 5–12. Every Node object contains three items: the item inside the Node, the next item, and the previous item. For the first item, the previous item will point to a nil object; similarly, for the last item, the next item will point to a nil object; see Listings 5–5 and 5–6.

Listing 5–5. *ListNode*

```
ListNode.h
// Structure representing a
// doubly-linked list node
@interface ListNode : NSObject {
 @private
    NSObject *value;
    ListNode *next;
    ListNode *pre;
}

@property (nonatomic, strong) NSObject *value;
@property (nonatomic, strong) ListNode *next;
@property (nonatomic, strong) ListNode *pre;
```

```objc
- (id)initWithObject:(NSObject *)object;

@end

ListNode.m
@implementation ListNode

@synthesize value;
@synthesize next;
@synthesize pre;

- (id)initWithObject:(NSObject *)object {
    if (self = [super init]) {
        self.value = object;
    }
    return self;
}

@end
```

Listing 5–6. *Linked List*

```objc
LinkedList.h
@interface LinkedList : NSObject {
 @private
    ListNode *head;
    ListNode *tail;
    ListNode *current;
}

@property (nonatomic, strong) ListNode *head;
@property (nonatomic, strong) ListNode *current;
@property (nonatomic, strong) ListNode *tail;

- (id)initWithHead:(NSObject *)value;
- (void)addToFront:(NSObject *)value;
- (void)addToBack:(NSObject *)value;
- (void)insertObjectAtIndex:(NSInteger)index;
- (NSObject *)first;
- (NSObject *)currentValue;
- (NSObject *)next;
- (NSObject *)previous;

- (NSUInteger)count;
- (NSObject *)objectAtIndex:(NSInteger)index;

- (BOOL)removeCurrent;
- (BOOL)removeObjectAtIndex:(NSInteger)index;

@end

LinkedList.m
```

```objc
@implementation LinkedList
@synthesize current;
@synthesize head;
@synthesize tail;

- (id)initWithHead:(NSObject *)value {
  // to be implemented and explained later
  return nil;
}


- (void)addToFront:(NSObject *)value {
  // to be implemented and explained later
}


- (void)addToBack:(NSObject *)value {
  // to be implemented and explained later
}


- (void)insertObject:(NSObject *)object atIndex:(NSInteger)index {
  // to be implemented and explained later
}


- (NSObject *)first {
  // to be implemented and explained later
  return nil;
}


- (NSObject *)currentValue {
  // to be implemented and explained later
  return nil;
}


- (NSObject *)next {
  // to be implemented and explained later
  return nil;
}


- (NSObject *)previous {
  // to be implemented and explained later
  return nil;
}


- (NSObject *)objectAtIndex:(NSInteger)index {
  // to be implemented and explained later
  return nil;
}


- (NSUInteger)count {
  // to be implemented and explained later
  return -1;
}
```

```objc
- (BOOL)removeCurrent {
    // to be implemented and explained later
    return NO;
}

- (BOOL)removeObjectAtIndex:(NSInteger)index {
    // to be implemented and explained later
    return NO;
}

@end
```

As you can see from Listing 5–6, the LinkedList object has the capability to get objects from the list in the forward or backward order, as well as to add to the first or the end of the linked list. I will show you only the main implementation methods because others are similar or easy to implement yourself.

There are six main methods that you will need to think about when implementing a linked list: init, add object, get object, count, remove object, and release the whole list.

Init

```objc
- (id)initWithHead:(NSObject *)value {
    if ((self = [super init]) != nil) {
        head = [[ListNode alloc] initWithObject:value];
    }
    return self;
}
```

You need to allocate the head of the list first; this head will hold the next item.

Add Object

```objc
- (void)addToFront:(NSObject *)value {
    ListNode *node = [[ListNode alloc] initWithObject:value];
    // new element becomes the head node
    node.next = head;
    head.pre = node;
    self.head = node;
}
```

Adding into the first spot of the linked list is easy and fast; you just need to relink the LinkedList object with the new node. Adding to the end is similar and I leave it as an exercise for you.

To add a new node the beginning, you need to remove the link of objects around the position you desire and relink them with the new element, as shown in Figure 5–16.

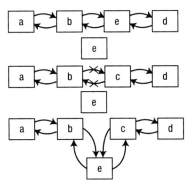

Figure 5–16. *Inserting new object to the middle of the array*

To insert an element into a current position in the list, you can use the following code snippet:

```
- (void)insertObject:(NSObject *)object atIndex:(NSInteger)index {
    ListNode *currentNode = self.head;
    ListNode *previousNode = nil;
    ListNode *nextNode = nil;

    // find two items around the place that you need to add an object in
    for (int i = 1; i <= index; i++) {
        currentNode = currentNode.next;
        if (i == index - 1) {
            previousNode = currentNode;
        } else if (i == index) {
            nextNode = currentNode;
        }
    }

    // add your object in
    ListNode *newNode = [[ListNode alloc] initWithObject:object];
    if (!previousNode) {
        self.head = newNode;
    } else {
        previousNode.next = newNode;
        newNode.pre = previousNode;

        nextNode.pre = newNode;
        newNode.next = nextNode;
    }
}
```

To insert an object at random position or in the middle of the linked list, you need to figure out where to put your node. Therefore, the first part of the code is to loop through the current linked list and find the previous node as well as the next node to insert an object in between. After that, you link nodes around the place with the new node.

Get Object

```
- (NSObject *)first {
    return self.head.value;
}
- (NSObject *)currentValue {
    return self.current.value;
}
- (NSObject *)next {
    self.current = self.current.next;
    return self.current.value;
}
- (NSObject *)previous {
    self.current = self.current.pre;
    return self.current.value;
}
- (NSObject *)objectAtIndex:(NSInteger)index {
    ListNode *currentNode = self.head;
    for (int i = 1; i < index; i++) {
        currentNode = currentNode.next;
    }
    return currentNode.value;
}
```

To get the current or next object of the linked list is easy; you use the current property. Methods like current, next, and previous are mainly used for iteration (looping through the whole linked list). I will leave the iteration for you as an exercise.

Another way to get random access to an object is to use objectAtIndex. It will loop until it reaches the correct index and return.

Count

```
- (NSUInteger)count {
    if (!self.head) {
        return 0;
    }

    ListNode *currentNode = self.head;
    int i = 1;
    while (currentNode.next) {
        currentNode = currentNode.next;
        i++;
    }
    return i;
}
```

To count the number of items inside the linked list, you just need to loop over the list until you find a nil object. Then you return the count.

Remove Object

This action is similar to the add object action, so I leave it as an exercise to practice. If you have any problems, you can look at the complete source code in my LinkedList sample project.

Performance Analysis

Insert/Delete:

▓ It depends on where you insert/delete and if you have the current node that you want to add after or before that node. If you need to traverse the whole list to find the place to add object in, the performance is the same as array: O(n). However, if you already have the current node, then the performance is really fast: O(1).

Search:

▓ For searching, you need to traverse the list, so the performance is O(n).

Access:

▓ For random access based on the index, you need to traverse the list until you read the node you want, so the performance is O(n).

Sort:

▓ You can sort the linked list the same way you sort an array. However, for a linked list, because it is not a built-in data structure, you have to write the sort method yourself. The best performance you can get is O(n * log(n)).

Stack and Queue

Stack and queue are special data structures to limit the permissible operations over the data that these data structures hold. These data structures can be implemented either by an array or by a linked list, as shown in the previous sections. These restrictions will help you manage your data better or make sure that the data is processed in the correct order.

Stack

Stack allows access to only one data item: the last item. If you insert, retrieve, or remove item from the stack, you have to do it from the last item. Figures 5–17 and 5–18 show you how a stack works.

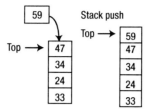

Figure 5–17. *Pushing a new item into the stack*

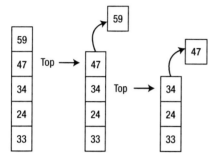

Figure 5–18. *Popping the latest item out of the stack*

There is an analogy that will help you to understand the concept of stack:

- *Washing dishes*: You wash the dish from the top to the bottom; you don't ever take out an arbitrary dish in middle or the whole dish stack will collapse.

Placing an item on the top of the stack is called *pushing* it. Removing it from the top of the stack is called *popping* it. The computer science term for this mechanism is Last-In First-Out (LIFO) because the last item inserted is the first one to be removed.

I will leave you with a small exercise to implement a stack yourself using both an array and a linked list. Your stack should support these necessary methods:

- init // to create the stack

- push

- pop

- peek // to retrieve an item from the stack without removing it out of the stack

- isEmpty

- isFull // if your stack can automatically grow its size, similar to the way NSMutableArray grows, this method always returns false.

Another practice exercise is to reverse a string by using a stack.

Queue

Queue is similar to stack in the way it restricts random access to the data. However, its mechanism is that the first one inserted to the queue is the first one get out of the queue; in other words, First-In First-Out (FIFO). A queue works like a line of people waiting to buy a ticket, as shown in Figure 5–19.

Figure 5–19. *Access to third last item in the linked list*

The way you manipulate data inside a queue is the opposite of the way you deal with a stack. Figures 5–20 and 5–21 illustrate the processes.

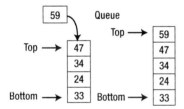

Figure 5–20. *Inserting the last item into a queue*

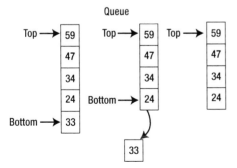

Figure 5–21. *Removing the first item out of a queue*

Again, I will leave you with a small exercise to implement a queue yourself using both array and linked list. Your queue should support these necessary methods:

- init

- insert

- remove

- peek // to retrieve an item from the queue without removing it out of the queue

- isEmpty

- isFull // if your queue can automatically grow its size, similar to the way NSMutableArray grows, this method always returns false

There may be no specific performance gain in using a stack or queue rather than an array or linked list. However, this can save you a ton of time thinking about restricting access to your data or an understanding concept that helps you to solve specific problems.

Binary Tree

Next, I will talk about binary trees. However, I will first take a short aside to discuss the main problems with sorting and searching algorithms; this will help you understand why you might want to use a binary tree.

Sorting Algorithms

In iPhone development, you shouldn't write the sorting algorithms yourself. You should understand how the sorting algorithms work and why they work that way. However, because of the abstraction and encapsulation of the frameworks and libraries, most of the time, you don't need to know which algorithms the Cocoa Touch framework is using. So, in this section I will just cover some famous algorithms and how to convert data structures into a sorted array of data.

Most of the time, you need to provide the framework a method to determine how to compare two objects inside your array. Here is a simple code snippet to take advantage of the sort algorithms inside NSArray:

```
MyItem
- (NSComparisonResult)compareWithItem:(MyItem *)item {
    return [self.name compare:item.name];
}
- (void)viewDidLoad {
    myArray = [myArray sortedArrayUsingSelector:@selector(compareWithItem:)];

}
```

Most of the time you will convert your current data structure into an array, sort this array, and use the results. This is one approach. The other approach to having a sorted array all the time is to use a binary tree, which I will discuss in later sections.

Search

Let's talk about the search strategy in data structures, such as array, linked list, set, and dictionary. As mentioned, set and dictionary are built based on a hash table, so searching for these data structures requires having an object that has a key and a hash value equal to the ones you are searching. Searching for these data structures is done in the time of O(1) (which means really fast).

For array and linked list, the problem is harder. If you want to search, you can use one of two strategies:

- Traverse through the array/linked list until you find the item you want. The performance is O(n).

- Sort the array or linked list and then use an optimal search strategy (binary search, which I will discuss later). The performance is O(n * log(n)) + O(logn), which means O(n * log(n)), because you only care about the fastest growing term.

So, as you can see, if you have an array that is always sorted, it takes you O(logn) to find the item you want. I will show you how to create a data structure that is always sorted in the "Binary Tree" section.

Binary Search

Remember the childhood game where a friend asks you to guess a number he's thinking of between 1 and 20? When you guess a number, he tells you three things: your guess is larger, equal, or smaller than the actual number in his head.

What's the best way to start? Do you start from 1 and continue to 20? Or should you start to 5 and then know which way to go next?

If you go with 10 and your friend says that your guess is smaller than the actual number, then you know that the actual number is between 10 and 20. Amazing! You just divided the set by half and now you only need to guess 10 more numbers. In three or four more steps you will figure out the number.

If you go sequentially from 1 to 20, in the worst case, you need to guess 20 times. In most cases, you will need to guess more than five times. There are only five times that you can guess correctly with less than five guesses. This is illustrated by Figure 5–22.

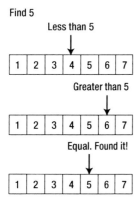

Find 5

Less than 5

| 1 | 2 | 3 | 4 | 5 | 6 | 7 |

Greater than 5

| 1 | 2 | 3 | 4 | 5 | 6 | 7 |

Equal. Found it!

| 1 | 2 | 3 | 4 | 5 | 6 | 7 |

Figure 5–22. *Binary Search in a sorted array*

That is binary search; it's really quite simple. Here is a code snippet for you to implement it on an array:

```
- (void)methodToCall {
    NSMutableArray *myArray = [NSMutableArray array];
    for (int i = 0; i < 20; i++) {
        [myArray addObject:[NSNumber numberWithInt:i]];
    }
    // find number 15.
    NSInteger index = [self indexForNumber:[NSNumber numberWithInt:15] inArray:myArray];
    NSLog(@"index: %d", index);
}

// Note that this method only works if the array is already sorted
- (NSInteger)indexForNumber:(NSNumber *)number inArray:(NSArray *)array {
    int firstIndex = 0;
    int uptoIndex = [array count];

    while (firstIndex < uptoIndex) {
        int mid = (firstIndex + uptoIndex) / 2;  // Compute mid point.
        if ([number intValue] < [[array objectAtIndex:mid] intValue]) {
            uptoIndex = mid;      // repeat search in bottom half.
        } else if ([number intValue] > [[array objectAtIndex:mid] intValue]) {
            firstIndex = mid + 1; // repeat search in top half.
        } else {
            return mid;      // Found it. return position
        }
    }
    return -1;    // Failed to find key
}
```

The main job of the algorithm is to look into the middle of the array. If the value of the middle element is less than the value of the data you are finding, the algorithm divides the array by half; it then takes the first half and continues with that first half until only one item is left. If the value of the middle element is greater than the value of the data you are finding, it will take the second half.

> **NOTE:** Binary search only works with sorted array or list. It assumes that the data in the right is always greater than the data in the left, so it can divide the data array by half.

Binary Tree

Binary tree combines two other structures inside: an ordered array, a linked list, and the binary search algorithm.

There are many uses for a binary tree:

- It is always sorted in a fast way. The performance to add in a new object is O (logn).

- It can always be used with binary search without any necessary calculations (because it is always sorted).

If you want an array/linked list that is always arranged in order (in other words, an ordered array/linked list), you may need to choose one of these approaches:

- For an already sorted array: When you need to insert new item in middle of the array, you need to look for the position and then shift all items to the right. This will take O(n) to run. The performance problem is when you need to shift all the items to the right to insert (or left to delete).

- For an already sorted linked list: With the insert/delete object inside, the linked list is really fast. However, although the linked list is already sorted, you have to traverse the list to find a place to insert the new object. The performance of this traverse is O(n).

- Adding to the end until you need to search or retrieve data, and then sort the array/linked list. The sort operation will take O(n * log(n)) to complete.

So, binary tree is a best way to implement a sorted collection so you can find the item easily within O(log(n)) performance.

I've discussed why you should use a binary tree, but you may still have some questions. What is a tree? What is a binary tree? Before I answer those questions, I want to introduce to you the concept of *node* and *edge*.

Node and Edge

Nodes are shown by the circles in Figure 5–23, while the lines show the edges. Nodes can be labeled with a name or number to make them unique in the tree. Each edge is bounded by the two nodes at its ends.

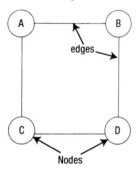

Figure 5–23. *Vertex and edge illustration*

Tree

A tree is a collection of points (usually called nodes) and connections (usually called edges) between these points. The tree has a node as the root, and nodes inside a tree are connected with each other by directed edges. Every node inside a tree must have at most one parent and no cycles are allowed. A simple illustration is shown in Figure 5–24.

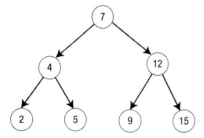

Figure 5–24. *Tree example*

A binary tree is a tree in which each node has 0, 1, or 2 children. Figure 5–24 also represents a binary tree. Figure 5–25 shows a non-tree because it creates a cycle inside it and node 5 has two parent nodes: 2 and 4.

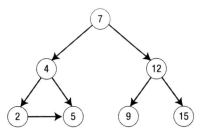

Figure 5–25. *Non-tree example*

The two children of each node in a binary tree are called the left child and the right child, as shown in Figure 5–26.

Figure 5–26. *Left and right child*

A binary search tree is a binary tree in which the right node is greater than the direct parent and the parent is greater than the left node for any three nodes that you pick from the binary tree. This is the technical name of the binary tree that I always talk about. For simplicity, I will use *binary tree* to talk about the *binary search tree*. Figure 5–27 illustrates an example.

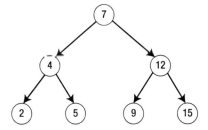

Figure 5–27. *Binary Search Tree*

How Does a Binary Tree Work?

The mechanisms for insert/delete and search in a binary tree are similar. All methods require you to traverse the binary tree until you find a place to insert/delete or search for the item that you want. Figure 5–28 shows an example that inserts the item into the correct place in the binary tree.

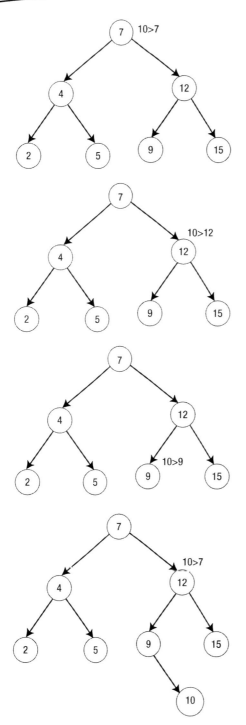

Figure 5–28. *Inserting an item into a binary tree*

The binary tree is implemented based on the idea of a linked list. Because I have already discussed how to implement a linked list, in this section I will only write the skeleton and APIs for the binary tree. Listing 5–7 only contains the interface file; you need to fill in the implementation file to make it work.

Listing 5–7. *Binary Search Tree*

```
TreeNode.h
@interface TreeNode : NSObject {
 @private
    NSObject *object;
    SEL compareSelector;
    TreeNode *leftChild;
    TreeNode *rightChild;
}

@property (nonatomic, strong) NSObject *object;
@property (nonatomic, strong) TreeNode *leftChild;
@property (nonatomic, strong) TreeNode *rightChild;
@property (nonatomic, weak) SEL compareSelector;

@end

Tree.h
#import "TreeNode.h"
@interface Tree : NSObject {
 @private
    TreeNode *root;
}
- (id)initWithObject:(NSObject *)obj compareSelector:(SEL)selector;
- (BOOL)find:(NSObject *)obj;
- (void)insertObject:(NSObject *)newObj;
- (void)deleteObject:(NSObject *)obj;

@end
```

To implement this code, you should understand a binary tree as a special linked list where you have a `tree` object that holds a `root` object, and then the `root` object hold its children itself. This is the same way a linked list works: you have a `LinkedList` object that contains the head node, and that head node contains the next node itself.

You should practice with binary tree by implementing the APIs that I gave you. You should also review binary search to make sure that you understand the concept well and know how to apply in this case. If you get stuck in any point, you can look at my sample project, `BinarySearchTree`.

Graph

Graph is a data structure that looks like tree but in a more general format. Currently, with the growing demand for data mining and data visualization, graph visualization problems are becoming more common to developers. In this section, I will show you the basic concept of a graph data structure and two algorithms to solve one of the most important problems with graph: searching. I will not go too deeply into the source code because you may not use this data structure and specific code that much. However, you really do need to understand the concepts of the graph because it can be used to solve many important problems.

Some common and popular terms:

- Vertex and edge: The vertex concept is the same as the node concept in the tree, and the edge concept for the graph is exactly the same as the edge concept in the tree. You can look back Figure 5–23 for the illustration of vertices and edges. The term "vertex" is mostly used in the graph concept while the term "node" is more frequently used in the tree concept.

- Path: A path is a sequence of edges that can go through a sequence of nodes. For example, in Figure 5–29, you can see two paths from the same pair of nodes: ACD and ABD.

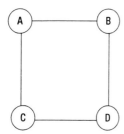

Figure 5–29. *Path*

- Connected graph: There is a path between any pair of vertices that you pick out from the graph. For example, Figure 5–30 shows a connected graph where if you pick every two vertices, you can go from one to the other by some path. However, in Figure 5–31, you can't go from A to C by any path, so it's not a connected graph.

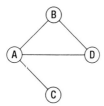

Figure 5–30. *Connected graph*

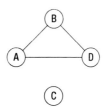

Figure 5–31. *Not a connected graph*

■ Directed graph: If every edge inside the graph has a direction, as shown by an arrow from one vertex to another vertex as in Figure 5–32, the graph is a directed graph. If the edges don't have any direction, you can go either way on them. However, if the edges have directions, you can only follow the path shown by the arrow.

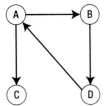

Figure 5–32. *Directed graph*

■ Weighted graph: If every edge inside the graph is given a weight, as shown by an edge with label as in Figure 5–33, the edge can show any cost or value of travel from one vertex to another vertex. The graph then is called weighted graph. Weighted graphs can be used to represent the airline flights between cities in the country with edge showing the cost.

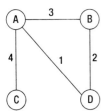

Figure 5–33. *Weighted graph*

Searching within the graph is important. There are many famous search problems in graph theory in computer science. Imagine a simple case: you want to travel from New York to California. You can travel directly by plane but it may cost a lot, or you can travel by train to many cities and finally reach your goal but the total cost was much cheaper than flying directly.

Here's another search problem. You want to travel to all the cities starting from your current city by moving along edges inside the graph. Common benefits are to get information on every city and to see every city. There are two ways to do this: depth-first search and breadth-first search.

Depth-First Search

As in Figure 5–34, you travel along the graph as shown by the arrow and when you reach the last node, you travel back by the dashed-line arrow.

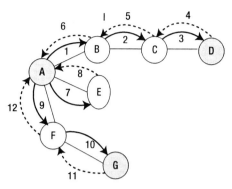

Figure 5–34. *Depth-first search traverse orders*

One of the common implementation of this depth-first search algorithm is using a stack and following these four steps:

1. Pick one vertex in the graph and push it into the stack as the initial vertex; also mark it as visited. You can track visited vertices by setting a property wasVisited as YES, as shown in Listing 5–7.

2. If possible, from the last vertex of the stack, visit any adjacent unvisited vertex, mark it as visited, and push it on the stack.

3. If you can't follow step 2, then if possible, pop a vertex off the stack, and then repeat step 2.

4. If you can't follow step 1 and step 2, you're done.

To make it easier to understand, follow Table 5–6 to see how the four rules are applied to Figure 5–34.

Table 5–6. *Steps in Depth-First Search Algorithm*

Step	Visited Vertices	Current Stack	Description
1	A	A	Pick vertex A as a start vertex.
2	A, B	A→B	Pick the next adjacent unvisited vertex, B, and push B into the stack.
3	A, B, C	A→B→C	Pick the next adjacent unvisited vertex, C, and push C into the stack.
4	A, B, C, D	A→B→C→D	Pick the next adjacent unvisited vertex, D, and push D into the stack.
5	A, B,C,D	A→B→C	There are no more adjacent unvisited vertices, so pop D out of the stack.

Step	Visited Vertices	Current Stack	Description
6	A, B, C, D	A→B	There are no more adjacent unvisited vertices, so pop C out of the stack.
7	A, B, C, D	A	There are no more adjacent unvisited vertices, so pop B out of the stack.
8	A, B, C, D, E	A→E	Pick the next adjacent unvisited vertex, E, and push E into the stack.
9	A, B, C, D, E	A	There are no more adjacent unvisited vertices, so pop E out of the stack.
10	A, B, C, D, E, F	A→F	Pick the next adjacent unvisited vertex, F, and push F into the stack.
11	A, B, C, D, E, F, G	A→F→G	Pick the next adjacent unvisited vertex, G, and push G into the stack.
12	A, B, C, D, E, F, G	A→F	There are no more adjacent unvisited vertices, so pop G out of the stack.
12	A, B, C, D, E, F, G	A	There are no more adjacent unvisited vertices, so pop F out of the stack.
13	A, B, C, D, E, F, G		You can't visit any adjacent unvisited vertices anymore, so you're done. Pop A out of the stack.

Listing 5–8 contains the code explanation.

Listing 5–8. *Depth-First Search*

```
@interface Vertex : NSObject {
 @private
   NSString *label;
   BOOL wasVisited;
   NSMutableSet *adjacentVertices;
}
@property (nonatomic,  copy) NSString *label;
@property (nonatomic, weak) BOOL wasVisited;
@property (nonatomic, strong) NSMutableSet *adjacentVertices;
```

The vertex object will have a label, a mark for visited or not, and a list of vertices around it.

```
@interface Graph : NSObject {
 @private
   NSMutableArray *vertices;
}
@property (nonatomic, strong) NSMutableArray *vertices;
- (void)addVertex:(Vertex *)vertex;
```

```
- (void)addEdgeForVertex:(Vertex *)vertex1 andVertex:(Vertex *)vertex2;
- (void)depthFirstSearch;
@end
```

The graph has a list of vertices. Because every vertex keeps a list of adjacent vertices,
graph doesn't need to take care of the edges.

```
- (void)depthFirstSearch {
    if ([self.vertices count] == 0) {
        NSLog(@"There is no vertex in graph");
        return;
    }

    Vertex *firstVertex = [self.vertices objectAtIndex:0];
    firstVertex.wasVisited = YES;
    [self display:firstVertex];

    Stack *stack = [[Stack alloc] init];
    [stack push:firstVertex];
    while (![stack isEmpty]) {
        Vertex *lastVertex = [stack peek];

        BOOL isAddNewVertex = NO;

        for (Vertex *adjacentVertex in lastVertex.adjacentVertices) {
            if (!adjacentVertex.wasVisited) {
                [stack push:adjacentVertex];
                adjacentVertex.wasVisited = YES;
                isAddNewVertex = YES;
                [self display:adjacentVertex];

                break;
            }
        }

        if (!isAddNewVertex) {
            [stack pop];
        }
    }
}
```

The main code for the depth-first search algorithm is in Listing 5–8. First, I checked to
make sure that there are some vertices inside the graph, and then I pushed the first
vertex into the stack. The loop code will continue the rules explained previously until it
gets out the last vertex and checks all the adjacent nodes. If there is a node that is not
visited, it pushes the nodes into the stack, marks that node, and prints that node out. If
it can't find any adjacent vertex, then it is popped out of the stack.

Breadth-First Search

As in Figure 5–35, you travel along the graph as shown by the arrow. You
travel by reaching the first layer and then the second layer and finally the last
layer. It is different than the order you traveled with the depth-first search.

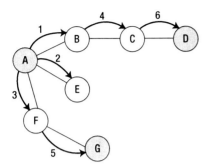

Figure 5–35. *Breadth-first search traverse orders*

One of common implementation for this breadth-first search algorithm is using queue and following these four steps, which are also explained in Table 5–7:

1. Pick one vertex in the graph as the current vertex; mark it as visited.

2. If possible, from the current vertex, visit any adjacent unvisited vertex, mark it as visited, and insert it into the queue.

3. If you can't follow step 2, then if possible, remove a vertex from the queue, make it the current vertex, and then repeat step 2.

4. If you can't follow step1 and step 2, you're done.

Table 5–7. *Steps in Breadth-First Search Algorithm*

Step	Visited Vertices	Current Vertex	Current Queue	Description
1	A	A		Pick vertex A as a current vertex.
2	A, B	A	B	Pick the next adjacent unvisited vertex, B, and insert B into the queue.
3	A, B, E	A	B→E	Pick the next adjacent unvisited vertex, E, and insert E into the queue.
4	A, B, E, F	A	B→E→F	Pick the next adjacent unvisited vertex, F, and insert F into the queue.
5	A, B, E, F	B	E→F	There are no more adjacent unvisited vertices, so remove B from the queue and let B be the current vertex.
6	A, B, E, F, C	B	E→F→C	Pick the next adjacent unvisited vertex, C, and insert C into the queue.

Step	Visited Vertices	Current Vertex	Current Queue	Description
7	A, B, E, F, C	E	F→C	There are no more adjacent unvisited vertices, so remove E from the queue and let E be the current vertex.
8	A, B, E, F, C	F	C	There are no more adjacent unvisited vertices, so remove F out of the queue and let F be the current vertex.
9	A, B, E, F, C, G	F	C→G	Pick the next adjacent unvisited vertex, G, and insert G into the queue.
10	A, B, E, F, C, G	C	G	There are no more adjacent unvisited vertices, so remove C from the queue and let C be the current vertex
11	A, B, E, F, C, G, D	C	G→D	Pick the next adjacent unvisited vertex, D, and insert D into the queue.
12	A, B, E, F, C, G, D	G	D	There are no more adjacent unvisited vertices, so remove G from the queue, and let D be the current vertex.
12	A, B, E, F, C, G, D	D		There are no more adjacent unvisited vertices, so remove D from the queue, and let D be the current vertex.
13	A, B, E, F, C, G, D			You can't visit any more adjacent unvisited vertices, so you're done.

For code, you should implement the breadth-first search algorithm yourself as an exercise.

Other Algorithms and Problem-Solving Approaches

I have introduced the most important data structures and their related algorithms; these will help speed up your code significantly. However, for an iPhone developer, there are a few more algorithms and problem-solving approaches you should know. You may already know about how to solve a problem with recursion. The second one is SAX/DOM parser for XML parsing. XML is heavily used in iPhone development when you need to download and get data from the network.

Recursion

Recursion is a programming technique in which a method (function) calls itself. This is one of the most interesting techniques in programming. I will show you scenarios that you can solve immediately using a recursion technique.

However, there is one drawback with recursion: the performance may be slower than using a direct loop. This performance loss may be insignificant if you only call recursion a few times, not thousands of times. It can cost you more memory when you need to store data and stacktrace if you are calling the methods over and over again.

The recursion technique can be used to implement many high performance algorithms like merge sort or binary search. To illustrate the technique in objective-C, I will show you two sample problems: a factorial calculation and a binary search. Then you can compare this version of binary search with the version using the loop that I showed previously.

What is a factorial? A factorial of n is found by multiplying n by the factorial of n-1. In other words, factorial (n) = n * factorial (n-1). This is perfect for a recursion because the definition already suggests to use recursion.

```
- (NSInteger)factorial:(NSInteger) n {
    if ( n <= 1 ) {
        return 1;
    } else {
        return n * [self factorial:(n - 1)];
    }
}
```

It is very simple and straightforward, right? Now, I will discuss a more difficult problem with binary search. Here is the original approach with a simple loop for a binary search:

```
- (NSInteger)indexForNumber:(NSNumber *)number inArray:(NSArray *)array {
    int firstIndex = 0;
    int uptoIndex = [array count];

    while (firstIndex < uptoIndex) {
        int mid = (firstIndex + uptoIndex) / 2;   // Compute mid point.
        if ([number intValue] < [[array objectAtIndex:mid] intValue]) {
            uptoIndex = mid;      // repeat search in bottom half.
        } else if ([number intValue] > [[array objectAtIndex:mid] intValue]) {
            firstIndex = mid + 1;  // repeat search in top half.
        } else {
            return mid;      // Found it. return position
        }
    }
    return -1;     // Failed to find key
}
```

Here is an implementation for recursion:

```
- (NSInteger)indexForNumber:(NSNumber *)number inArray:(NSArray *)array
lowerBound:(NSInteger)lowerBound upperBound:(NSInteger)upperBound {
    int mid = (lowerBound + upperBound) / 2;
```

```
        if([[array objectAtIndex:mid] intValue] == [number intValue]) {
            return mid; // found it
        } else if (lowerBound > upperBound) {
            return -1;  // can't find it
        } else { // divide range
            if ([[array objectAtIndex:mid] intValue] < [number intValue]) {
                // it is in upper half
                return [self indexForNumber:number inArray:array lowerBound:(mid + 1)
        upperBound:upperBound];
            } else {
                // it is in lower half
                return [self indexForNumber:number inArray:array lowerBound:lowerBound
        upperBound:(mid - 1)];
            }
        }
    }
}
```

SAX/DOM Parser for XML Parsing

XML parsing is important for iPhone developers when they need to retrieve data from network; much of it will return in the XML format. There is one important consideration when dealing with XML: SAX vs. DOM. I will discuss the two main differences between SAX and DOM and when you should choose one over the other.

SAX is a way to read the file or the XML string line by line to find or parse the data you need. Parsing through the whole XML file with SAX can be done very quickly. The problem is that the logic can be really complicated if you need to find a simple piece of data inside the XML file. It does not consume much memory as well.

DOM is opposite to SAX: you store the whole XML structure in memory, making it very easy to retrieve the data that you need. However, it takes more time and memory to store the data structure in memory than the SAX approach.

Now let's compare the two methods in code. To use SAX Method, I choose to use NSXMLParser; I also need to implement two methods so that I can receive the XML events: the start element event and end element event.

```
@interface XMLParser : NSObject <NSXMLParserDelegate> {
 @private
    NSMutableArray* strings;
}

@property (nonatomic, strong) NSMutableArray *strings;
- (NSString *)parseDemonstration;

@end


#import "XMLParser.h"



@implementation XMLParser
@synthesize strings;
```

```objc
- (void)parser:(NSXMLParser *)parser didStartElement:(NSString *)elementName
 namespaceURI:(NSString *)namespaceURI qualifiedName:(NSString *)qName
   attributes:(NSDictionary *)attributeDict {
  // you need to implement this method to get the element out
}


- (void)parser:(NSXMLParser *)parser didEndElement:(NSString *)elementName
 namespaceURI:(NSString *)namespaceURI qualifiedName:(NSString *)qName {
  // you need to implement this method to get the element out
}


- (void)parser:(NSXMLParser*)parser foundCharacters:(NSString*)string {
  // you need to implement this method to get the element's content out
}



- (NSString *)parseDemonstration {
    self.strings = [[NSMutableArray alloc] init];
    NSString *filePath = [[NSBundle mainBundle] pathForResource:@"books" ofType:@"xml"];
    NSString *text = [[NSString alloc] initWithContentsOfFile:filePath
encoding:NSASCIIStringEncoding error:nil];
    NSData*      data       = [text dataUsingEncoding:NSASCIIStringEncoding];
    NSXMLParser* parser     = [[NSXMLParser alloc] initWithData:data];
    parser.delegate = self;
    [parser parse];

    NSString* result = [self.strings componentsJoinedByString:@""];

    return result;
}

@end
```

For the DOM method, all you need to know is the element names:

```objc
[myXMLDoc nodesForXPath:[NSString stringWithFormat:@"//%@:links", @"myNameSpace"]
                    namespaceMappings:namespaceDic error:nil];
```

Summary

In this chapter, I covered the main data structures and algorithms, both theoretically and practically. The theoretical way is used as a benchmark when talking about the concept of algorithms or data structures. I used it to compare the different algorithms and data structures. However, in practice, don't forget to use the instruments to get a real benchmark.

You also know how to use three main important data structures, which are built in to the Cocoa Touch framework. Knowing how to use them properly will help you boost the performance of your app without reinventing the whole wheel. However, when you really need better performance, you should consider good alternatives like linked list, binary search tree, and other abstract concepts like stack and queue. Recursion and XML parsing are more important skills that you will need.

EXERCISE

1. Finish the exercise in the chapter:

    You are given two lists: one of people who play tennis and one of people who play football. Now, you need to find three lists:

    People who play both tennis and football.

    People who only play tennis.

    People who only play football.

    You should try to implement both ways, using a NSMutableSet and a NSMutableArray.

2. Implement the remove item in the linked list.

3. Implement the insert item into the end of the linked list.

4. Implement iteration for the linked list and give sample code.

5. Implement the binary search tree.

6. Implement the breadth-first search algorithm.

7. Parse the following XML document two ways: SAX and DOM to get the title, the price, and the author's full name of every book. You can use the project XMLParser to get the XML file without the need to retype it. For DOM, you can use TouchXML (via https://github.com/mrevilme/TouchXML) and for SAX, you can use NSXMLParser (built-in Apple Library):

```xml
<?xml version="1.0"?>
<catalog>
   <book id="bk101">
      <author>
         <firstName>Gambardella</firstName>
         <lastName>Matthew</lastName>
      </author>
      <title>XML Developer's Guide</title>
      <gcnre>Computer</genre>
      <price>44.95</price>
      <publish_date>2000-10-01</publish_date>
      <description>An in-depth look</description>
   </book>
   <book id="bk102">
      <author>
         <firstName>Ralls</firstName>
         <lastName>Kim</lastName>
      </author>
      <title>Midnight Rain</title>
      <genre>Fantasy</genre>
      <price>5.95</price>
      <publish_date>2000-12-16</publish_date>
      <description>A former architect battles corporate</description>
```

```
    </book>
    <book id="bk103">
        <author>
            <firstName>Galos</firstName>
            <lastName>Mike</lastName>
        </author>
        <title>Visual Studio 7: A Comprehensive Guide</title>
        <genre>Computer</genre>
        <price>49.95</price>
        <publish_date>2001-04-16</publish_date>
        <description>Microsoft Visual Studio 7</description>
    </book>
</catalog>
```

## Chapter 6

Improve Parallel Data Access using Multithreading Techniques

In this chapter, you will learn about:

- Threads and multithreading.
- How to write and manage threads with locks in iPhone applications.
- General concepts related to the multithreading environment.
    - Safety: The program should generate the expected result.
    - Liveness: The expected result has to be finally generated at some point.
    - Performance: The expected result has to be quickly generated.
- Knowing when to use threads.
- Knowing many different alternatives between threads and some other built-in solutions provided by Apple.

Today's computing devices have more and more processors. The iPhone is no exception; sooner or later, the iPhone will have multiprocessors; in fact, Android already had some devices with dual-core. Therefore, the need to know how to exploit the multiprocessor system is increasing. This is just one of the reasons for learning about multithreading. Thread canals help you with other issues such as asynchronous code, file and network I/O, or slow calculating processes.

What Are Threads and Multithreading?

A thread, in its simplest form, is a sequence of commands for the operating system (OS) to run. Different threads can run in the same processor (CPU) or in different processors; this is determined by the OS, as shown in Figure 6–1.

Normally, the OS starts a new application with only one thread—in other words, one sequence of commands from the beginning to the end. Multiple threads are when the system has more than one sequence of commands running in parallel or concurrently. In a multi-processor system, each thread can be executed at the same time in each processor, as shown in Figure 6–1.

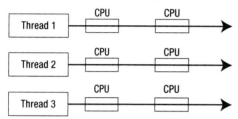

Figure 6–1. *A three*-processor system running with three threads

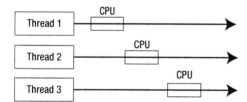

Figure 6–2. *A single-processor system running with three threads*

However, in a single-process system, the CPU will process some commands in one thread before switching to another thread. In Figure 6–2, the CPU executes some commands in thread 1 before jumping into thread 2. Then the CPU executes commands in thread 2 before jumping into thread 3.

Along the processing road, different threads can call different methods from different objects, as in Figure 6–3. Thread 1 and thread 2 can use the same object and call the same method at the same time as thread 1 and thread 2 call Method 1 of Object 1 and Method 3 of Object 3. However, thread 1 and thread 2 can call different methods and different objects when thread 1 calls Method 2 of Object 2 and thread 2 calls Method 4 of Object 4.

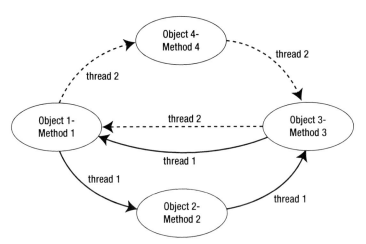

Figure 6–3. *Two threads call different methods from different objects*

There are some advantages and disadvantages to having multiple threads inside the same application. The following sections will discuss all of them. One of the most important advantages of multithreading applications is the decoupling of other tasks from the main User Interface (UI) process so that the UI isn't blocked or frozen.

Threading Terminology

Here are the important threading terms defined:

- The term **thread** is used to refer to a separate sequence of commands/execution for code.

- The term **process** is used to refer to a running executable, which can encompass multiple threads.

- The term **task** is used to refer to the abstract concept of work that needs to be performed.

What is the difference between a thread and a process if both of them are used to execute logic concurrently? A process is different than a thread in the following aspects:

- A process is a unit of allocation; it has its own resources, heap memory, and privileges. A thread is only a unit of execution with its own stack and program counter.

- A process contains many threads, and each thread can belong to only one process.

- A thread shares data with other threads inside the process that these threads belong to. Two processes do not share data with each other; they usually use interprocess communication to transfer data. (Interprocess communication is out of the scope of this chapter.)

■   An OS has to allocate a specific resource, and processes can't share resources, so a process is considered heavyweight. Threads, though, share resources, so an OS can create as many threads as it wants inside the same process.

First Example

This example will demonstrate some problems with IO performance. I will speed up the code later by using some multithreading techniques. My sample code is simple:

■   In the first benchmark, I will load and display a list of images inside a table view. Then, I will show you how the scrolling experience suffers: you can't scroll the table until all images in the current state are returned.

■   In the second benchmark, I will use multithreading to speed up the program. You can see that the scrolling experience while you're waiting for the image loading process is much better.

> **NOTE:** For both cases, my sample project will not cache the images to let you see the differences between two cases clearly.

Table 6–1 shows the benchmark results of each test based on the Core Animation instrument so you can see the application of the instrument into a real world situation.

Table 6–1. *Results of Multithreading and Non-Multithreading Samples*

Time	First Benchmark (non-multithreading)	Second Benchmark (multithreading)
1	2	54
2	1	59
3	3	54
4	0	54
5	0	46
6	10	42

Table 6–1 shows you the frame per second (fps) that the iPhone OS loads when processing and running the application. You can see that using multithreading significantly speeds up the loading process. The problem with not using multithreading

in this case is that the loading process will block the UI and your application will appear to have hung.

I will give you a look at the source code and offer a few explanations before I explain the concepts in-depth. Listing 6–1 shows the code for the first benchmark.

Listing 6–1. First Benchmark; This Code Runs Inside the UITableViewDataSource's Method.

```
- (UITableViewCell *)tableView:(UITableView *)tableView
cellForRowAtIndexPath:(NSIndexPath *)indexPath {

 static NSString *CellIdentifier = @"Cell";

 UITableViewCell *cell = [tableView dequeueReusableCellWithIdentifier:CellIdentifier];
 if (cell == nil) {
     cell = [[UITableViewCell alloc] initWithStyle:UITableViewCellStyleDefault
reuseIdentifier:CellIdentifier];
 }

 NSURL *imageURL = [NSURL URLWithString:[self.imagesArray objectAtIndex:indexPath.row]];
 cell.imageView.image = [UIImage imageWithData:[NSData dataWithContentsOfURL:imageURL]];

 // Configure the cell.
 return cell;
}
```

The Listing 6–2 only shows the general approach to retrieving the image in the asynchronous code and sending the image into the UIImageView after it finishes retrieving it. For simplicity, the actual asynchronous code is not displayed or discussed here.

Listing 6–2. Second Benchmark—Getting the Image Through a Background Thread

```
// Customize the appearance of table view cells.
- (UITableViewCell *)tableView:(UITableView *)tableView
cellForRowAtIndexPath:(NSIndexPath *)indexPath {

    static NSString *CellIdentifier = @"Cell";

    ImageCell *cell = (ImageCell *) [UIUtilities getCellWithTableView:tableView
                                                cellIdentifier:CellIdentifier
                                                nibName:@"ImageCell"];

    // Configure the cell.
    NSURL *imageURL = [NSURL URLWithString:[self.imagesArray
objectAtIndex:indexPath.row]];
    [cell.contentImage displayImageWithURL:imageURL];

    return cell;
}
#import <Foundation/Foundation.h>
#import "ImageFetcher.h"

@interface UIImageView (Network) <ImageFetcherDelegate>

- (void)displayImageWithURL:(NSURL *)url;
```

```
@end

#import "UIImageView+Network.h"
#import "ImageFetcher.h"

@implementation UIImageView (Network)

- (void)imageFetcherFinished:(ImageFetcher *)fetcher {
    self.image = fetcher.image;
}

- (void)displayImageWithURL:(NSURL *)url {
    self.image = nil;
    if (url) {
        // This code will run in the background thread and callback when it retrieves
        //    image
        [ImageFetcher loadImageWithURL:url delegate:self];
    }
}

@end
```

In the first benchmark, inside the method to return the cell for the table view, I put in code to get the image there. With this line of code, the iOS will stop and wait until the image is returned from the network. After that, it continues to return the cell and display that cell to the UI. This waiting makes the whole application stop and that is the reason why you can't quickly scroll the table view in the first benchmark.

For the second benchmark, I use asynchronous code, which is actually another form of multithreading, but the low-level library will handle the multithreading code for you. With this code, the main process is free from waiting for the downloading process to be finished. Therefore, in the second benchmark, you can scroll the table view without any problem.

Benefits of Multithreading

There are some cases where you might consider using threads inside an iPhone application.

- *Exploiting all the cores and processors*: (One processor can always have multiple cores inside and the core is the actual computing unit.) Currently, the iPhone 4 only has one processor and one core but iPhone 5 may have more than one core and you will want your app to utilize all available processors to speed up performance.

- *Modeling*: You may try to model real behaviors from the real world. For example, consider a situation where you have 12 different types of tasks to do (fix bugs, interview candidates for system administration, and create slides for your next product presentation, etc.) versus having only one complicated task (fix 12 bugs). The latter situation is easier to do when you only have a queue of work to finish. The first case is a sophisticated situation where you can assign each thread to handle with each task.

▨ *Handling I/O processing task*: Usually, I/O (both file and networking I/O) takes time to return data back to the application. Therefore, if you use only one thread to handle it, your application may stop working and spend time waiting for the data. Using multithreading helps you split the I/O thread out until it receives all data and merges back to the main thread.

▨ *More responsive UI*: GUI applications like iPhone applications start with only one thread, which means that all application code executes through a *main event loop* (also called a *main run loop*). An event loop is when an application receives an input event (such as a tap, a swipe, or a double-tap) from a user and then runs the logic corresponding to that input event. The longer it takes for an application to execute within an event loop, the less responsive the UI.

▨ *Working in some logic processing in background*: This is also an important part of iPhone application code. There may be some cases where you need to process data heavily, such as running an XML parsing algorithm to extract out some data inside. This is related to the responsiveness of the UI; less work in the UI thread will make the program offer a better user experience.

How to Write Multithreaded Applications

So now that you know how good a multithreaded application can be and how it can help you solve many problems, how do you write a good multithreaded application? I will show you the main techniques to write/handle a good multithreaded application for the iPhone.

Create a Thread

To create a thread, you can use any of the following:

▨ NSThread

▨ POSIX Threads

▨ NSObject to create a new thread

▨ NSOperation and NSOperationQueue

I will go over each of them and give you examples because each has its own advantages and disadvantages. At the end of this section I will give you a table comparison to make sure you can differentiate between them and pick the right one for your particular needs.

NSThread

To create a new thread with NSThread, you can simply call:

```
[NSThread detachNewThreadSelector:@selector(threadMethod:) toTarget:self
withObject:nil];
```

This method will create a new detached thread for your application. A *detached thread* is one that will have all of its resources reclaimed by the system when that thread exists.

There are some attributes that you need to know.

```
+(void)detachNewThreadSelector:(SEL)aSelector toTarget:(id)aTarget withObject:(id)anArgu
ment
```

- aSelector: The method that will be called on the target object when the thread begins. According to Apple documentation, this selector takes only one parameter and has no return value.

- aTarget: The object that will execute the method specified in the aSelector parameter.

- anArgument: The only argument; it will be passed to the aSelector method when the thread begins.

If you want to create a thread but don't want to start it yet, you can use the following mechanism:

```
NSThread* myThread = [[NSThread alloc]
                        initWithTarget:self
                            selector:@selector(myThreadMainMethod:)
                                object:nil];
[myThread start];  // Actually create the thread
```

As you can see, in the first line, you can create a new thread and then later, whenever you choose, you can call start on that object to create and start a new thread. This is good if you only want to pass the myThread object around instead of passing the selector, target and argument around.

Another good way to use a NSThread object is to send a message to that thread object using

```
-(void)performSelector:(SEL)aSelector onThread:(NSThread *)thr
withObject:(id)arg waitUntilDone:(BOOL)wait
```

This method will queue the selector on another thread. When the system automatically runs that thread, the thread will dequeue the message and call the desired method specified inside aSelector variable.

Using POSIX Threads

This mechanism is mainly used for C programming in iPhone applications. In Chapter 9, I will cover C programming in depth and how it can help you improve your iPhone apps performance in many situations. So this part may not help you much if you don't already know C programming. If you do know C programming, Listing 6–3 shows the code and an explanation follows.

Listing 6–3. *POSIX Thread*

```
#include <assert.h>
#include <pthread.h>

void* ThreadMethod(void* data)
{
   // Your main logic comes here.
   return NULL;
}

void LaunchThread()
{
   // Create the thread using POSIX routines.
   pthread_attr_t  attr;
   pthread_t       posixThreadID;
   int             returnVal;

   // init and check if init a new thread successful
   returnVal = pthread_attr_init(&attr);
   assert(!returnVal);

   // set attribute detach state for new thread
   returnVal = pthread_attr_setdetachstate(&attr, PTHREAD_CREATE_DETACHED);
   assert(!returnVal);

   // create and run the new thread
   int    threadError = pthread_create(&posixThreadID, &attr, &ThreadMethod, NULL);

   returnVal = pthread_attr_destroy(&attr);
   assert(!returnVal);
   if (threadError != 0)
   {
      // Report an error.
   }
}
```

NSObject

All objects have the ability to create and detach a new thread to execute these objects' selectors. You can use the following line of code to run the method doSomething in a background thread:

```
[myObj performSelectorInBackground:@selector(doSomething) withObject:nil];
```

The effect of calling this method is the same as the following line of code:

```
[NSThread detachNewThreadSelector:@selector(doSomething) toTarget:myObj withObject:nil]
```

This method is good as a short form for detaching and creating a new thread to run the background task.

NSOperationQueue

NSOperationQueue class is a mechanism to manage and run tasks concurrently. A good thing about NSOperationQueue is that it can restrict the number of concurrent operations inside the system within a given limit to keep the system load at an acceptable level. Because of this restriction of the maximum number of threads, a higher number of instances of NSOperationQueue may not lead to more concurrent threads running in the system at the same time.

You can add operations into the queue but you can't remove them. However, you can cancel all of the existing and non-running operations inside the queue. Table 6–2 shows some other methods that you will find really useful when using NSOperationQueue.

Table 6–2. *Descriptions of Methods*

Method	Description and Note
-(void)addOperation: NSOperation *)operation	Whenever an operation is added into the queue, it remains there until it finishes executing.
-(NSArray *)operations	An array contains operations in the order these operations are added into queue. This array only contains operations that have not finished (running and waiting to be executed).
-(NSUInteger)operationCount	Number of operations that have not finished.
-(void)cancelAllOperations	Sends a cancel message to all operations inside the queue. Waiting operations will be canceled before running. Running operations can determine their actions by themselves.
-(void)setMaxConcurrent OperationCount:(NSInteger) co	The maximum number of concurrent operations that can be executed at the same time within the queue.
-(void)setSuspended:(BOOL) suspend	Suspends or resumes operations inside the queue. It is different than cancel because later you can resume operations within the queue.
+(id)currentQueue	If you call this method from within an NSOperation object, you get the queue that started the operation.
+(id)mainQueue	The operation queue bound to the main thread.

You can use NSOperationQueue with three different classes.

- NSInvocationOperation: This is a simple wrapping if you already have an object and a method to put into a concurrent thread. It also requires no subclassing, so you can create a simple NSOperation object by this class. NSInvocationOperation is a subclass of NSOperation.

- NSBlockOperation: This is another wrapping to execute one or more blocks without having to create a separate NSOperation object to have each of blocks executed. When executing more than one block, the NSBlockOperation is considered finished only when all of the inside blocks have finished executing.

- Custom NSOperation Object: NSOperation is a base class. By subclassing it, you can have complete control over the whole implementation of the NSOperation objects, including the default way in which your operation executes and reports its status.

To make a multithreading app with NSOperationQueue, you need to create a specific object by one of these three methods and add the newly created NSOperation into your queue. Then the queue will maintain and run those operations for you.

Here is a code snippet that will help you to create a NSOperationQueue and add separate operation objects into it to create a multithreading environment:

```
NSOperationQueue* myOperationQueue = [[NSOperationQueue alloc] init];
[myOperationQueue addOperation:myOperation]; // Add a single operation
[myOperationQueue addOperations:arrayOfOperations waitUntilFinished:NO]; // Add multiple
operations
[aQueue addOperationWithBlock:^{
  /* Do Something. */
}];
```

Now I will go into details of how you create new operations using each of the previously mentioned methods.

NSInvocationOperation

The NSInvocationOperation object is run to execute the method that was specified when a new NSInvocationOperation object was created. You may want to use this object if

- You want to avoid creating too many custom operation classes inside your application.

- You are adding or maintaining an existing application in which the classes are well defined and you don't want to modify that class to subclass NSOperation.

- The selector can change depending on the user input. In this case, you just create a new NSInvocationOperation object with the selected selector.

The code to create an NSInvocationOperation object is as following:

```
NSInvocationOperation* theOp = [[NSInvocationOperation alloc] initWithTarget:self
selector:@selector(myTaskMethod:) object:data];
```

It is similar to when you create and detach a new thread using NSThread. You pass the target object, the selector that you want to call, and an argument that you want the selector to have when it is executed.

NSBlockOperation

The NSBlockOperation is another subclass of NSOperation. When you create a block operation, you have to add at least one block inside this operation object. Then later you can add more blocks to be executed within this operation object. When the operation queue executes this block operation, it will execute all the blocks inside the block operation before this block operation finishes. Therefore, you can use this operation object to keep track of a group of blocks and then you can merge or deal with related results.

To create a block operation object, you can use the following code:

```
NSBlockOperation* theOp = [NSBlockOperation blockOperationWithBlock: ^{
    NSLog(@"Beginning operation.\n");
    // Do some work.
}];
```

You then later add another block into this operation by calling

```
[theOp addExecutionBlock:[NSBlockOperation blockOperationWithBlock: ^{
    NSLog(@"Beginning operation.\n");
    // Do some work.
}];
```

NSOperation

NSOperation is a class for you to customize by subclassing. To subclass NSOperation, you create a class with two recommended (but not compulsory) methods.

- *Custom initialization method*: To receive data and necessary attributes for logic processing within the class. For example, you can have an init method to receive a url to download an image, like so:

```
- (id)initWithData:(id)data {
    if ((self = [super init]))
        myData = data;
    return self;
}
```

- Main *method*: A necessary method and will be called when the task is started.

To make a concurrent NSOperation subclass, you have to override more methods to help the NSOperationQueue object handle multithreading requests from caller.

- **start** *or* **main**: You will need to either override this method or the main method in order to execute your logic when the thread starts your operations. By default, this method does nothing except call the main method. Therefore, you can override this method or the main method.

- **isExecuting** *and* **isFinished**: Your operation must report its current status to outside clients. The two most important status states are if your operation has started executing and if it has finished its operation. So you need to keep track of your current operation status by using properties or instance variables and report these statuses here.

- **isConcurrent**: You have to override this method to return YES.

Other methods are not compulsory but you will usually need them.

- *Other logic processing methods*: Unless you want to put all of your code inside the main method, you will need other methods to contain your logic processing code as well.

Listing 6–4 shows the complete code example for a custom and concurrent NSOperation class.

Listing 6–4. *A Custom and Concurrent NSOperation Class*

```
@interface ConcurrentOperation: NSOperation {
    BOOL        executing;
    BOOL        finished;
    NSURL       *url;
}

@property (nonatomic, strong) NSURL *url;
@property (nonatomic, weak) id delegate;

@end

@implementation ConcurrentOperation

@synthesize url;

// put your necessary data and arguments in the custom initilization code
- (id)initWithURL:(NSURL *)aURL operationDelegate:(id)aDelegate {
    self = [super init];
    if (self) {
        executing = NO;
        finished = NO;
        self.url = aURL;
        self.delegate = aDelegate;
    }
    return self;
}
```

```
// remember to always override this method and return YES
- (BOOL)isConcurrent {
    return YES;
}

- (BOOL)isExecuting {
    return executing;
}

- (BOOL)isFinished {
    return finished;
}


// here, we choose to override the main method to download the image and send it back to
// the main selector.
- (void)main {
    NSData *loadedData = [[NSData alloc] initWithContentsOfURL:self.url];
    UIImage *myImage = [UIImage imageWithData:loadedData];

    [self.delegate performSelectorOnMainThread:@selector(imageLoaded:)
                                    withObject:myImage
                                 waitUntilDone:YES];
}

@end
```

Listing 6–4 shows how you can write a custom NSOperation to download an image from the web using multithreading

> **NOTE:** If you have done Java programming before, you may see that there is a similarity between NSOperation and Thread class or Runnable interface. In Thread class, you can extend the Thread class and override the run method. It is the same for the Runnable interface, where you implement the Runnable interface and override the run method as well. You can see the main method of NSOperation as the run method in Thread class and Runnable interface in Java.

Configuring a Thread

There are a few options that you can use to configure your thread properly to utilize your system resources well without overloading them, especially in a restricted runtime environment like iPhone.

■ *Stack size*: Whenever a new thread is created, the OS allocates a default amount of memory as a stack for that thread to execute. If you don't know what a stack is, you can look at Chapter 5. A stack inside the thread will store local variables and the methods called when the thread operates. To set up the stack size for a thread, you have to set that size before detaching the thread. In case of NSThread, this means that you use the initialize method as follows:

```
NSThread* myThread = [[NSThread alloc]
                      initWithTarget:self
                          selector:@selector(myThreadMainMethod:)
                          object:nil];
[myThread setStackSize:40960]; // 40KB here, the size is in bytes and multiple of 4KB
[myThread start];  // Actually create the thread
```

- *Thread-local storage*: Every thread has a dictionary of key-value pairs to store data that can be accessed from anywhere inside the thread. You can use this dictionary to store data that you want to be persistent across the thread execution without creating a global variable inside the code. You can call the dictionary by using [aThread threadDictionary]

- *Thread priority*: Thread priorities are about the likelihood a thread is chosen to execute by the OS. The higher the priority, the more likely thread runs. However, the priority does not guarantee you anything like the time the thread executes before the OS switches to another thread. It also does not guarantee that a higher thread will always be chosen rather than other low priority thread.

Your Thread Entry

When you start your thread, you need to have some code to manage the current state of that thread, the memory that thread creates when it executes, and any exception that can be thrown inside the thread. The reason is that your newly created thread will have its own stack, which is different than the default stack, as illustrated in Figure 6–4. Therefore, the memory that your thread uses is different than the memory area that the main thread uses. The exception is similar; it will only be stored in your stack and not returned back to the main stack and main thread.

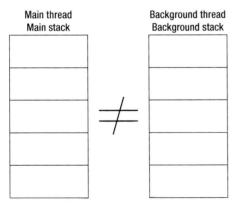

Figure 6–4. *Two threads have different stacks to manage their execution*

There are couples of things that you need to remember:

- **Autorelease Pool**: To manage autoreleased object.
- ExceptionHandler: To manage exceptions thrown when the thread runs.
- RunLoop: To create event-handling code.

I will discuss why you need to implement each of them and how to do it properly.

Table 6–3 provides a short summary to let you review the main techniques of creating and configuring threads plus their advantages and disadvantages.

Table 6–3. *Comparison of different ways to create and configure threads*

Mechanism	Advantages	Disadvantages
NSThread	Reuse code. Just need to pass a selector and object. Can set up some basic properties like thread priority and stack size.	Can't restrict/manage threads easily.
NSObject	Really easy to write and create a new thread.	Can't set up properties. Can't restrict/manage threads.
NSOperationQueue	Create and manage threads automatically. Make sure the number of running threads is not too much.	More complicated mechanism. Need to have this layer to manage operations inside.
NSInvocationOperation	Doesn't need to create new class or modify existing class. The selector can change depending on the user input by creating a new invocation operation object.	Hard to customize behavior of the thread.
NSBlockOperation	Can be used to keep track of a group of blocks together. Block operation object can manage and merge returned results.	Also hard to customize behavior of each thread.
NSOperation	Can customize the whole code in the way you want. Can manage and decide important actions such as finishing, pausing, and continuing your thread.	Need a new class to subclass the NSOperation class. More complicated, so it's easy to make mistakes.

Autorelease Pool

In every thread of the application, you should always have an `Autorelease Pool`, by putting the code inside the @autoreleasepool block. This pool contains all autoreleased objects when that thread is running. If you have never called a method that returns an autoreleased object, it is still better to include it because the underlying frameworks and libraries can create and return autoreleased objects. If you have an @autoreleasepool and you never use autorelease, everything still runs correctly.

If you look at the `main` method of any application template provided by XCode, you will see the following code:

```
int main(int argc, char *argv[]) {
    @autoreleasepool {
        int retVal = UIApplicationMain(argc, argv, nil, nil);
    }
    return retVal;
}
```

This @autoreleasepool will handle all autoreleased objects inside that thread. As you may already know, an autoreleased object is an object that you don't need to use anymore but you don't want to release it yet. It can also be returned as an autoreleased object by a factory method like [NSMutableArray array];. These objects will be released with the pool at the end of the run loop.

So, if you create a new thread, make sure you wrap your code inside the @autoreleasepool block, like so:

```
- (void)myThreadMethod {
    @autoreleasepool { // Top-level pool
        // Do thread work here.

    }
}
```

ExceptionHandler

Exceptions are important when dealing with threads. Because each thread has its own stack, when an exception is raised, it will travel over the stacks' methods to reach to the top. This can cause your thread to stop running. Any exception handler in the main thread will also be ignored.

Here is some basic code to handle an exception:

```
NSObject *myObject = nil;
@try {
   // access to some objects inside an array
   myObject = [myArray objectAtIndex:2];
}
@catch ( NSException *e ) {
 NSLog(@"Array has fewer than 3 items");
}
```

```
@finally {
    // clean up code here
}
```

Run Loop

When you create a new thread, you have two ways to execute that thread.

- You write code to execute the logic inside the thread until the task performed is finished with little or no interruption, such as the code to download the image from a URL, shown previously. This is easy, as you can see.

- You want your thread to respond when there dynamic events come into your thread, such as listening to some socket from the network or some events triggered at certain time. This is different than the first situation and requires you to write code to create a new run loop.

The following is some simple code for a RunLoop to listen to an input stream:

```
NSRunLoop *runLoop = [NSRunLoop currentRunLoop];
[iStream setDelegate:self];
[iStream scheduleInRunLoop:runLoop forMode:NSDefaultRunLoopMode];
```

> **NOTE:** If the method [NSRunLoop currentRunLoop] is called on a thread without a run loop, this method will cause a new run loop to be created.

And if you want a runloop to wait for an interval of time before start running, you can use NSTimer for this task:

```
[NSTimer scheduledTimerWithTimeInterval:2.0
                          target:self
                          selector:@selector(doStuff)
                          userInfo:nil
                          repeats:YES];
```

However, there are some cases when you should not use RunLoop, such as if in your main thread you have event-handling code such as NSInputStream or NSTimer work on some intensive task that takes too long to finish. Because event-handling code like my example will finally work on the thread that created it, your thread can't continue to work with other event-handling code until the old event has been processed and finished. This can harm your main UI thread if you create timer or input stream run loop inside that thread. The main problem is that it makes your UI less responsive.

Risks of Threads

When running in a multithreaded environment, there is something you always need to be careful about: you can't control the order of thread execution. For example, if you have two threads, thread 1 and thread 2, the CPU will work on thread 1 for a certain time and then it will switch to thread 2 and continue to run another amount of time. The problem is that you don't know when the CPU will switch and how much time it will allocate to a specific thread. These amounts of time are not equal for every thread and for every run.

To demonstrate the danger of output that can't be controlled easily, I will show you an example. The example will contain two threads: thread 1 and thread 2. Thread 1 prints the odd integer and thread 2 prints the even integer. These integers range from 1 to 20. Thread 1 will start first and then thread 2 will start. The example will run three times.

Listing 6–5 shows the sample code.

Listing 6–5. *Uncontrolled Output and Multithreading*

```
- (void)printOddIntegers {
    for (int i = 0; i < 20; i++) {
        // print odd integers
        if (i % 2 == 1) {
            NSLog(@"%d", i);
        }
    }
}

- (void)printEvenIntegers {
    for (int i = 0; i < 20; i++) {
        // print even integers
        if (i % 2 == 0) {
            NSLog(@"%d", i);
        }
    }
}

- (void)viewDidAppear:(BOOL)animated {

    [NSThread detachNewThreadSelector:@selector(printOddIntegers) toTarget:self
withObject:nil];

    [NSThread detachNewThreadSelector:@selector(printEvenIntegers) toTarget:self
withObject:nil];

}
```

As you can see, I called to print odd integers first and then called to print even integers. So you may have expected to see

- Some odd integers printed first.

- The odd and even integers printed evenly, such as two odd integers and then two even integers.

However, both of these assumptions are not correct, as you can see in Table 6–4, which shows the results of the three runs.

Table 6–4. *Output from Three Runs of the Odd/Even Integer Code*

Time	Results
First time	1, 0, 3, 2, 4, 5, 6, 7, 9, 8, 11, 10, 13, 12, 15, 14, 17, 16, 19, 18
Second time	0, 1, 2, 3, 4, 5, 6, 7, 8, 9, 10, 11, 12, 13, 14, 15, 17, 16, 19, 18
Third time	1, 0, 3, 2, 5, 4, 7, 6, 9, 8, 11, 10, 13, 15, 17, 19, 12, 14, 16, 18

As you can see in the second time, the number 0 is printed first while in other times number 1 is printed first. The printing of odd and even integers are not distributed evenly; moreover, there is no pattern of how many odd integers are printed before even integers are printed.

So, in multithreading environment, you can't control the order in which the threads will be executed. Multithreading is a double-edged sword. Developers implementing a multithreading application must be aware of three main risks.

- *Safety*: This criteria means that under the multithreading environment, the output should be correct as expected. In other words, the program can be run in different order many times, but the final output should be as expected and correct. "Nothing bad ever happens."

- *Liveness*: This is different than safety. One definition is "something good finally happens." For example, say thread A has to wait for the results from thread B, and somehow those results are never returned. So thread A can never calculate the final result. The term you usually hear for this problem is *deadlock*.

- *Performance*: One of important goals for iPhone apps is to have a better performance and a more responsive UI. So, your performance goal has to be reached. Liveness is only concerned with something good finally happening; it doesn't care about how fast that good result will occur.

I will cover each criterion in following parts with examples so you can understand what leads to a bad criterion and how you can fix it to make sure your application runs with high performance.

Safety

Safety refers to the requirement that a program running within the multithreaded environment should produce a correct and expected result as if it is running within a single threaded environment. I will discuss a potential problem that usually happens in a multithreaded environment when two or more threads access to the same data.

Problem

Figure 6–5 describes how two threads trying to retrieve the same item can cause an application crash. In Figure 6–5, thread 1 tries to push the item into the current stack. Then both thread 2 and thread 3 want to get that item out and do a check to make sure that there is an item inside the stack. However, after both threads check, thread 2 runs in first and gets the item out. Oops! As you can see, there is no item left for thread 3 to get out. This can lead to a crash for your application.

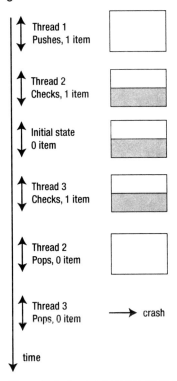

Figure 6–5. *A crash happens when running multithreading checks*

You can get the sample code from the project ThreadSafety, but Listing 6–6 shows a code illustration for the problem. Notice that this problem does not always happen but it will happen if you run the code for enough time. The code uses a NSMutableArray variable, storages, so client's code can add in and remove data from it.

Listing 6–6. *Thread Safety*

```
- (void)pushData {
    @autoreleasepool {
        while (YES) {
            // The storages property is a NSMutableArray used to store data
            [self.storages addObject:[[NSObject alloc] init]];
            [NSThread sleepForTimeInterval:0.1];
        }
    }
}
```

```
    }

- (void)popData {
    @autoreleasepool {
        while (YES) {
            if ([self.storages count] > 0) {
                NSObject *object = [self.storages objectAtIndex:0];
                NSLog(@"object: %@", object);
                [self.storages removeObjectAtIndex:0];
            }
            [NSThread sleepForTimeInterval:0.1];
        }
    }
}


- (void)viewDidAppear:(BOOL)animated {
    self.storages = [NSMutableArray array];
    [NSThread detachNewThreadSelector:@selector(pushData) toTarget:self
withObject:nil];
    [NSThread detachNewThreadSelector:@selector(popData) toTarget:self withObject:nil];

    [NSThread detachNewThreadSelector:@selector(popData) toTarget:self withObject:nil];
}
```

When you run the above code for a couple time, you will receive the below messages:

```
2011-05-19 18:53:15.540 ThreadSafety[2130:7103] object: <NSObject: 0x4e1d5e0>
2011-05-19 18:53:15.540 ThreadSafety[2130:6b03] object: <NSObject: 0x4e1d5e0>
2011-05-19 18:53:15.546 ThreadSafety[2130:6b03] *** Terminating app due to uncaught
exception 'NSRangeException', reason: '*** -[NSMutableArray removeObjectAtIndex:]: index
0 beyond bounds for empty array'
*** Call stack at first throw:
(
    0   CoreFoundation      0x00dc75a9 __exceptionPreprocess + 185
    1   libobjc.A.dylib     0x00f1b313 objc_exception_throw + 44
    2   CoreFoundation      0x00dc049f -[__NSArrayM removeObjectAtIndex:] + 415
    3   ThreadSafety        0x000022b1 -[ThreadSafetyViewController popData] + 251
    4   Foundation          0x00021cf4 -[NSThread main] + 81
    5   Foundation          0x00021c80 __NSThread__main__ + 1387
    6   libSystem.B.dylib   0x95486819 _pthread_start + 345
    7   libSystem.B.dylib   0x9548669e thread_start + 34
)
terminate called after throwing an instance of 'NSFxception'
```

The error message is

```
2011-05-19 18:53:15.546 ThreadSafety[2130:6b03] *** Terminating app due to uncaught
exception 'NSRangeException', reason: '*** -[NSMutableArray removeObjectAtIndex:]: index
0 beyond bounds for empty array'
```

What this tells you is that you tried to remove an object in an empty array, which should not happen when you already checked for empty array before removing the first object. And you even printed it out to see that there was a last object there.

Now, if you look at the Figure 6–4 again, you should understand why this creates a crash—because after the first thread checks and prints out the last object, the first thread stops and the second thread runs.

Solution

My solution for this problem is to lock the method until the thread is done. A lock is the mechanism to guarantee that only one thread has access to the specific block of code at a time. Imagine that you are now in a contest that requires direct competition with many people. You and your competitors are given a question and whoever rings the bell first can answer. After the first one finishes, another can ring the bell. The bell is locked while the first one is giving answer. It is the same for the thread here. You can create a lock that works like your bell: the thread that first gets the lock (similar to ringing the bell) blocks all other threads until it is finished. After the first thread finishes, the lock is opened (similar to when everybody else can ring the bell); the other threads can try to get to the lock first and the process repeats.

The basic point is that the lock mechanism makes sure that when one is working on the task, nobody else can interrupt. For example, if thread 1 is getting the object and printing it out, thread 2 will have to wait until thread 1 finishes getting and removing the object out of the array.

The lock will be created on an object. If thread 1 gets the lock for object A, no other threads can get the lock for object A anymore and these later threads have to wait until thread 1 finishes and returns the lock back to object A.

The simplest way to get a lock for an object A is using @synchronized(objA), as in the code in Listing 6–7.

Listing 6–7. *Code for Locks*

```
@synchronized(anObj) {
  // Everything here is locked by the @synchronized directive on object A
}
```

And our code will become:

```
- (void)pushData {
   @autoreleasepool {
      while (YES) {
         @synchronized(lockedObj) {
            [self.storages addObject:[NSObject new]];
         }
         [NSThread sleepForTimeInterval:0.1];
      }
   }
}


- (void)popData {
   @autoreleasepool {
      while (YES) {
         @synchronized(lockedObj) {
            if ([self.storages count] > 0) {
               NSObject *object = [self.storages objectAtIndex:0];
               NSLog(@"object: %@", object);
               [self.storages removeObjectAtIndex:0];
            }
         }
      }
```

```
            [NSThread sleepForTimeInterval:0.1];
        }
    }
}

- (void)viewDidAppear:(BOOL)animated {
    self.storages = [NSMutableArray array];
    self.lockedObj = [NSObject new];
    [NSThread detachNewThreadSelector:@selector(pushData) toTarget:self
withObject:nil];    [NSThread detachNewThreadSelector:@selector(popData) toTarget:self
withObject:nil];
    [NSThread detachNewThreadSelector:@selector(popData) toTarget:self withObject:nil];
}
```

> **NOTE:** In many cases you can use `self` as the lock for, things will work the same way. You only
> need to be sure that you use the same lock object for places that you want to lock them together.
> For example, if you have 2 different `storages` variable, you may consider using separate locks
> for separate `storages`.

Figure 6–6 visualizes how the @synchronized works on threads.

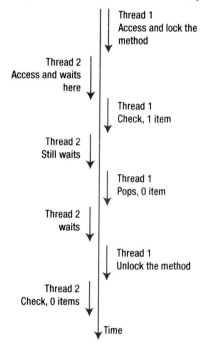

Figure 6–6. *How lock works in multithreading*

You synchronized both the push and pop data methods because if you only lock one
method, there's a risk that when you are checking for a pop, the storage pushes more
data in and you won't get the correct object that you want. To prevent this, you need to

lock both of them by using the same lockedObj so that only one method at the time can run.

Your code is safe, but there are still two more important attributes of multithreading to discuss.

Liveness

Liveness is when "a good thing finally happens." For example, if your code's goal is to make sure that you can continuously push and pop objects out of the array, the question is whether this process will work forever. The problem with locking is the lock can cause all threads that are working in your system to keep waiting—in other words, deadlock. If you can guarantee the liveness of your application, deadlock should never happen.

Problem

Imagine that you have two threads: A and B. A is waiting for B to finish its work before A can start. However, thread B is waiting for thread A to finish its work before it can continue.

For an actual example, you can look back the code in Listing 6–7. Note that the push and pop threads are locked by the same object, lockedObj. Figure 6–7 shows how two threads that are locked on the same object can wait for each other forever.

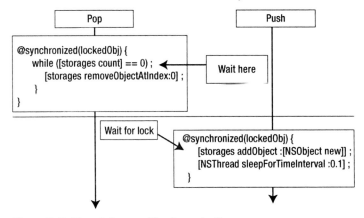

Figure 6–7. *Threads keep waiting for each other*

As you can see in this new example, the pop thread keeps waiting on the while loop because the storages count is 0. And the push thread can't add another object into the array because that code is locked by the object lockedObj. The push thread now has to wait until the pop thread gets done and gives the lock back to the lockedObj. Therefore, these two threads stop and wait for each other forever. Here are some possible solutions to solve this deadlock issue.

If your code is prone to deadlock, you can't use @synchronized(lockedObj) anymore because this directive doesn't support any mechanism to avoid the deadlock issue. There are two other possible mechanisms that you can use to avoid deadlock.

- NSLock: You can use this to protect concurrent access to sections of code, like the way @synchronized(obj) is used, but you can control when to lock and unlock that section of code.

- NSCondition: This is useful for the producer/consumer model like the push/pop example shown previously.

NSLock Solution

You can use it in two ways, lock or tryLock. With the lock method, the method that can't acquire the lock will stop and wait until it gets the lock. With the tryLock, method, however, if the tryLock method returns NO, that means lock is already owned by another thread and can't be acquired by the calling thread.

Lock example:

```
NSLock *testLock = [[NSLock alloc] init];
[testLock lock];

if ([self.storages count] > 0) {
  NSObject *object = [self.storages objectAtIndex:0];
  NSLog(@"object: %@", object);
  [self.storages removeObjectAtIndex:0];
}
[NSThread sleepForTimeInterval:0.1];
[testLock unlock];
```

This section of code works just like the @synchronized(obj) at the previous example where you acquire the lock at the beginning of the code and unlock it at the end. However, the tryLock method will run differently.

TryLock example:

```
NSLock *testLock = [[NSLock alloc] init];
if([testLock tryLock])
  // storages is a NSMutableArray member variable property to store data.
  if ([self.storages count] > 0) {
    NSObject *object = [self.storages objectAtIndex:0],
    NSLog(@"object: %@", object);
    [self.storages removeObjectAtIndex:0];
  }
  [NSThread sleepForTimeInterval:0.1];
}
[testLock unlock];
```

It tests if you can acquire the lock and then continues. If you don't acquire the lock, everything is fine and the thread just continues to run the rest of the code without getting blocked.

NSCondition Solution

With `NSLock`, you can see that after you acquire a lock by using `[testLock lock];` you can't stop or suspend your thread to wait for some condition. The only way you can do so is to continue until you unlock so other threads can come in.

Take a look back at the push/pop example. Keep running the thread over and over again to check if there is an item in the array that is not efficient. In a loop, if the thread sees that there is no item in the array, it should stop and wait there until there are some items and then go in and get that item out. The good thing about this approach is that you can suspend your thread and not waste too many system resources for nothing.

To let a thread stop, wait, and return the lock at the same time you need to use `NSCondition`. Listing 6–8 demonstrates how you can use `NSCondition` for a push/pop sample.

Listing 6–8. *NSCondition Example*

```
- (void)pushData {
    @autoreleasepool {

        while (YES) {
            // condition is a NSCondition member variable of the class so you can share
            //  this condition with other methods/blocks of code
            [condition lock];

            // storages is a NSMutableArray member variable property to store data.
            [self.storages addObject:[NSObject new]];
            [NSThread sleepForTimeInterval:0.1];
            [condition signal];
            [condition unlock];
        }
    }
}

- (void)popData {
    @autoreleasepool {
        while (YES) {
            // condition is a NSCondition member variable of the class so you can share
            //  this condition with other methods/blocks of code
            [condition lock];

            // storages is a NSMutableArray member variable property to store data.
            while([self.storages count] <= 0)
                [condition wait];
            NSObject *object = [self.storages objectAtIndex:0];
            NSLog(@"object: %@", object);
            [self.storages removeObjectAtIndex:0];
            [condition unlock];
        }
    }
}
```

There are other locking mechanisms, such as NSRecursiveLock and NSConditionLock, but using NSLock and NSCondition is usually enough for most cases. For threading, you should always try to make it simple because multithreading can introduce subtle bugs in your code.

> **NOTE:** NSRecursiveLock is useful if you have a thread that wants to acquire the lock multiple times without causing any deadlock. NSRecursiveLock still blocks other threads to access into the block of code

Deadlock

Using these locks can raise the issue of deadlock in your code. Deadlock looks like the first issue I introduced to you, but it is more related to the scenario when you have two or more locks and the threads are waiting for each other.

Figure 6–8 demonstrates a situation where thread 1 acquires the lock on the object 1 and thread 2 acquires the lock on object 2. Then thread 1 wants to acquire the lock for object 2 but has to wait for thread 2 to release the lock. At the same time, thread 2 wants to acquire the lock for object 1 but has to wait for thread 1 to release the lock. As you can see, both threads end up waiting for each other and no thread can continue to work.

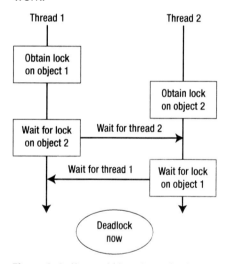

Figure 6–8. *How multithreads can be deadlocked*

There are some methods that you can use to fix this deadlock situation, such as reordering threads; minimize locking; a bigger lock; tryLock; and time out for locking. These mechanisms are not hard to implement; the figures that follow will help you understand how to do it.

In Figure 6–9, the simplest way is to reorder the thread and locking order so that only when a thread is done with locking on lock 2, the other thread can get the lock and continue its work.

However, if your method structure is fixed and some code belongs to a third-party library, it is hard to reorder the lock or modify the code.

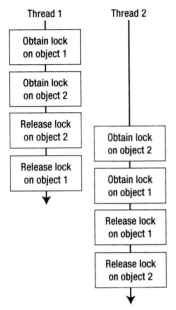

Figure 6–9. *Thread reordering*

The next way is to try to only lock when you really need to lock that part. This way you will minimize the locking part, as shown in Figure 6–10.

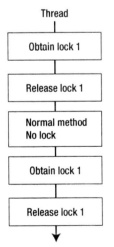

Figure 6–10. *Minimize locking*

This can only be done easily if you have the code or you can find some way to separate out the part that you don't need to lock. Note that it may also make your code look more complicated.

Another way for you to do this is to implement another bigger lock over the other locks. This will allow other threads to try to access the same lock at the same time. For example, in Figure 6–11, due to the new bigger lock, thread 2 now has to wait for thread 1 to finish before it can obtain any lock or run any necessary code. In normal code, if you can remove smaller locks and replace them with a bigger lock, you should do so when it reduces code complexity. This mechanism is usually used in cases where you need to prevent deadlock in libraries that you can't or don't want to modify the library code.

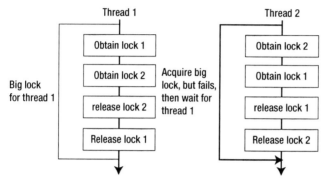

Figure 6–11. *A bigger, master lock*

You could also try the aforementioned `tryLock`. Using `tryLock`, if a thread can't obtain the lock, it will not stop and wait. That thread can just continue to run the other logic inside the thread. Here is sample code for using `tryLock`:

```
NSLock *testLock = [[NSLock alloc] init];
if([testLock tryLock])
  if ([self.storages count] > 0) {
    NSObject *object = [self.storages objectAtIndex:0];
    NSLog(@"object: %@", object);
    [self.storages removeObjectAtIndex:0];
  }
  [testLock unlock];
}
[NSThread sleepForTimeInterval:0.1];
```

The last method that I will mentioned here (although there are many other methods to prevent deadlock) is to use timeout. In objective-C, you can specify the thread to wait until it can acquire the lock or the time for it to wait ends. Using the `lockBeforeDate` method will help you achieve this goal. The thread that calls this method will be blocked until it can obtain the lock. If the specified `NSDate` instance in the argument happens but the thread still can't obtain the lock, it will just continue. This will help in case you have deadlock; your thread can continue with a little bit of risk but no deadlock will ever happen.

Performance

Performance is the main reason to use multithreading in applications. However, as you can see, if you don't use it properly, your application will have many problems. Your application will crash frequently if you can't control the safety risk of multithreading, as I showed you previously. Moreover, some of the functions won't work because some of threads are blocked or have to wait for each other forever. So if you integrate multithreading into your application, you must make sure that your application runs properly before you worry about the performance.

With the aforementioned issues in mind, you should considering carefully if your application needs to have multithreading to run faster. To determine if a calculation or a computation needs to work on many separate threads, you need to ask yourself if that calculation is a CPU-bound or I/O-bound task.

A CPU-bound task is one that works most or all of the time on the CPU and keeps the CPU busy. The following are some examples of CPU-bound tasks:

- Complex algorithms, such as merging two arrays together when calculating some logic for a game.

- Scanning the big string from memory (already loaded and stored in memory) for a given string.

In contrast, an I/O-bound task is one that spends most of the time waiting for data from other sources. For example, if you need to read and load an image from a file or remote server, most of the time your thread will sit there doing nothing but waiting for data from a remote server. These tasks are called I/O tasks and they need to be called on a separate thread.

Why should you not separate a CPU-bound task into many threads? Does it help to calculate things faster? Let Figure 6–12 explain this in detail.

As you can see in Figure 6–12, when a CPU needs to switch from a thread to another thread, it takes some time and resources for it to do so. Therefore, there is an overhead cost for any multithreading application. If your task is just a CPU-bound task, it would take more time for the CPU to finish the whole task because the number of tasks is the same but CPU needs to deal with overhead cost. However, if, in the future, iPhone does have additional CPU cores, it would make sense to separate a task out.

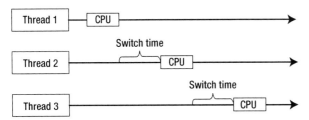

Figure 6–12. *Switching the thread cost time from CPU*

In I/O tasks, the situation is different. If CPU doesn't switch to another thread, it just sits there, waiting for data and doing nothing at all. Therefore, in the case of I/O tasks, you should always put it into another thread so that CPU can do something else instead of waiting for data.

In other words, imagine a supermarket. Your task is to serve all customers. Here are two scenarios that will help explain both concepts:

- If all customers are the same, and they come in frequently, you can choose to put them in many similar checkout lines or put them in the same queue. If you put your customers into many lines and you have only one cashier, he needs to switch from counter to counter to serve all the customers. However, if you allow them to be in the same queue, then your cashier doesn't need to move around. This is a CPU-bound task.

- However, it's different if you have different kinds of customers and they don't come in frequently. For example, you can have a customer service booth, an area for self-checkout, and an area for checkout lines. Now, if the customers don't come to checkout lines often, your cashier will have to stand there, wait, and do nothing. Or he can switch frequently from area to area, answering questions at the customer service booth and assisting others at the self-checkout counter. You don't need to hire three cashiers and you can't put your customers into the same queue. This is similar to an I/O-bound task where your data is not the same and does not come frequently into one queue.

You also need to take into account user responsiveness. If your CPU-bound calculation takes too much time to finish, the whole UI will be blocked and become unresponsive. Therefore, if it's the main thread (or UI thread), you need to put off any heavy calculations, either CPU-bound or I/O-bound, out of this thread.

There are other performance issues that you may need to be careful about when you design your multithreading application. Look at the following code and see if you can figure out what's wrong with it:

```
+ (void)saveImage:(NSData *)imageData {
    @synchronized (self) {
        @autoreleasepool {
            NSString *filePath = @""; // some default path here
            [imageData writeToFile:filePath atomically:YES];
        }
    }
}

+ (void)caller {
    NSData *imageData = nil;
    [NSThread detachNewThreadSelector:@selector(saveImage:) toTarget:self
withObject:imageData];
}
```

As you may or may not see, the problem is with @synchronized (self); line. You are doing multithreading and you block only one thread to access to that piece of code at the time. What is the benefit of multithreading in this case? So, you have to be careful with locks. You are doing multithreading to make sure that your I/O-bound tasks get the benefit of not waiting or blocking a thread for a long time. If you don't use threads in a proper way, all your threads still need to wait for each other before they can start their tasks.

Thread Synchronization

Now, let's move to some other important parts of multithreading. Since every thread runs in its own stack and create its own objects, how can your threads communicate and share data between different threads inside your application? As mentioned, when you share your data structure or objects between multiple threads, there's a risk that many threads are trying to change that object or data structure.

First, I want to introduce a new term called *thread-safe*. Thread-safe classes (or functions) are classes where you don't have to worry about any of the previously mentioned safety issues. These classes will either take care of the locking process or they are immutable classes (they can't be changed). Here is a list of thread-safe classes or functions:

- NSArray
- NSConnection
- NSData
- NSDate
- NSDictionary
- NSNumber
- NSObject
- NSSet
- NSString

And other, usually mutable, thread-unsafe classes:

- NSMutableArray
- NSMutableAttributedString
- NSMutableCharacterSet
- NSMutableData
- NSMutableDictionary
- NSMutableSet
- NSMutableString

Why should you prefer thread-safe classes to thread-unsafe classes? Why don't you just use mutable classes but make sure about locking? Let me give you an example of locking issues that you may have with changing objects when accessing by threads:

```
NSMutableArray* myArray = GetSharedArray();
id anObject;

if ([myArray count] > 0) {
```

```
    anObject = [myArray objectAtIndex:0];
}

[anObject doSomething];
```

This example is very simple but it will help you understand a very important concept. Do you see what's wrong with this code? After your code checks for the length of the array, another thread can modify that array, and there may be no object in the array anymore because the other thread can remove all the objects out. So, you improve it a little bit by adding lock in, but this is not a perfect solution yet.

```
NSLock* arrayLock =[[NSLock alloc] init];
NSMutableArray* myArray = GetSharedArray();
id anObject;

[arrayLock lock];
if ([myArray count] > 0) {
    anObject = [myArray objectAtIndex:0];
}
[arrayLock unlock];

[anObject doSomething];
```

That's better, but there are still some issues, such as the fact that the object you get out can be changed or modified by some other thread. Therefore, the next step is to put the line [anObject doSomething]; into the lock area as well.

```
NSLock* arrayLock =[[NSLock alloc] init];
NSMutableArray* myArray = GetSharedArray();
id anObject;

[arrayLock lock];
if ([myArray count] > 0) {
    anObject = [myArray objectAtIndex:0];
    [anObject doSomething];
}

[arrayLock unlock];
```

If the myArray object you have is an NSArray without an NSMutableArray, you may not need the lock at all. You can just call them normally.

```
NSArray* myArray = GetSharedArray();
id anObject;

anObject = [myArray objectAtIndex:0];
[anObject doSomething];
```

This is the good thing about using immutable objects rather than mutable objects. You can be sure that while you are processing these objects, nobody else can change or modify their properties.

Alternatives to Threads

Sometimes you don't want the headache of threads or you don't want to create and manage separate threads yourself. For example, if you want to have a timer to call your method every 2 seconds, you may have to write a thread that keeps looping, sleeps 2 seconds, and then calls the methods. Or you may want to write code to handle asynchronous behaviors like downloading a file to the network. Or you simply want to continue a heavy calculation process when your iPhone is free from working. These are not easy to implement properly or with decent performance. I will discuss some solutions.

NSTimer

NSTimer doesn't promise to be really precise; if you set a firing time to be 0.5 seconds, the timer can fire at 0.55 or even 0.6 seconds. However, it is a good mechanism if you only want a relatively precise mechanism for scheduling.

Repeating vs. Non-Repeating Timers

You can schedule a repeating timer or a non-repeating timer. For a repeating timer, the timer will fire after every interval of time that you specify and never get invalidated. You need to manually invalidate the repeating timer if you want it to stop. For a non-repeating timer, it will only fire the event once and then get invalidated automatically. For both cases, once a timer is invalidated, it can't be reused; you will need to create another timer.

To create a timer, you may choose to call either

```
+ scheduledTimerWithTimeInterval:target:selector:userInfo: repeats:
```

or

```
+ timerWithTimeInterval:target:selector:userInfo:repeats:
```

The first line will create a new timer, add it to the current run loop, and return the timer object back to you. The second method will just create a new timer; you'll need to add it the run loop yourself by calling `[runLoop addTimer:forMode:]`.

To invalidate a timer when using the repeating timer, you need to use `invalidate` method as in the following: `[aTimer invalidate];`

> **NOTE:** On a thread without the runloop, NSTimer doesn't work at all.

Asynchronous Functions

In many cases, asynchronous functions can be more lightweight than threads. For example, the iPhone environment can reuse threads from the thread pool to handle the asynchronous functions. Moreover, if you need to handle 100 asynchronous functions, the OS may only need to create 10 threads because one thread can handle multiple asynchronous functions. The only problem is that sometimes it may look more complicated than if you just create some threads and a synchronous request to handle them.

Listing 6–9 is a block of code to create an asynchronous request to the server and merge result back to create a complete data object.

Listing 6–9. *Asynchronous Calling*

```
MyFetcher.h

#import <Foundation/Foundation.h>

@interface MyFetcher : NSObject {
 @private
    NSURLRequest *request;
    NSMutableData *data;
    UIImage *image;
    NSURL *imageURL;
}

@property (nonatomic, strong) NSURLRequest *request;
@property (nonatomic, strong) NSMutableData *data;
@property (nonatomic, strong) IBOutlet UIImage *image;
@property (nonatomic, strong) NSURL *imageURL;


- (void)loadImageWithURL:(NSURL *)url;


@end


MyFetcher.m

#import "MyFetcher.h"

@implementation MyFetcher
@synthesize request;
@synthesize data;
@synthesize image;
@synthesize imageURL;


- (void)loadImageWithURL:(NSURL *)url {
    self.request = [NSURLRequest requestWithURL:url];
    NSURLConnection *connection = [NSURLConnection connectionWithRequest:self.request
delegate:self];
    if (connection) {
        self.data = [NSMutableData data];
    }
}

- (void)connection:(NSURLConnection *)conn didReceiveResponse:(NSURLResponse *)response_
{
    [data setLength:0];
```

```
}

- (void)connection:(NSURLConnection *)conn didReceiveData:(NSData *)data_ {
    [data appendData:data_];
}


- (void)connectionDidFinishLoading:(NSURLConnection *)connection {
    self.image = [UIImage imageWithData:self.data];
}


- (void)connection:(NSURLConnection *)connection didFailWithError:(NSError *)error {
    self.data = nil;
    self.image = nil;
}


@end
```

Compare that with this simple threading and synchronous solution:

```
@autoreleasepool {
    NSData *imageData = [NSData dataWithContentsOfURL:imageURL];
}
```

You can see that in some cases, you may need to write more code to have better performance. You just need to make sure what you are doing will actually benefit you.

If you are doing synchronous HTTP request, you have to run it on a background thread. It is the iOS's policy to kill your application if it becomes non-responsive for a long time. That would certainly create a bad impression about your application.

> **NOTE:** If you have too many simultaneous HTTP calls, you may consider creating a separate thread to handle asynchronous calls to avoid any impact on the main thread.

Idle-Time Notifications

There are things you want to do only when the system is idle. For example, if you want to send some feedback from the iPhone to your server, you may not want to send it when other processes are running or other users are still interacting with the device. You should only send it if the user or the device has nothing else to do. This would be a really hard job to do it on your own. Happily, Apple has provides a function for it. You can use NSNotificationQueue to post a notification with the style NSPostWhenIdle, as in the following code:

```
- (void)notificationMethod {
    // do something here
}

- (void)registerForNotification {
    [[NSNotificationCenter defaultCenter] addObserver:self
                                    selector:@selector(notificationMethod)
```

```
                                    name:@"my_notification"
                                 object:nil];
    NSNotification *notification = [NSNotification
notificationWithName:@"my_notification" object:nil];
    [[NSNotificationQueue defaultQueue] enqueueNotification:notification
postingStyle:NSPostWhenIdle];
}
```

As you can see, it works just like the normal way you use NSNotificationCenter; you add the object and method as observer and selector. Then you can post a new notification to the queue so that the method is processed when the system is in the idle state.

Thread Instrument for iPhone

The thread instrument was discussed in Chapter 2 so Figure 6–13 is just a simple figure to remind you about the instrument.

Figure 6–13 *Thread Instrument for iPhone*

The instrument doesn't give you much information except the current state of running threads inside your application. This can help you know if you are overloading the system by having too many running threads or any threads that suspend and wait for too long, which is a signal of a deadlock.

Summary

In this chapter, you learned how to improve the performance of your app using multithreading. The concept is really simple: you create a new thread to handle some calculations. However, to make it correct and safe for the application, you need to be aware of many different pitfalls. You also need to know about the concept of CPU-bound tasks and I/O-bound tasks to make sure what you are doing will really boost the performance of your application up, not make it slower. You learned how to create, manage, and run threads in different ways. You also learned objective-C style and its syntax to deal with lock and thread synchronization issues, which are really important.

EXERCISES

1. Write a complete program to download and display an image from the Internet into a UIImageView. You can use the template called View-based application in XCode.

2. Rewrite the ThreadLock example using NSLock so that it doesn't have the deadlock issue.

3. Rewrite the sample project MultiThreadingSample to use threading with synchronous requests instead of asynchronous requests.

## Chapter 7

Optimize Memory Usage for Better Performance

In this chapter, you will learn the following:

- Review the old manual memory management policies

- Object ownership policy

- The new Automatic Memory Management bases on the old manual memory management.

- What object copying is and how to use it.

- How to use `autorelease` and `release` methods properly.

- A review of memory instruments.

iPhone is a constrained environment with a limited amount of memory. However, many developers either underestimate or overestimate that fact, so they don't take advantage of all the available memory in the iPhone to boost performance. Others are so scared of memory and performance in iPhone that they do lots of premature optimization, which harms the readability of the code and makes it hard to maintain the code base later.

To utilize the memory for better performance and better readability without making the application crash, you need to understand the memory structure of the iPhone environment. You need to learn how to avoid holding too many objects in memory, which can cause a memory warning and then a crash. You also need to learn when you should retain an object or release an object; if you hold too few objects in memory, it can make your calculation run slower because you need to reconstruct the object or load it from the file system.

A Little Review

This part gives you a good transition to the new automatic reference counting (ARC) mechanism. Some people got confused about the transition to a new learning experience. I hope that this part can help you to move smoothly without any problems to the new ARC mechanism.

Old Object Ownership Policy

This old concept relates to if your object A has a strong reference to another object B, your object A needs to manually release this object B. Object A has a strong reference to object B if object A **alloc, copy, mutableCopy, new or retain** object B. On the other hand, if your object A does not call those methods in object B, object A only has a weak reference to object B.

For the old memory management mechanism, if your object or method has a strong reference to another object B, it is responsible to **release** or **autorelease** that object B. Every strong reference to object B will increase its retain count by 1. If no object has a strong reference to object B anymore, in other words, the retain count is 0, object B is deallocated (Listing 7.1).

Listing 7.1. Release the Object if You Have a Strong Reference

```
- (void)doSomething {
  NSObject *obj = [[NSObject alloc] init];
  NSLog(@"obj: %@", obj);
  [obj release];
}
```

Autorelease

The autorelease method's job is to send the object to a pool and declare that this object will later be released. Using this method, you don't want to have a strong reference to the object anymore but you don't want it to be deallocated. Take a look at Listing 7.2.

Listing 7.2. Memory Issue

```
- (NSObject *)getObj {
  NSObject *obj = [[NSObject alloc] init];
  return obj;
}

- (void)anotherMethod {
  NSObject *myObj = [self getObj];
  // do something
  // Should I release the object here?
  [myObj release];
}
```

Now, after you have finished working with the object, you should ask yourself if you should release your myObj now or not. Basically, you will think you have to release it;

otherwise, nobody will release that myObj and a memory leak will happen. However, because your anotherMethod does not have a strong reference to myObj, it cannot release myObj. The only way is to use autorelease as in Listing 7.3.

Listing 7.3. Use Autorelease to Solve the Problem

```
- (NSObject *)getObj {
  NSObject *obj = [[NSObject alloc] init];
  return [obj autorelease];
}

- (void)anotherMethod {
  NSObject *myObj = [self getObj];
  // do something
}
```

> **NOTE:** The method anotherMethod does not have a strong reference

Autorelease Pool

I will give a quick overview of autorelease pools and then explain the concept in depth so you can understand the differences between autorelease pool and release explicitly.

The autorelease pool is where all of your autoreleased objects are stored. When this autorelease pool is released, all the autoreleased objects will also be sent a release message. If the retain count of an object is 0, that object will be deallocated.

An autorelease pool will be released at the end of the event life cycle. For example, when user taps into the UI, a new event life cycle is created to process the tap event, then it processes all the logic related to that tap event, and finally it displays the results back to user. This is one event life cycle. For that event life cycle, you will have an autorelease pool.

The main autorelease pool, which is created in the main method as the following code shows:

```
int main(int argc, char *argv[]) {

    @autoreleasepool {
        int retVal = UIApplicationMain(argc, argv, nil, nil);
    }
    return retVal;
}
```

As you can see in the code, at the beginning of the method, a new autorelease pool is created, then the main logic is executed using the UIApplicationMain; after that event loop, the pool is released. This cycle is shown in Figure 7–1.

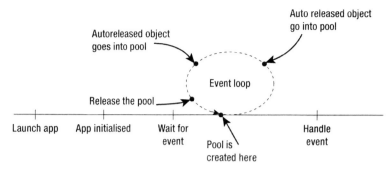

Figure 7–1. *Autorelease cycle*

Automatic Reference Counting

The problem with the above process is that it gets more complicated when you always need to remember the rules and when you need to put `retain, release or autorelease` in. So, in the new Xcode (Xcode 4.2), Apple released a new mechanism, which makes the process of `retain, release and autorelease` to be automatic. All policies above still apply to the code in the new version. But Xcode will append all the necessary code for you to manage the memory.

To give you a quick picture, I will write the code in Listing 7.1 and Listing 7.3 again.

Listing 7.4. Rewrite Code for the New ARC mechanism

```
For Listing 7.1:
- (void)doSomething {
        NSObject *obj = [[NSObject alloc] init];
        NSLog(@"obj: %@", obj);
}

For Listing 7.3:
- (NSObject *)getObj {
        NSObject *obj = [[NSObject alloc] init];
        return obj;
}
```

That's it! No more `release` or `autorelease` is necessary. When you compile the code, Xcode will automatically add all the necesary release/autorelease calls for you. After the compiler adds these calls, the code will be exactly the same as Listing 7.1 and Listing 7.3.

How to Set Up Your Project in Xcode?

Go into your project settings, find if the line **Objective-C Automatic Reference Counting** is set to **YES** or not. You can see figure 7–2 for the position of the setting line:

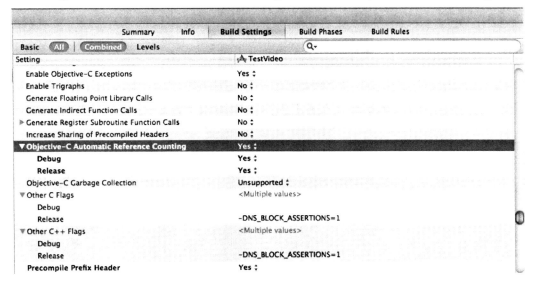

Figure 7–2. *Set up your project for ARC*

If your project is an existing project with the old `retain/release/autorelease` call, you can use a migration tool of Xcode to remove those unnecessary calls for your project as shown in Figure 7–3.

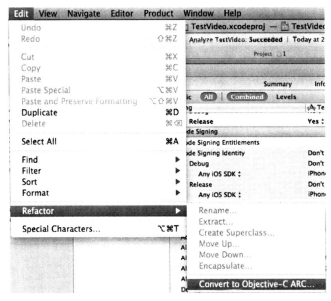

Figure 7–3. *Convert the old code to Objective-C ARC*

ARC Policy

You need to follow some new rules to make sure that your project is compatible with ARC:

- You cannot use or call the old memory management methods: retain, release, autorelease and retainCount. You can override the dealloc method to do any clean up that you need, but you must not call any dealloc method, for example [super dealloc] is not allowed.

  This rule also enforces you when setting up your properties:

  @property (nonatomic, retain) NSString *myName; // This is not allowed.

- You cannot use object pointers in C, this may create some problems for you if you want to integrate C code into your project, as described in Chapter 9.

- You cannot use NSAutoreleasePool objects, and you must use @autoreleasepool.

  Instead of using:

  ```
  NSAutoreleasePool *myPool = [[NSAutoreleasePool alloc] init];
  // your code here
  [pool release];
  ```

  You have to use:

  ```
  @autoreleasepool {
      // your code here
  }
  ```

New Qualifier for ARC

As the new ARC policy, you now need to include new lifetime qualifiers to enforce new rules of ARC into the codebase.

- strong : This is to indicate that you want to keep a strong reference to this variable. As long as there is a strong reference to an object A, object A will not be deallocated.

- weak : This works like assign, if you just want a reference to the object, without explicitly own that object. Therefore, you do not need to manage the lifetime of that object. The good thing is that if object A has a weak reference to object B and object B is deallocated, the reference becomes nil. This makes it safer when you will not have a reference to a deallocated object.

- ▨ unsafe_unretained: This is similar to weak, the difference is that if the object B, which is referenced by object A, gets deallocated, the reference will point to a deallocated object, which can cause a crash for your application.

- ▨ autoreleasing: If you have a method that needs to have a pass-by-reference argument, you can consider using this qualifier. The method will be responsible to autorelease the argument when it returns.

Object Property

Now, you need to change the object property declaration. Instead of using old memory management mechanism: @property (retain) NSString *myString as in the previous version, you now have a new set of rules.

If you want to have an ownership to the object

```
// This is similar to @property (retain) NSString *myString
@property(strong) NSString *myString;
```

If you just want a reference to the object, without the ownership

```
// This is similar to @property (assign) UIViewController *myViewController;
//   except that if myViewController object is deallocated,
//   the reference becomes nil.
@property(weak) UIViewController*myString;
```

> **NOTE:** If you want your application to run in iOS4, you cannot use weak, you need to use unsafe_unretained and set the reference to nil yourself.

Variable Declarations

To use the qualifier inside the methods, you need to add __ into the beginning of it. For example, you will have __strong or __weak. In methods, __strong qualifier is the default qualifier.

Using __strong qualifier guarantees that your object is still alive until the end of the method, and be careful with using __weak or __unsafe_unretained. If there is no strong reference to your object, your object will be deallocated immediately. For example:

```
NSString __weak *myString = @"hello world";
NSLog (@"myString: %@", myString);
```

Will print out (null) because at the time the myString object is printed, there is no strong reference to it.

The __autoreleasing qualifier is used for methods receiving a pass by reference argument.

```
- (BOOL)performTaskWithError:(NSError *__autoreleasing *)error;
```

You can call that method normally using:

```
NSError *error = nil;
[self performTaskWithError:&error];
```
By default, the `error` object is declared with `strong` qualifier, but the compiler will add code in to make the method call `[self performTaskWithError:&error];`

> **NOTE:** For all methods that return an object, and the name does not contain `new`, `alloc`, or `copy`, the object will automatically be autoreleased on return.

Advanced Memory Issues

Now that you have learned the most basic memory techniques, I will introduce you to some advanced memory topics.

Retain/Relationship Cycles

In the old memory management world, if object A owns object B, then object A has to release object B when object A gets deallocated. However, what happens if object A owns object B and objects B also owns object A?

You want to release object A by calling `release` method on it and setting your reference to `nil`. However, because object B still owns object A, the retain count of object A is greater than 0. It's the same when you release object B; its retain count is still greater than 0 because object A still owns object B.

This sequence keeps going on like this without any object getting deallocated, as illustrated by Figure 7–4.

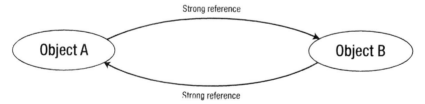

Figure 7–4. *Retain cycle*

This still holds true for the new ARC mechanism, if you have 2 objects having strong reference to each other, both objects get leaked.

So what do you need to do if you want both objects to own each other? You need weak references.

Weak References

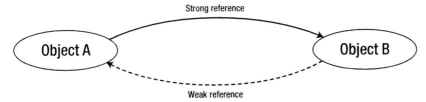

Figure 7–5. *Weak reference cycle*

So, to avoid a retain cycle, only object A holds a strong reference to object B and object B can only hold a weak reference to object A.

UIViewController

All iPhone apps require that you work with the UIViewController (how else can you have your UI?). Therefore, understanding the UIViewController life cycle will help you with many important things, such as:

- Utilizing your memory better.

- Avoiding any memory leaks.

- Improving responsiveness.

From my observation when teaching and conduct training for many developers, many of them make a serious mistake by not understanding the management life cycle of a view controller object. There are some main management processes in the iPhone environment to control the life cycle of a view controller object, such as:

- Loading the view.

- Unloading the view when the system needs to reclaim memory.

- Releasing the view.

- Displaying or hiding the view from the UI.

Load View Process

When a view controller is asked for its view, it checks if its view is loaded into the memory or not. If not, then it will load that view and then the method viewDidLoad is called. Figure 7–6 shows the process of loading the view.

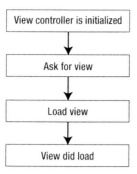

Figure 7–6. *Loading view process*

There are some notes about performance that you should remember about this loading view process:

- If you override the `loadView` method, you need to create the view hierarchy to display to the UI. This can lead to slightly better performance because it doesn't need to load the view from a nib file.

- If you don't override the `loadView` method, the iOS environment will automatically look for the nib file that you specify or a nib file that has the same name as the view controller file. Using a nib file is better for maintenance and is a drag and drop feature.

- If nothing is matched, the iOS environment will create a new and empty view and return that empty view.

Unload View Process

This process is really important for memory and performance. The main reason is that this process is running when your application has a memory warning and needs to reclaim the memory resource. In this process, the `didReceiveMemoryWarning` method will be called first and then the `viewDidUnload` method is called. Views that are on the screen will not get unloaded. You can see the process in Figure 7–7.

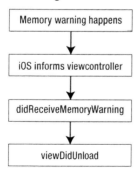

Figure 7–7. *Unloading view process*

In this unloading view process, there are a couple of performance and memory issues you need to remember:

- Make sure that when the method `didReceiveMemoryWarning` is called, you clear the memory cache for your heavy objects, such as all image cache. If you don't do so, the iOS environment can force your app to close, which is a really bad user experience.

- You shouldn't clear or release any view here because it may be unsafe to do so. Instead, you should call [`super didReceiveMemoryWarning`] so the superclass can check if it is safe to release the subview or not.

- If it is safe to release its view, the method `viewDidUnload` will be called. You can choose to override this method to do any clean up required for your views and hierarchy.

> **NOTE:** When you override loading methods such as `init`, `loadView`, and `viewDidLoad`, the call to the superclass must be at the beginning of the method. However, if you override cleaning methods, such as `didReceiveMemoryWarning`, `viewDidUnload` or `dealloc`, the call to the superclass has to be at the end of the method.

There are some key points in `viewDidUnload` that confuse many developers.

- `viewDidLoad` and `viewDidUnload` do not correspond to each other. The `viewDidLoad` method is called after the view controller object is initialized and a view is requested. `viewDidUnload` is called after a memory warning is received. After calling `viewDidUnload`, there is no call to the `dealloc` method of the view controller object. The view that is unloaded will be deallocated.

- In `viewDidUnload`, you only clean up your views; all other objects will be cleaned up or released in `didReceiveMemoryWarning`.

Displaying and Hiding Views in the User Interface

The process of displaying and hiding views in UI has very little to do with memory. However, it is related to the performance and the user's experience of the performance of an iOS app.

There are four main methods in the view controller life cycle to represent the four different states of a view when it is being displayed and being hidden.

- `viewWillAppear`: This method is called before your view is displayed. Only after this method finishes is your view displayed. To create a good experience of a fast application, all calculations here have to be really fast. Otherwise, what the user perceives about your navigation and animation is really weak. A good practice is to setup views' attributes (for example, background color or text color).

- For example, a user presses a Back button to go back to a view A. However, inside the method `viewDidAppear` of view A, there is a calculation that takes time. The result takes a few seconds, but in the meantime the UI thread is blocked to process the logic inside view A and can't display view A.

- `viewDidAppear`: This method is called right after your view is displayed, so you can put logic processing here. However, if your process changes the view quite a bit after it finishes, the user can get confused, which is not a positive experience.

  - For example, you have a sort algorithm to sort your table view. When user gets sees view A, the old table is still displayed. And then suddenly all rows change without any warning or an explanation as to why this just happened.

- `viewWillDisappear`: This is called right before the view disappears from the UI. Anything belonging to the view that you want to show to your users should be put here. Note that you should not put too much logic processing code here. If you do put a lot of processing code here, it will take too much time for a new view to be displayed.

- `viewDidDisappear`: This is called right after your view disappears. You can't show any view or any UI effects to user.

There is no hard and fast rule as to where you should put your logic processing. I give you all basic concepts and you can use them to create the best user perception about your app's performance.

Object Copy

So why do you need to know about object copying and why do you need to it? Copying an object is useful if you don't want to change the old object because it could affect other parts of the program. In some cases, you can't change the object at all, so you copy the content of that object in order to modify it.

Shallow vs. Deep Copy

Shallow copying actually means the same as *retaining* in objective-C. Because shallow copying means copying the pointer of the object to a new variable, there is no difference between shallow copying and retaining.

Deep copying, on the other hand, means you actually create a new object, and copy all data and instance variables from the old object into the new object.

To illustrate the differences between shallow copy and deep copy in objective-C, consider these code examples for each case:

Shallow copying:

```
- (void)setMyObj:(NSObject *)newObj {
  if (newObj != myObj) {
    myObj = newObj;
  }
}
```

Deep copying:

```
- (void)setMyObj:(NSObject *)newObj {
  if (newObj != myObj) {
    myObj = [newObj copy];
  }
}
```

In the first case, you assign the variable to the new object and retain the object. In objective-C, this is a shallow copy. In the deep copy case, the code actually copies the value and instance variables inside the newObj into myObj.

Implementing a Deep Copy

If you want to do a truly deep copy, you have to follow the whole hierarchy of the object.

- You need to create a new object.
- You copy all instance variables of the old object into the new object.
- If the instance variable is a primitive data type like float, int, or double, you just need to copy that value. Boolean is not a primitive data type but you also only copy the value of a Boolean instance variable.
- For each instance variable that is a pointer type, you will need to copy their instance variable as well.
- The process continues to the end.

This process can be long and hard to implement. Some built-in objects and libraries don't support deep copying. Therefore, you should always find a compromise between shallow and deep copying. For example, you won't want to deep copy a delegate, which can cause a retain cycle, discuss previously, where object A owns object B and object B also owns object A. Moreover, you usually don't want to copy your delegate because at the end you want to callback to that delegate, not the new delegate.

This is an example of a mixed approach between shallow and deep copy:

```
@interface Item : NSObject {
   NSString *itemName;
   CGFloat price;
   id delegate;
}

@property (nonatomic,  copy) NSString *itemName;
@property (nonatomic, weak) CGFloat price;
@property (nonatomic, weak) id delegate;

@end
```

In this example, you can see that there are three instance variables. The first one is itemName (which is a pointer object), the second one is a primitive data, and the last one is a delegate.

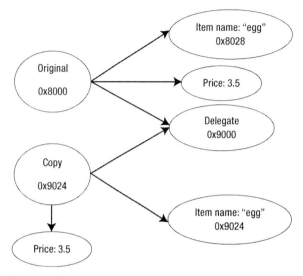

Figure 7–8. *Deep copy of an object*

As you can see in Figure 7–8, the delegate object will be kept the same and shared between the original item and new item. The itemName object will be copied and have a new memory address (0x9124 instead of 0x8028) but have the same value of "egg". The primitive variables, such as price, will be copied over and have no memory address.

Integrating a Copy Method into an Object

To have a deep copy of an object, you will usually have to override the method copyWithZone:. When an object is sent a copy message, this method will be called. Here is some code for overriding this method. You will need to create a new object by alloc and init and then use the set method to set the value for instance variables.

```
- (id)copyWithZone:(NSZone *)zone {
    Item *copy = [[Item allocWithZone: zone] initWithName:self.itemName];
    copy.price = self.price;
    copy.delegate = self.delegate;
    return copy;
}
```

As stated previously, if there are other custom type instance variables inside your Item class, you need to implement the copy for those as well. In my example, for the sake of simplicity, the code doesn't create a new itemName object.

Advanced Autorelease Pool

You learned several basic techniques about memory in the previous sections of this chapter. This section will cover more advanced techniques for using the autorelease pool and show you where you should use it to have high performance in restricted cases.

In every thread, you must have an autorelease pool to collect and store all autoreleased objects. If you don't have an autorelease pool in every thread, all autoreleased objects will be leaked and you will have a big memory leak. The autorelease pool is organized inside stacks; this is explained in the following section.

Autorelease Pool and Stacks

Autorelease pools are stored inside a stack and are commonly understood to be nested. Whenever you create a new autorelease pool, it will be pushed on the top of the stack. And all new objects that are autoreleased will be pushed into that new autorelease pool.

As you can see in the following code, the objects (such as myArray and myString) inside the method doSomething will be stored in myPool, not the main pool of the application:

```
- (void)doSomething {
  @autoreleasepool {
    NSArray *myArray = [NSArray array];
    NSString *myString = [NSString string];
  }
}
```

Here is the main pool is inside the main method, as usual:

```
int main(int argc, char *argv[])
{
  @autoreleasepool {
    int retVal = UIApplicationMain(argc, argv, nil, nil);
  }
  return retVal;
}
```

At the end of the @autoreleasepool block, all autoreleased objects are stored inside that pool will be released when the event life cycle ends.

Figure 7–9 demonstrates this concept. This is an important concept for good performance—knowing to release the object as soon as possible.

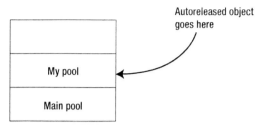

Figure 7–9. *Autorelease pool in stacks*

Autorelease Pools and Threads

When a new thread is created, you need to create a new autorelease pool object and associate that pool with the new thread. So when the thread stops, your autorelease pool gets deallocated and all the autoreleased objects are deallocated as well. I covered this topic in depth in Chapter 6, so please review it if you need some help understanding this concept.

Autorelease Pool's effects on Performance

The old rule of memory management still applies for code that is written with ARC If you call a method that does not have new, alloc and copy in its name, that object is already autoreleased. If you run a loop that creates too many autoreleased objects, you will soon run out of memory.

This code demonstrates the best way to do memory management in looping:

```
- (void)doSomethingWithAutoRelease {
    for (int i = 0; i < 1000; i++) {
        @autoreleasepool {
        Product *product = [Product productWithItemID:@""];
        // process and display the product here
        }
    }
}
```

After the loop finishes and at the end of the @autoreleasepool block, all of autoreleased objects are released. This way you can control and release all unused objects and take your memory back.

Instruments

Instruments were covered in Chapter 2 when I discussed benchmarking using devices and simulators. In this section, I will briefly discuss common problems plus some more advanced problems that can affect what memory management approach you should choose.

There are four main instruments that you need to use most of the time.

- Static Analyzer
- Leaks Instrument
- Zombie
- Object allocation

Static Analyzer

Static Analyzer is a good to quickly check for small and obvious memory leaks. For example, if you alloc a new object and you don't release it inside that method, as shown in Figure 7–10, the Static Analyzer can figure it out quickly.

```
- (void)applicationDidFinishLaunching:(UIApplication *)application {
    NSString *str = [[NSString alloc] init];
    NSLog(@"str: %@", str);
    // Override point for customization after app launch
    [window addSubview:viewController.view];    Potential leak of an object allocated on line 19 and stored into 'str'
    [window makeKeyAndVisible];
}
```

Figure 7–10. Static Analyzer shows a memory leak

Leak Instrument

The Leaks Instrument is more complicated and takes some time to run and analyze but it gives you the best results according to your actions. It can detect most of memory leaks when it keeps track of all data in running time

Leaked Object	#	Address	Size	Responsible Library ▼	Responsible Frame
UIImage		0x8026020	16 Bytes	LeaksViewController	–[RootViewController
UIImage		0x4b2a250	16 Bytes	LeaksViewController	–[RootViewController
Malloc 9.00 KB		0x5026a00	9.00 KB	ImageIO	initImageJPEG

Figure 7–11. *Leak results from the instrument*

The Leaks Instrument can give you detailed results of list of leaked objects, as shown in Figure 7–11.

```
- (void)tableView:(UITableView *)tableView didSelectRowAtIndexPath:(NSIndexPath *)indexPath {
    NSString *avatarFile = [NSString stringWithFormat:@"a0"];
    NSString *avatarName = [[NSBundle mainBundle] pathForResource:avatarFile ofType:@"jpeg"];
    UIImage *image1 = [[UIImage alloc] initWithContentsOfFile:avatarName];
    NSLog(@"image: %@", image1);
    image1 = [[UIImage alloc] initWithContentsOfFile:avatarName];
    NSLog(@"image: %@", image1);
```

Figure 7–12. *Leak details shown by Leaks Instrument*

It can also show the exact line of code that causes the leaks (Figure 7–12).

Zombie

Zombie helps you check for the part of the code that caused a crash, EXEC_BAD_ACCESS for your application. This is really useful if your application keeps crashing but you can't discover the problem through logging or verifying your code.

As shown in Figure 7–13, Zombie will show you a list of actions, including malloc, autorelease, retain, and release when the app crashes. You can track the autorelease and release methods using Zombie.

⊞ Statistics ⬦	Object Summary		History: 0x4b047b0					≡
#	Category	Event Type	RefCt	Timestamp	Address	Size	Responsible Li...	Responsible Caller
0	CFNumber	Malloc	1	00:14.433	0x4b047b0	16	Foundation	–[NSPlaceholderNumber ...
1	CFNumber	Autorelease		00:14.433	0x4b047b0	0	ZombieDebug	–[ZombieDebugViewCon...
2	CFNumber	CFRetain	2	00:14.433	0x4b047b0	0	ZombieDebug	–[ZombieDebugViewCon...
3	CFNumber	CFRelease	1	00:14.433	0x4b047b0	0	ZombieDebug	–[ZombieDebugViewCon...
4	CFNumber	CFRelease	0	00:14.433	0x4b047b0	0	Foundation	–[NSAutoreleasePool rel...
5	CFNumber	Zombie	–1	00:14.977	0x4b047b0	0	Foundation	–[NSCFString appendFor...

Figure 7–13. *Results from a crash tracked by Zombie Instrument*

Zombie can show you the place for each action, such as where the object is allocated and where the object is autoreleased or released.

Object Allocation

Object allocation is the last tool related to memory that I want to introduce here. It shows all the memory usage over time when your application is running. This tool is really helpful when the memory usage grows so much and you need to trace back to the group of lines that created so much memory.

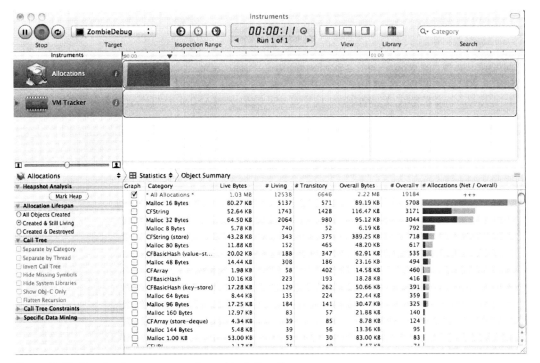

Figure 7–14. *Results of memory usage from object allocations*

Figure 7–14 shows you the line of code, time the object is created, and the caller that creates the object.

Memory Warning Levels

The last thing I want to discuss about memory is memory warnings. When your memory usage grows to a certain point, the iOS environment will try to tell you this by calling the didReceiveMemoryWarning method on view controller objects. You will have to react to this memory warning by freeing some memory.

> **NOTE:** There are other ways to receive memory warnings from inside your application: the application delegate receives the memory warning and calls appropriate methods in other objects or your objects can register to receive memory warning via NSNotification.

The first memory warning (memory warning level 1) is the most important one: it means that your code has to reduce memory usage fast. Otherwise, your app will receive a memory warning level 2 and it will almost certainly crash.

Summary

Memory has a big effect on the performance of your app. It can also make your app crash if you don't use it properly. In this chapter, you learned important concepts about memory management in objective-C that will help you avoid memory leak issues and application crashes. The UIViewController life cycle is also important as it relates to managing and controlling memory usage. It also affects how users feel about the performance and experience of the application. Finally, you learned the differences between autorelease and release when dealing with memory and when you should use one instead of the other.

EXERCISES

1. 1. List the differences between the autorelease and release methods.
2. 2. Use the instruments covered in this chapter in a real-world situation.
3. 3. Implement the copy method for an existing object in your project.

Integrate Multithreading and Efficient Memory Usage for Multitasking Apps Performance

In this chapter, you will learn about:

- What Apple means by multitasking.

- The multitasking life cycle and how to handle the benefits and costs

- Different background services, such as

  - Audio

  - VOIP

  - Location

  - Background processing

- What you should know to make your app multitask well.

In this chapter, you will learn how to take advantage of multitasking in iPhone so that the application can process data in background without the user's notice. This must be balanced with using as little CPU processing time or memory as possible; otherwise, you may severely impact the battery life or worse—be killed by the iOS.

What is Multitasking in iPhone?

From the user's perspective, multitasking means that she is using several applications at the same time and can switch from one to another at will. In iOS 3.2 and below, whenever a user quit an app, the app closed, and when user opened it again, the app needed to reload. This was a problem for two reasons: the wait was long and the app forgot whatever she just did (Figure 8–1).

Before quit   After relaunch

Figure 8–1. *How an app in older versions of iOS behaves when a user quits and reopens*

Since iOS 4.0, the app is not loaded again from the start so it doesn't take much time for the user to switch from one app to another. Apple hopes that the user will perceive the multitasking feature to be as powerful as that of a desktop app. From the developer's side, the app is actually put into the background and all states are saved. As you can see in Figure 8–2, when the user opens the app again, the state and data are quickly loaded and restored to the previous position.

Before quit   After relaunch

Figure 8–2. *How an app in iOS 4.0 behaves when a user quits and reopens*

Multitasking Life Cycle

It would be useful for you to know the process of the old iOS, which can help you to understand about the current mechanism of the iOS4 and above. I will first explain the previous mechanism where multitasking didn't exist. The app is started by calling `application:didFinishLaunchingWithOptions:`, and then the event loop is run to catch all the events and to display the UI (see Figure 8–3). When the user quits the application, the whole app is closed and the method `applicationWillTerminate` is called. The next time the user opens the application, the method `application:didFinishLaunchingWithOptions:` is called again.

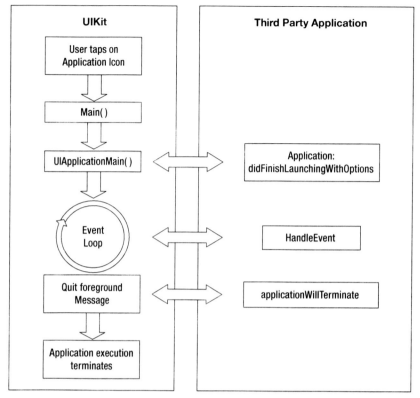

Figure 8–3. *Application life cycle for the old iOS environment*

iOS4 requires a more complicated implementation and it's easy to misunderstand this whole process. As shown in Figure 8–4, when the user quits the app, it enters the background and method `application:didEnterBackground` is called. The application is in foreground state when users can see it running; users don't see the application when it is in background. When it relaunches, many methods and notifications are involved and you have to understand different states of the application to respond properly to them. Here are the application states that you need to know about.

- Not running: Never opened, or opened and then terminated.

- Inactive: The app is in foreground but not receiving events, such as when the user locks the screen.

- Active: The app is in foreground and is receiving events.

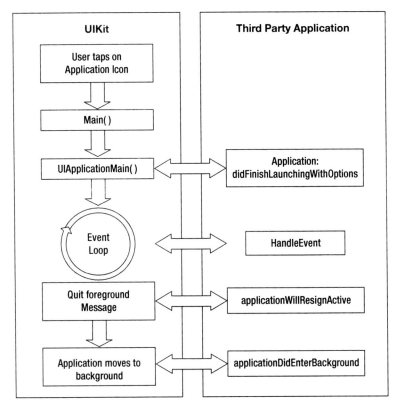

Figure 8–4. *Application life cycle for iOS4*

Developers often confuse these last two states: background and suspend.
The background state happens before the suspend state. When the user quits the app
or jumps to another app, the application is brought into the background state. It stays
there for a short period of time, after which the application is suspended. The period of
time depends on the application and what it wants to do in the background. I will explain
in more detail what the application can do in this state.

There are two main situations for which the application life cycle will be different. The
first situation is when user quits the app by answering a phone call or another
interruption from the operating system. The second situation is when users press the
Home button and the app goes into the background. Each situation has its own
application life cycle.

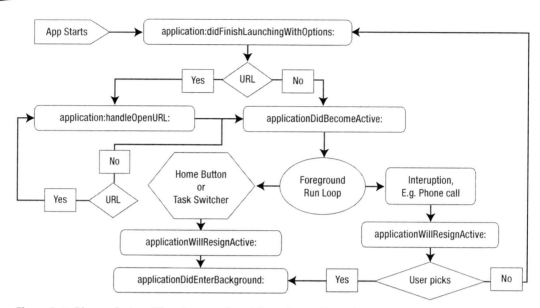

Figure 8–5. *Diagram for two different cases: phone interruption and home button.*

As you can see in Figure 8–5, in the first case, when the user receives a phone call or SMS message, the app is put into inactive mode with the applicationWillResignActive: method. If the user chooses No (doesn't answer the phone) the method applicationDidBecomeActive is called; otherwise, applicationDidEnterBackground is called. So, in the applicationDidBecomeActive section, you may not need to reload all data and views again. You should be careful with this part when comparing it to clicking on the Home button.

When users press the Home button, the application goes directly into the background and the delegate method applicationDidEnterBackground: is called.

Multitasking Handler Methods

Figures 8–4 and 8–5 showed you when certain methods are called in the lifecycle. Table 8–1 provides a complete list of methods to handle in your application delegate and other view controller classes to respond properly to the life cycle events.

Table 8–1. *List of Methods and Notifications that the Application Will Receive in the Life Cycle*

Application Delegate Methods (and Object Notifications)	Description
Launching	

`application:didFinishLaunchingWithOptions:`
Notification:
`UIApplicationDidFinishLaunchingNotification`
	Use this method to initialize important data. At this point, the app has been launched and the Window nib file is loaded.

`application:didReceiveRemoteNotification:`
`application:didReceiveLocalNotification:`
`(No notification for this method)`
	This method is called when the app is launched corresponding to the notification (both remote and local notifications). You can process the notification and make the app behave based on the notification.

Active State	

`applicationDidBecomeActive:`
Notification:
`UIApplicationDidBecomeActiveNotification`
	The method is called when the app moves from an inactive to active state (see Figure 8–5). Use this method to restart any activities like timers and to refresh the UI.

`applicationWillResignActive:`
Notification:
`UIApplicationWillResignActiveNotification`
	This method is used when the app moves from an active to inactive state. This can be due to a phone call, locking of the device, or moving to the background. For ongoing tasks and games, this should pause these actions.

Background State	

`applicationDidEnterBackground:`
Notification:
`UIApplicationDidEnterBackgroundNotification`
	The method is called when the user quits the application.
	
	Use this method to release shared resource, save the user's data, and invalidate timers. You should store enough user information. Disable update to the UI.
	
	You have up to five seconds to finish and return this method. Other work should be done in the background processing.

`applicationWillEnterForeground:`
Notification:
`UIApplicationWillEnterForegroundNotification`
	You can restore all data and view controller activities that are stopped and saved from the `applicationDidEnterBackground:` method.

Application Delegate Methods (and Object Notifications)	Description
Terminate	
applicationWillTerminate: UIApplicationWillTerminateNotification	When the operating system stops your app and removes the app from the memory, use this method to store any unsaved data, and release the final resources that you are using. This is your last chance.

NOTE 1

To receive the notification for events, your view controller or object can register it as shown in the following code snippet:

```
[[NSNotificationCenter defaultCenter] addObserver:self selector:@selector(someMethod:)
name:UIApplicationDidBecomeActiveNotification object:nil];
```

Don't forget to clean up after yourself! In dealloc, remember to remove yourself as the observer, like so:

```
[[NSNotificationCenter defaultCenter] removeObserver:self];
```

The method someMethod: may (but is not required to) accept an NSNotification as a parameter. Inside this NSNotification, you may find more user information or data to process. You can work with this NSNotification as usual; there is nothing special here.

NOTE 2

- The method applicationDidBecomeActive: will always be called, either when users first launch your application or launch it again from the background.

- The method applicationDidFinishLaunching: will always be called on the first launch, not on launches from background.

- The method applicationWillEnterForeground: will always be called when the application comes back from the background.

You can use these facts to integrate multitasking into your application so that you can respond properly to different states of the application.

Multitasking Benefits and Costs

What should you do if you don't want to have multitasking in your application? What are the benefits and costs if you have to maintain all these different states and complex code in order to make sure your application works well?

There are many benefits of using multitasking. Here are two:

- Users can continue working with the existing state of your application without navigating back from the beginning any more.

■ Your application can continue to work in parallel with background services like downloading data from the Internet, playing audio, or receiving GPS location notification.

As you already learned, over the whole life cycle of multitasking, there are couple of costs that you have to pay for:

■ More complicated logic while walking through the application life cycle, as shown previously.

■ Your app may be forced to quit in the background and leave the application data inconsistent. Due to this inconsistency, your app can crash when user reopens it.

So, in some cases, you may not want to use multitasking in your application. In these cases, you can configure your `info.plist` file to not use multitasking. Here are the steps to do so:

■ Open your info.plist file.

■ Add the key `UIApplicationExitsOnSuspend` or select `Application does not run in background`.

■ Set the new key to `YES` or tick in the tick box.

You can see this in Figure 8–6.

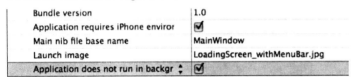

Bundle version	1.0
Application requires iPhone enviror	☑
Main nib file base name	MainWindow
Launch image	LoadingScreen_withMenuBar.jpg
Application does not run in backgr ⬍	☑

Figure 8–6. *How to set up the no multitasking option*

Background Services

As shown in the previous sections, there are many services that you can run in the background to process data and provide services to the user. Here is a list of things you can do in the background in iOS4:

■ Audio: Your app can play audio while it is in the background.

■ Privacy: Let the OS show a splash screen when your application is relaunched. This is useful if your app is showing some sensitive information.

■ Location: Your app can receive significant changes in location while in background.

■ VOIP: The user can make phone calls while your app is in background.

■ Local notifications: Your application can ask the system to schedule a specific time to pop up a message to the user.

■ Task completion: Your app can ask the system for extra time to complete a given task. This is an important feature that I will cover in more detail later in this chapter.

These are specific services that can help you speed up your program by utilizing the multitasking features of the iOS. Audio and VOIP don't speed up your app but they help make the user feel better and make your application more usable. Location, task completion, and local notifications are good tools for your application's performance when done properly. Considering that location is one of the most powerful features in mobile technology, many apps now want to incorporate it in order to serve the user better.

Audio Service

The most trivial way to enable your audio service in background is to include a key in the info.plist and then set up the audio settings properly to let the audio keep playing in the background after your application enters background.

You need to add a new key called UIBackgroundModes with the value audio, as shown in Figure 8–7. The result will show "Required background modes" in the array.

| ▼ Required background modes | (1 item) |
| Item 0 | App plays audio |

Figure 8–7. Set the audio to play in the background.

If you look at Apple's documentation, it doesn't say anything about configuring your audio setting so that it can keep playing. Many developers complain about this, so you should be aware of this issue. You need to add the following code snippet before you can play the audio:

```
[[AVAudioSession sharedInstance] setCategory:AVAudioSessionCategoryPlayback error:nil];
AVAudioPlayer *backgroundMusicPlayer = [[AVAudioPlayer alloc]
                                initWithContentsOfURL:YOUR_AUDIO_URL
                                                error:nil];
[backgroundMusicPlayer play];
```

> **NOTE:** You need to add the AVFoundation framework and import it in your file to make this code compile.

The problem with this approach is that you can only play one song in the background. After that song ends, your application enters into background mode. To play a list of songs in the background, you have to write code to implement a long-running background job.

Sometimes you want to stop downloading/streaming audio/video in the background to save the traffic for the user. You can use the `applicationDidEnterBackground` method to stop all video/audio streaming, like so:

```
- (void)applicationDidEnterBackground:(UIApplication *)application {
  [backgroundMusicPlayer stop];
}
```

Show Splash Screen

When your application enters the background, the iOS environment will take a screenshot of its current view. When the user relaunches your application, the iOS environment will display this screenshot while your application is still loading. This creates a perception within the user's mind that your application is loading really quickly, which boosts the user experience. However, in some cases, there is some sensitive information that you may want to hide until all the data is loaded. Here is a simple method to support this (you can also do this by directly manipulating your views in the `applicationDidEnterBackground`, but it's a more complicated process):

```
- (void)applicationDidEnterBackground:(UIApplication *)application{
    if (appHasSecret) { // if your application has something to hide
        UIImageView *splashView = [[UIImageView alloc] initWithFrame:CGRectMake(0,0,
320, 480)];
        splashView.image = [UIImage imageNamed:@"YOUR_DEFAULT_PICTURE"];
        [window addSubview:splashView];
    }
}
```

Your `Default.png` can be anything that the user can view while he is waiting for your app to load its view and data. So, when the user relaunches your app, he sees this `default` image first and then your view.

Location Service

Location-based social networking is hot these days, and there are plenty of services that need the user's location. The problem is that your user won't want to keep your application open all the time to let your app knows her current location. Therefore, Apple provides you a mechanism so your application can find the latest location while staying in background.

To get the user's current location, here are some ways your app can choose to implement:

■ Use Standard Location Service: Your application can ask the iOS environment for the current user's location whenever the app wants. This approach consumes a lot of battery power and takes time for the application to query data. Another problem is that the app can't get a location using this service if it's running in background.

▓ Register for significant location changes: Your application can also register for location events and notifications. Your application will be notified whenever the user changes his location significantly. This often gets called when the device moves from one cell tower to another. Using this approach is more passive but it saves battery life. Another benefit of this approach is the iOS notifies your application even if your application is in background.

▓ Continuous background location update: This approach is the best for your application but the worst for your user's battery life. Your application can constantly get location updates from the iOS, whether in the background or foreground.

Standard Location Services

This is a common location service that most apps use because it was available in the old iOS. To use this service, you may want to set the accuracy and filter properties before calling startUpdatingLocation. If you don't have a configuration set, the iOS will simply use these default configurations:

```
CLLocationManager *locationManager = [[CLLocationManager alloc] init];
locationManager.delegate = self;
[locationManager startUpdatingLocation];
```

> **NOTE:** You need to add the CoreLocation framework and import CoreLocation in your file. The class represented by self object must implement the CLLocationManagerDelegate.

The code is really straightforward. You can set some configuration parameters to get better location data. These properties belong to CLLocationManager class:

```
@property(nonatomic, weak) CLLocationAccuracy desiredAccuracy
```

Set the accuracy level for the location detection. The default value is best; however, if your application accepts the lower accuracy level, you should go with that. The problem with the "best" configuration is that it takes more time and more battery energy to request the location. It offers the following accuracy levels (these names are self-explanatory):

▓ kCLLocationAccuracyBestForNavigation

▓ kCLLocationAccuracyBest (Default Value)

▓ kCLLocationAccuracyNearestTenMeters

▓ kCLLocationAccuracyHundredMeters

▓ kCLLocationAccuracyKilometer

▓ kCLLocationAccuracyThreeKilometers

Another property of class CLLocationManager that you can set is

@property(nonatomic, weak) CLLocationDistance distanceFilter

You can set either kCLDistanceFilterNone (default) or any double value that you want. The property specifies the distance (measured in meters) that your users have to move before your application receives notification about the new location. The kCLDistanceFilterNone means your application can receive all notifications whenever user has a movement.

This section only describes how you can ask the operating system for a location update. The details about the return value and what to do will be briefly described later.

Significant Location Changes

There are two different mechanisms to update based on certain conditions:

- When there are significant changes in the user's location.

- When the user enters or quits a specific region.

The first mechanism is really like the Standard Location Update and happens by initializing the object and then setting up configurations. The only difference is that now you call startMonitoringSignificantLocationChanges.

One important note is that if you use this Significant Location Change mechanism, your application will be invoked or will wake up when new location data arrives. This will also happen if your application is already suspended or terminated. Because your app can be awakened with this mechanism, you don't need to handle background processing code or worry about missing location data. However, your application is only given a small amount of time in background to process this location data. Your application may not have time to process very much network data but you can still do a lot of other useful stuff.

Before moving to the region mechanism, the following code will explain how to receive the location update and process this location data:

```
// Delegate method from the CLLocationManagerDelegate protocol.
- (void)locationManager:(CLLocationManager *)manager
    didUpdateToLocation:(CLLocation *)newLocation
    fromLocation:(CLLocation *)oldLocation {

    NSLog(@"latitude %f, longitude: %f\n",
            newLocation.coordinate.latitude,
            newLocation.coordinate.longitude);

}
```

As you can see, all you need to do is to include a delegate method, (void)locationManager:didUpdateToLocation:fromLocation:. Inside the newLocation object, you have two important data points, latitude and longitude.

The Region-based mechanism is also similar to the Significant Location Change mechanism in that you register for a specific circular region by a center and its radius. The code block is as simple as the following:

```
// Create the region and start monitoring it.
// radius is measured in meters
 CLRegion* region = [[CLRegion alloc]
initCircularRegionWithCenter:destinationLocation.coordinate
                    radius:radius identifier:@"YOUR_REGION_ID";

[self.locationMananager startMonitoringForRegion:region
                desiredAccuracy:kCLLocationAccuracyHundredMeters];
```

Usually, this mechanism is integrated with a MapKit so users can register for their destination and get notified when they are around that region.

You also need to implement the following two methods to receive events about the regions:

```
- (void)locationManager:(CLLocationManager *)manager didEnterRegion:(CLRegion *)region
- (void)locationManager:(CLLocationManager *)manager didExitRegion:(CLRegion *)region
```

Continuous Background Location Update

The last mechanism is for applications that require a continuous update from the iOS environment. This is a good mechanism for an application that requires every new location update even when the app is in background and not running. To do this, you need to add the key UIBackgroundModes with the value location, similar to the audio playing in background (covered in previous sections).

▼ Required background modes	(2 items)
Item 0	App plays audio
Item 1	App registers for location updates
Application requires iPhone enviror	☑

Figure 8–8. *App registers for location updates*

As you can see in Figure 8–8, your application now is registered with location updates. There are many advantages and disadvantages with this mechanism. Here are two.

Advantage:

▓ You can get updates to the location service frequently, even with small changes.

Disadvantages:

▓ It can consume lots of your user's battery power.

Local Notification

This is a new feature of iOS4 that allows applications to set up notifications at a specific time. This feature is useful for time-based application like alarms or calendars. This can be helpful if the user needs to wait for a specific time for some specific events. The events can be based on user settings or server settings. This also helps to get the user's attention to the application.

You need to have a new local notification object and set up the date and time properly, like so:

```
// Create a new notification.
UILocalNotification* alarm = [[UILocalNotification alloc] init];
if (alarm) {
    alarm.fireDate = theDate;
    alarm.timeZone = [NSTimeZone defaultTimeZone];
    alarm.repeatInterval = kCFCalendarUnitDay;
    alarm.alertBody = @"Time to wake up!";
    [[UIApplication sharedApplication] scheduleLocalNotification:alarm];
}
```

Voice Over IP (VOIP)

Voice Over IP is mainly used for voice chat applications like Skype. This is another feature of multitasking in the new iOS4; however, it's beyond the scope of this chapter, so I won't cover it here. Most applications don't need to use VOIP at all.

Background Execution

Background execution is an important technique for iOS developers. This technique is new as of iOS4 and helps developers get more time to finish critical tasks, so the app can control its lifetime a little bit more.

For example, imagine that you are uploading an image/video to your server. In the middle of the uploading process, the user suddenly quits the app, leaving the image half uploaded. The next the user goes back to your app, she will have to wait again for the whole uploading process. The other option is to force the user to wait for the image to finish uploading before the app closes, but this is not a great user experience.

In another scenario, there are important posts or downloads from your server, which you definitely want to complete. Background execution is important to in helping developers with these tasks. You can wrap your uploading process within the background task and start that task, like so:

```
UIApplication* app = [UIApplication sharedApplication];
UIBackgroundTaskIdentifier bgTask = [app beginBackgroundTaskWithExpirationHandler:^{
    [self.imageUploadService uploadImage:image];
    [app endBackgroundTask:bgTask];
}];
```

```
// Start the long-running task and return immediately.
dispatch_async(dispatch_get_global_queue(DISPATCH_QUEUE_PRIORITY_DEFAULT, 0), ^{
  // Do the work associated with the task.
  [app endBackgroundTask:bgTask];
});
```

As shown in the code, to initiate a new background task, you will need to call method
beginBackgroundTaskWithExpirationHandler:, which will return a background task
identifier that you can use to end the background task later. With method
beginBackgroundTaskWithExpirationHandler:, you tell iOS that your app would like this
task to complete even if the app is moved into the background state, before the app
becomes suspended. The endBackgroundTask: method tells iOS that your app's task has
completed, allowing it to move your app to the suspended state if necessary. If the app
remains in the foreground the whole time then these calls have no effect, so it doesn't
hurt to use them.

You need to be aware that background tasks don't get an unlimited amount of time to
run in the background; in other words, the application has to finish its tasks in a limited
time (usually up to 10 minutes). Otherwise, the iOS will suspend the app without waiting
for the task to finish. The expiration handler part
of beginBackgroundTaskWithExpirationHandler: is a block (it's just like a method without
the name) specifying your cleanup code if the task outlives its lifetime. Code executing
as a background task must not make any UI updates or openGL calls (as the app is
offscreen).

You can use this beginBackgroundTaskWithExpirationHandler: method to initiate a new
background task in any place in your code. I use it to wrap an upload image process
that makes sure that, even if the user quits the app immediately, the uploading process
is still successful. Many people also use this method along with
applicationDidEnterBackground: to make the app run for a little longer in order to finish
all the final calculations or networking processes.

As mentioned, you can also use background services to play audio. Using this
background service, you can play a list of songs instead of only one. You can use the
following code skeleton to implement this; note that you may need to fill in other
necessary parts of the code to make it work. You should do this as an exercise to
understand more about how the background task works.

```
UIBackgroundTaskIdentifier bgTaskId;
// AVAudioPlayer *backgroundMusicPlayer
if ([backgroundMusicPlayer play]) {
  bgTaskId = [[UIApplication sharedApplication]
beginBackgroundTaskWithExpirationHandler:NULL];
}

- (void)audioPlayerDidFinishPlaying:(AVAudioPlayer *)player successfully:(BOOL)success
{
    UIBackgroundTaskIdentifier newTaskId = UIBackgroundTaskInvalid;

    if (self.haveMoreAudioToPlay) {
        newTaskId = [[UIApplication sharedApplication]
beginBackgroundTaskWithExpirationHandler:NULL];
        [self playNextAudioFile];
```

```
    }

    if (bgTaskId != UIBackgroundTaskInvalid) {
        [[UIApplication sharedApplication] endBackgroundTask: bgTaskId];
    }

    bgTaskId = newTaskId;
}
```

As you can see in the code, by using background services you can register the delegate events; then inside that delegate method, you can simply play the next file. (Note that the total time your application can play audio is up to 10 minutes.) I hope this is a helpful demonstration of how to use background services efficiently.

What to Notice when Running in Background

The following is a small checklist from Apple to make sure that your application behaves and runs well in the background and doesn't affect any other apps:

- Reduce your stored memory to the lowest level.

- Release all shared resources, such as Calendar.

- Respond properly to the application life cycle events.

- Don't update your UI or call code that consumes CPU and battery excessively.

- Run in the background correctly.

- Respond to system changes in background.

If your application can strictly follow these guidelines, it will run well and it will get the most out of the multitasking feature. It also won't get killed in the background. Keeping your application alive in the background so it relaunches quickly is an important part of a good user experience.

Memory

As mentioned, in iOS4, your application can run in background services and will still reside in the RAM while the application is in background. However, the RAM system has its limits and these are even worse in limited environments like iOS, as you learned in Chapter 7. Therefore, Apple has a strict policy about the memory usage of an application when it is in background. Because there will be several apps residing in the background at the same time, these apps could eat a huge amount of memory quickly. When the device runs out of memory, iOS will find the application that consumed the most memory and kill that app first.

To reduce your memory usage, you need to clear your caches in memory, especially image caches. You may also need to remove unnecessary subviews because these subviews also are saved into memory when your application goes into background.

Actually, you need to save your critical data and clear out all unnecessary data to avoid your application being suspended by the iOS.

Shared Resources

There are some applications that share data, such as the calendar database and the address book. If your application uses this resource while running, it has to stop while it enters the background. If your application is found to use or has not yet released these shared resources when the application enters the background, it is killed immediately. The reason is that all these shared resources belong to the foreground application.

Application Life Cycle Events

As mentioned, you are responsible for handling and responding correctly to the application life cycle events. If you don't test to make sure that your life cycle is correct, you run the risk of data loss or improper behavior. For example, you need to save your application data before it goes to background and you need to pause the current flow when the application moves to inactive state.

You can't depend too much on the memory storage in the background. Because the iOS can suspend your app whenever the it runs out of memory, and you may not have a chance to react to that event, you should always save all the necessary data before you go into background.

You may have a little bit time to run in background, but the iOS can also stop your background process whenever it runs out of memory or CPU cycles. So, in the background process, you need to act fast and use multithreading if possible. You are running against the iOS time.

At this point, when moving into the background, the iOS will take a snapshot of your view. The purpose of this is to briefly show that snapshot to the user while your view and data are loading, which improves the user experience. However, you should hide sensitive information that you don't want to be captured as part of the screenshot, such as date of birth, a password, or your user's private photos.

User Interface Update and Process in Background

A general rule when your application is in background is to avoid unnecessary processes. And UI update is one of those processes. If you need extra time or extra CPU processing while in background, you may need to explicitly request permission . Here is a short list of things that you should address if your application is in background:

- Don't make OpenGL ES calls from your code.

- Cancel any Bonjour-related services.

▓ Handle any connection or networking failures while your application is in background. You can always resume these connections later when your application becomes active again.

▓ Avoid updating windows and views. Users can't see your views, so there's no reason to update them. Your application should not update windows and views in background because this consume CPU cycles and may affect foreground applications.

▓ Clean up any alerts or pop up messages before moving to background to avoid confusing the user. You should dismiss your alerts and show them again later if necessary.

▓ Do minimal work in background. Try your best to use services provided by Apple, such as audio in background or monitoring significant location changes.

System Changes Notification

While your application is in background, the system can experience many changes and it will notify you of these, so you should be prepared for changes. These changes include device orientation, time changes, battery changes, or locale changes while the application is in background. Table 8–2 shows a list of important notifications.

Table 8–2. *List of Notifications That Can Be Sent to Your Application While It's in Background*

Event – Notification	Description
The device orientation changes `UIDeviceOrientationDidChangeNotification`	Usually the view controllers will update the orientation properly as the application is in the foreground.
Significant time change `UIApplicationSignificantTimeChangeNotification`	Use this if the time is past midnight or the user has changes time zone or is moving to Daylight Saving Time. You can use this to update your local notification or any data related to date time.

Battery level or state changes
`UIDeviceBatteryLevelDidChangeNotification`
`UIDeviceBatteryStateDidChangeNotification`
	Your application may need to act according to the battery level. If you are writing a game that consumes lots of battery power, you need to be careful with the battery level and may need to stop some activities.

Application settings change `NSUserDefaultsDidChangeNotification`	You may need to change your UI or data settings according to the new changes in the settings.
Locale change `NSCurrentLocaleDidChangeNotification`	If your application supports internationalization, don't forget to change your user interface and data according to the new locale.

You will receive a queue of notifications when your app resumes from background. You may need to quickly deal with these notifications, especially the settings and locale changes, because the user always want to see these changes happen immediately.

Dealing with iOS Versions

It's estimated that anywhere from 5 to 20% of devices are still using iOS3, including iPad 1, old iPod, and iPhone devices. So how do you make sure that nothing goes wrong with your application when it runs in iOS3?

You need to store all data and user information in `applicationDidTerminate` and correctly reinstruct all data in the method `application:didFinishLaunchingWithOptions:`. Because in iOS4, the method `applicationWillTerminate:` is called only when the application is terminated, you should be okay.

You won't have support for background executions, so you can't rely on this mechanism to save the user's data. If you have any important data to save, upload, or download from server, you can do it in either the termination or launching methods.

In old devices, you can try to create the feeling of multitasking (or fast app switching) by using an archiving approach. In this approach, you save all the view controllers' states when the application closes and restore all of them when the application relaunches. This is a complicated process and I don't recommend you spend your valuable time and effort on it.

If your application was previously released for iOS3, you will need to support both iOS versions; otherwise, your users might react poorly and give you one star rating in the Apple App Store. If your application is newly released, you can go straight to iOS4 without worrying.

Summary

Multitasking is a new concept in iOS4. Most of the time, you will need to keep track of your states and life cycles to make sure that your application is responding correctly.

You can choose to remove the multitasking support from your application by changing some properties in the `Info.plist` file. You can also request special permissions for some background services by adding `UIBackgroundModes` key into the `Info.plist` file.

You can request an extra amount of time to process important calculations and services (up to 10 minutes). You need to clean up all resources and cache data to reduce the memory footprint; otherwise, iOS can kill your application in the background. This generally means you lost all the benefits of a multitasking application.

EXERCISES

1. Write an application to play audio in the background.

2. Write an application to monitor significant location changes of the user.

3. Write an application to post data into a web service before your application moves to background. You can put your code in `applicationDidEnterBackground`.

## Chapter 9

Improve Performance with Native C/C++

In this chapter, you will learn about:

- The benefits and costs to integrating C/C++ code into your iPhone application.

- Basic concepts in C programming

    - Data types

    - Pointer

    - Memory management

- Basic concepts in C++ programming

    - Class

    - Memory management

    - Inheritance

    - Template

- How to work through a real example with SQLite, a database that has a C API.

- How to integrate C++ and Objective-C++ into your iPhone application.

In this chapter, you will learn about low-level programming with C/C++, which is important for high performance applications. It's true that Objective-C is a superset of C and also a native programming language, but Objective-C adds a wrapper over the C language that reduces performance. If you have ever worked with games and animations, you know that using OpenGL with C/C++ provides much better performance.

C++ is also supported by Apple. Most of your basic applications will not need to touch any C/C++ code; however, when your application requires better performance, you should consider this option. Moreover, you don't need to write lots of C/C++ code but you do need to understand C/C++ code to call the library correctly. You may also need to modify open source libraries to fit your needs.

Because Objective-C is a superset of C, everything you can do in C, you can do in Objective-C. There are syntax differences and new concepts, but I'll cover them in this chapter. C++ and Objective-C have many differing concepts as well, so it may be harder for you to learn C++ than C.

Actually, the concept of Objective-C is limited, and most of the classes and supports you see in the iPhone development environment come from Cocoa Touch. For simplicity, I will use Objective-C as a symbol for Objective-C and all the supports from Cocoa Touch Frameworks.

Benefits and Costs

Before going into the ideas of C/C++ programming, I want to quickly analyze the benefits and costs of using C/C++ code inside your iOS application.

Benefits:

- There are specialized libraries written in C/C++ such as animation or sound libraries. These libraries are usually written in C/C++ for high performance and portability.

- Your application can be ported to Android without much effort.

- You may improve application performance by using C/C++ code.

Cost:

- C/C++ has a different syntax than Objective-C, and mixing them up makes the code harder to understand.

- C/C++ has a different memory management mechanism than Objective-C, so you need to be careful about memory leaks or application crashes.

So, knowing both benefits and costs, you can make the decision if you want to integrate C/C++ into your iPhone application or not. Even if you are using another open source library or write your own code, you should understand C/C++ before doing so. Many of the problems that arise can be so subtle that iPhone instruments can't help you much. It's easy to spend an hour integrating a library—and then spend the whole day fixing a bug inside.

Objective-C is already a native programming language, so you may not get much better performance if you try to write all code in C/C++. However, there are many high performance libraries written in C/C++ that you can take advantage of and integrate into your application.

Basic C and C++ programming

I will guide you through some simple lessons in C/C++ to give you a good basic understanding of the language. Objective-C and C/C++ have many things in common, so you may not need to learn many new concepts in this chapter. Knowing C/C++ also helps you to write better Objective-C code because Objective-C is a superset of C.

C Programming

C++ is also a superset of C so you will learn how to use C first and then learn about C++ in the next section. I will only discuss the parts in C programming that are not commonly used in iPhone programming.

Basic Data Types and Functions

C has very few data types: integer, floating point, double precision floating point, and characters. The number of bits used for each data type is different in every operating system, even in the iOS family. The following is a sample of range value for each data type, but you should not depend too much on this information to make important decisions:

- `char`: -128 to 127

- `integer`: -32768 to +32767

- `float`: 3.4 e-38 to 3.4 e+38

- `double`: 1.7 e-308 to 1.7 e+308

There are a number of qualifiers that can be applied to these basic types; for example, short and long are applied to integer.

```
short int sh;
long int counterLong;
```

The intent of these qualifiers is to provide a shorter or longer value range for `integer`; for example `short` can be 16 bits and `long` can be 32 bits. The iOS compiler guarantees that `short` is not longer than `int`, which is not longer than `long`.

You can also apply `signed` and `unsigned` qualifiers. If you don't specify any `signed` or `unsigned` qualifiers, the compiler will default to `signed`. Using `unsigned` qualifier will let you have a double data range. For example, `integer` can have from 0 to 65535.

Usually you just need to use `integer`. If you need to store a really big `integer`, add the `long` quantifier. Using `short` over `int` is such a small memory optimization that you can just skip it.

> **NOTE:** if you use Objective-C, you should use NSInteger, NSUInteger, and CGFloat. These are built-in wrappers of Apple to encapsulate the real underlying data structure.

C does not have a Boolean data type, but Objective-C does. In C, if a Boolean statement returns true, the value is 1; otherwise, it is 0. For example 2 == 2 will return 1, while 2 == 3 will return 0. To have readable code, you may need to define two Boolean values, like so:

```
#define TRUE 1
#define FALSE 0
int t = (1 == 1);
if (t == TRUE) {
    // do your work here
}
```

Although C functions look different from Objective-C methods, you still need to return value and accept parameters. Here are two examples of functions in C:

```
int pi_value() {
    return 3.14;
}


int add_number(int n1, int n2) {
    return n1 + n2;
}
```

Pointer

Pointers are an important concept in C programming. In Objective-C, you usually see the same pointer concept and syntax in Objective-C, for instance NSMutableArray *myArray = [NSMutableArray array]. However, you don't usually need to work at a low level with memory so the pointer concept in Objective-C is easy to understand as an object. However, you can do more with C, and the concept of pointers is more complicated.

Memory Pointing Concepts

Main memory can be viewed as an array of cells, each cell as a byte, and every data item is stored inside a group of cells. A char is stored in one cell, an integer can be stored in two cells, and long can be stored in four cells. Each cell can be numbered so every variable will have a memory address to store data.

Figure 9–1. *Memory pointer concept*

A pointer is a variable that can hold the memory address of another variable. For example, data inside variable p in Figure 9–1 stores the memory address of variable c.

So if p is said to point to c, you can represent it with the statement p = &c;. The & operator returns the memory address of c and assign that to p. The & operator only applies to variables, arrays, and objects in memory, not expression or constants. Another pointer operator is *; when it applies to a pointer, the pointer operator returns the contents of the memory at the given address. This process is commonly called de-referencing. Here is some source code to show how this works:

```
int x = 1, y = 2, a[3];
int *ip; // ip is a pointer that can only point to integer

ip = &x; // ip now points to x
y = *ip; // y is now 1, because you return the data pointed by ip
*ip = 0; // x is now 0, I set the data pointed by p to be 0
ip = &a[0]; // ip now points to the first element of array a
```

Pass by Value and pass by Reference

In C programming, you can pass arguments to functions by value or by reference. By value is the normal way you pass arguments into functions.

```
int add(int t1, int t2) {
  return t1 + t2;
}
```

However, pass by value will not work if you want to swap the value between two variables in the following swap function:

```
void swap(int x, int y) {
    int temp;
    temp = x;
    x = y;
    y = temp;
}

int main() {
  int x = 3, y = 4;
  swap (x, y);
}
```

The problem is that after the method returns, the value inside the variable will not be swapped. When the method swap is called, the values inside x and y are copied and passed into the function as swap (3, 4). Thus, the original variable does not change.

If you want to change the data stored inside the variables x and y, you need to pass by reference. With passing by reference, the memory address of x and y are passed in. Having the memory address of x and y, you can simply change the value stored inside these addresses.

```
void swap(int *px, int *py) {
  int temp;
  temp = *px; // temporarily store the value inside the memory of x
  *px = *py; // set the value inside the memory of x.
  *py = temp; // set the value inside the memory of y.
}

int main() {
  int x = 3, y = 4;
```

```
    swap (&x, &y);
}
```

Figure 9–2 gives you a better understanding of the process.

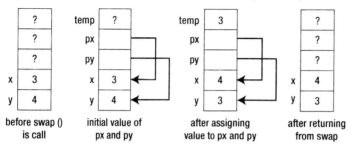

Figure 9–2. *Pass by reference*

Advanced Data Types

There are some advanced data structures in C: array, string, and struct. These all are supported in Objective-C but you should use them sparingly because they make the code harder to understand and maintain in future. All these data structures in Objective-C have corresponding wrappers to make the code more object-oriented. However, in many cases you still need to use C data structures to improve performance or process the result from calling C/C++ libraries.

Array

In Objective-C, you will usually use an NSArray or NSMutableArray object to represent an array. However, in C, you don't have those concepts, so you focus entirely on the primitive array concept. To define an array in C, you need to know the length of the array ahead of time and define it like this:

```
int a [10]; // an array with maximum ten elements
```

a[0], a[1], a[2] … a[9] is the first, second … tenth elements of the array

Pointer has a close relationship with array.

```
int *pa;
pa = &a[0];
```

This pointer assignment code will set pa to point to the first element of the array. As explained in the pointer part, the assignment x = *pa will set x to the value contained inside the a[0].

You can move the pointer to different elements inside the array by using simple arithmetic operators: (pa + 1) will return the address of the next element and (pa - 1) will return the address of the previous element. Figure 9–3 demonstrates the pointer arithmetic inside the array.

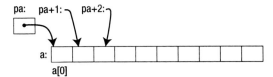

Figure 9–3. *Pointer arithmetic*

These calculations don't depend on the type or the size of variables inside array a. So (pa + i) will always return the address of ith element. Another important relationship between array and pointer is you can refer the data inside a[i] by using *(a + i).

There is one difference between an array name and a pointer: a pointer is a variable so pa = a and pa++ is acceptable. However, a = pa and a++ are unacceptable.

String

A string constant in C, such as "I am Khang," is an array of characters terminated by a null character '\0' so that programs can find the end of an array. Because string is an array of characters, you can assign it to the pointer easily.

```
char *pmessage;
pmessage = "I am Khang";
```

You can manipulate the string as a normal array or with pointers, as in this source code:

```
void my_string_copy (char *s, char *t) {
    while (*s++ = *t++) ;
}
```

The my_string_copy function is simple; it just takes two character pointers and assigns the value of each character in string t (represented by character pointer t) to its own character element.

> **NOTE:** When you pass an array into a function as a parameter, C will automatically convert that array to be a pointer of the same type.

Here is another example using an array of characters, but not using a pointer, to illustrate the interchangeable nature of array and pointer:

```
int my_string_length(char *s) {
    int i = 0;
    while (s[i] != '\0') {
        i++;
    }
    return i;
}
```

Struct

C has no concept of object-oriented programming. So to create a complex data structure (rather than just primitive types and arrays), you use struct. In some Objective-C code, you can even see the struct used intensively in areas that need to save memory.

For example, CGPoint, CGRect, and CGSize are structs. Apple developers put them as struct because they are used intensively for building views in iPhone. You can use struct as in Objective-C.

```
struct point {
  int x;
  int y;
};

struct point add_point(struct point p1, struct point p2) {
  p1.x += p2.x;
  p1.y += p2.y;
  return p1;
}
```

If you pass a big data structure into a function, you may consider passing the pointer to that struct to the function, which will avoid copying the whole structure (because of passing by value). You use the struct pointers as in other normal cases.

```
struct point origin;
struct point *porigin;
porigin = &origin;
printf("origin is (%d, %d) \n" , (*porigin).x , (*porigin ).y );
```

Dynamic Memory Allocation

Memory management in C has some similarities and differences to that in Objective-C. In C, you can also create and allocate memory to objects; if you allocate an object to memory, you need to manually deallocate/free that object to reclaim the memory. There is no concept of autorelease or Autorelease Pool in Objective-C.

There are four functions to remember to have a good memory management mechanism in C, as shown in Table 9–1.

Table 9–1. *Functions to Manage Memory in C*

Function	Task
malloc	Allocates memory requested in size of bytes and returns a pointer to the first byte of allocated space. The contents of the allocated memory are indeterminate (i.e., garbage data).
calloc	Allocates space for an array of elements, initializes all elements to zero, and returns a pointer to the first element of the array. The initialization process helps with the garbage data problem of malloc.
free	Deallocates previously allocated space.
realloc	Modifies the size of previously allocated space.

■ **Malloc**: You can request a block of memory of specific size and return a pointer of type void. You then can cast this pointer to your specific type and use it, like so:

```
my_ptr = (cast_type *)malloc(number_of_bytes); // General format
my_ptr = (int *)malloc (100  * sizeof(int)); // allocate a pointer of integer with size
    //  of 100 integer
```

■ **Calloc** is usually used to request multiple blocks of memory, each of the same size, and then set all bytes to zero.

```
my_ptr = (cast_type *)calloc(number_of_elements, size_of_element); // General format
my_ptr = (int *)calloc (100, sizeof(int)); // allocate a pointer of integer with size
    //  of 100 integer
```

■ **Free**: The memory management mechanism here is similar to Objective-C: the memory you allocate, you need to release. You can use the free method in C to do so.

```
free(my_ptr);
```

■ **Realloc**: Sometimes the memory you allocated for the object or array is insufficient, so you may need to change the memory size with the help of function realloc.

```
realloc(my_ptr, 200 * sizeof(int));
```

> **NOTE:** You can't use the function malloc/calloc again because that will erase all data stored in the memory that your pointer points to.

Linked List Example
It's time to take a break from all the theory and start coding. You will apply what you learned to a problem using linked list to store data. You already learned the linked list implementation in Objective-C in Chapter 5. Now, you will learn how to write a linked list in C, which can provide much higher performance in many cases.

```
#include <stdio.h>
#include <stdlib.h>

struct Node {
 int number;
 struct Node *next;
};
```

To have a linked list, you need a struct that can reference itself. In your case, the Node struct needs to have a link to the next struct inside the linked list. In C, you can declare the method interface in both the header or implementation files.

```
void append_node(struct Node *list, int num);
void display_list(struct Node *list);

int main(void) {
 struct Node *list;
```

```
    list = (struct Node *)malloc(sizeof(struct Node));
    list->number = 0;
    list->next = NULL;

    append_node(list, 1);
    append_node(list, 5);
    append_node(list, 3);

    display_list(list);

    // delete a list here. free(list) will not work
    return(0);
}

void delete_list(struct Node *list) {
    // do it as your exercise
}

void display_list(struct Node *list) {
    // loop over the list to print the value out.
    while(list->next != NULL) {
     printf("%d ", list->number);
     list = list->next;
    }

    printf("%d", list->number);
}

void append_node(struct Node *list, int num) {
    // go into the end of the list
    while(list->next != NULL)
     list = list->next;

    // set the next property for the last Node object.
    list->next = (struct Node *)malloc(sizeof(struct Node));
    list->next->number = num;
    list->next->next = NULL;
}
```

You can see that because your linked list doesn't have a fixed size, you always need to use malloc to allocate new element. After you finish with the linked list, delete your list. You need to remember the memory management rule: for every malloc or calloc you call, you need to call a free function; otherwise, you have a memory leak. As the comment in the code warns, a simple call to free (list) will cause some memory leaks in your program. I will leave the implementation for delete_list as your exercise.

Function Pointers

In C, a function is not a variable but you can define pointers to functions as you define pointers to integer or struct. You can put these function pointers into an array, and pass these function pointers as arguments into other functions. It is really similar to selector in Objective-C.

Next you will look at a simple example to implement a comparison method to fill in the quick sort algorithm. The qsort is a built-in function in C that can accept a function pointer and uses the quick sort algorithm to sort the array.

Here is the qsort interface:

```
void qsort (void *array, int number_of_elements, int size_of_element, int (* comparator)
(const void *, const void *) );
```

So, you need a comparator function that accepts two pointers and returns an integer indicating what value is bigger.

```
int compare (const void * a, const void * b) {
  return ( *(int*)a - *(int*)b );
}
```

And then you can pass it as a parameter to your qsort function.

```
int main () {

  int values[] = { 40, 10, 100, 90, 20, 25 };
  qsort (values, 6, sizeof(int), compare); // pass in the compare function here.
  return 0;
}
```

Bitwise Operators

Bitwise operators can be slightly faster than addition and subtraction operators and significantly faster than multiplication and division operations. You may see code using bitwise operators a lot in libraries, especially ones written with the old microprocessors.

Knowing bitwise operators can help you to manipulate the bits and boost the performance much faster in intensive calculations. There are a few bitwise operators and bit shift operators that you need to remember: NOT, AND, OR, XOR, left shift, and right shift.

- NOT is a complement operator that make bits with 0 become 1 and vice versa.

  NOT 0111 = 1 000

- AND takes two binary representations of equal length and performs the AND operation on each pair of corresponding bits. The result is 1 if bit 1 and bit 2 are 1; otherwise it is 0.

  ```
  0 1 0 1
  AND    0 0 1 1
         = 0 0 0 1
  ```

- OR takes two binary representations of equal length and performs the OR operation on each pair of corresponding bits. The result is 1 if either of them is 1 or both are 1; otherwise it is 0.

  ```
          0 0 1 0
  OR      1 0 0 0
        = 1 0 1 0
  ```

- XOR takes two binary representations of equal length and performs the XOR operation on each pair of corresponding bits. The result is 1 if two bits are different; otherwise it is 0.

```
         0 1 0 1
  XOR    0 0 1 1
     = 0 1 1 0
```

Using these bit operators, you can change the bit value quickly. This may all look strange if you are not used to explicit bit operators. I will give you an illustration in Objective-C. Here is an application of bitwise operators inside Cocoa Touch framework that you are already familiar with: NSCalendar.

In an NSCalendar, you can get a list of date components of a specific date based on an input parameter. For example, if you want to have an NSDateComponent object that contains only date components you want, you can use this source code:

```
NSUInteger unitFlags = NSYearCalendarUnit | NSMonthCalendarUnit | NSDayCalendarUnit;
NSDateComponents *dateComponents = [calendar components:unitFlags
                                    fromDate:startDate
                                      toDate:endDate
                                     options:0];
```

When the method [calendar components:fromDate:toDate:options] is called with the unitFlags, it will check to see what components of a date the caller needs and return exactly those ones. It is convenient to read and write code like this, with only OR operator needed.

Within the method [calendar components:fromDate:toDate:options], it will check the unitFlags by using an AND operator.

```
BOOL hasYear = (unitFlags & NSYearCalendarUnit) != 0;
BOOL hasMonth = (unitFlags & NSMonthCalendarUnit) != 0;
BOOL hasWeek = (unitFlags & NSWeeCalendarUnit) != 0;
…
```

Now, I will explain to you in detail what happens inside these operators and how this works. Firstly, each flag (NSYearCalendarUnit, NSMonthCalendarUnit, etc.) is assigned with a unique binary representation with format: 0100, 1000.

When you do an OR operation over three flags, you will receive something like 1011. You pass this to the method [calendar components:fromDate:toDate:options]. Inside this method, it will do an AND operator with each flag to see what flag is stored inside.

```
1011 & 0100 = 0100 → there is a NSYearCalendarUnit.
1011 & 1000 - 1000 →  there is a NSMonthCalendarUnit
```

Using this approach will improve your application's performance compared to other normal approaches, which either pass in too many arguments, use a big enum to store case, or need a big loop to check for data.

> ▨ **Bit shift**: You can shift the bit to left and right when you multiply or divide your number by a factor of 2. For example, if you multiply or divide your number by 2, 4, 8, 16…, you can consider using bitshift, which has higher runtime performance than doing the multiply or divide directly. You can only do bit shift on integers.

There are two bit shift operators: left shift and right shift. Integers are stored in binary, with a series of bits such as 0000 0110 (6 in decimal). The results for applying the bit shift operations vary on each operation:

- **Left shift**: You move all the bits to left and fill with zeros from the right. If you shift n bits to the left, it also means you multiply with 2^n.

  0000 0110 << 1 = 0000 1100 (12 in decimal)

- **Right shift**: You move all bits to the right and fill with zeros from the left. If you shift n bits to the right, it also means you divide the number by 2^n.

  0000 0110 >> 1 = 0000 0011 (3 in decimal)

C++ Programming

C++ is a superset of C, so you will learn a couple more techniques here. C++ has some different concepts and syntax than Objective-C, although both of them are object-oriented programming language. There are a couple of important differences: class, pointers, multiple inheritance, memory management, and template.

Class

It is similar to Objective-C in that you have two files for one class: one for header and one for implementation. You can also specify the private and public members/methods. Here is a standard way to declare a class header:

```
class Cat {
  public:
      // public accessors
    unsigned int GetAge();
    void SetAge(unsigned int Age);

    Cat ();
    Cat (int initialAge);      // constructor
    ~Cat();                    // destructor

    // public member functions
    void Meow();

    // private member data
  private:
    unsigned int  itsAge;
};

// GetAge, Public accessor function
// returns value of itsAge member
unsigned int Cat::GetAge() {
    return itsAge;
}
```

```
// returns sets itsAge member
void Cat::SetAge(unsigned int age) {
    // set member variable its age to
    // value passed in by parameter age
    itsAge = age;
}

// action: Prints "meow" to screen
void Cat::Meow() {
    cout << "Meow.\n";
}

int main() {
    Cat cat;
    cat.Meow();
}
```

You can see that to declare public and private, you separate them out into areas and put qualifiers private and public in, just as in Objective-C with the same qualifiers @private and @public when you define your header. For the class implementation, you need to put class name before the method implementation to declare that the method belongs to the class.

For the accessors and mutators, you need to explicit declare them as

```
unsigned int GetAge();
void SetAge(unsigned int Age);
```

To create a new object of Cat, you can just declare Cat cat; and then call the method cat.Meow(); The object, though, only exists inside the local scope of the function.

For memory management, you may need to declare both constructor and destructor. If you don't declare your own constructor, the compiler assumes that it will use the default constructor without any argument.

> **NOTE:** If you declare your own constructor, please remember to declare your destructor as well, even if it doesn't do anything. It is a good convention to follow. To create a new object of Cat with Cat cat, you need a default constructor.

Pointers and Memory Management

If you want to use the newly created object elsewhere in your program, you need to allocate memory on the free store in C++. The object will always stay in the memory area until you explicitly call to delete that memory, similar to programming in C. To declare a pointer to a memory address containing integer you can do as this code does:

```
int *pInt;
pInt = new int;
*pInt = 72;
```

To allocate and delete for an object, you can use the new and `delete` keywords.

```
Cat *pCat = new Cat;
pCat->SetAge(5);
delete pCat;
pCat = 0;
```

> **NOTE:** If you call delete twice in the same pointer, your application will crash. If you don't delete the pointer before reallocating it, you will have a memory leak.

Inheritance

The inheritance in C++ has some complicated concepts compared to Objective-C. You can have inheritance, overriding, and polymorphism as normal. The only difference is the concept of virtual and pure virtual methods.

```
class Dog : Mammal {
}
```

The Dog class will inherit all the attributes and methods of the Mammal class, and it can have its own attribute and methods. When a Dog object is created, the constructor of the Mammal is called first before any other code inside the constructor of the Dog class.

There is an important concept in C++ inheritance: you can only override the methods that are virtual. With other methods, you can only inherit without overriding that method. You can have two methods with the same name in superclass and subclass but there is no overriding and no polymorphism. With virtual methods, your subclass is suggested to override the method if necessary. The default qualifier for C++ method is non-virtual. There are two kinds of virtual methods: virtual methods and pure virtual methods.

```
#include "stdafx.h"
#include "stdio.h"

using namespace System;

class Animal {
 public:
  virtual void Speak() = 0;
  virtual void Eat();
  void Run();
};

void Animal::Eat()
{
        printf("Animal eats\n");
}

void Animal::Run()
{
        printf("Animal runs\n");
}
```

```
class Dog : Animal
{
public:
        void Eat();
        void Speak();
        void Run();
};

void Dog::Eat()
{
        printf("Dog eats\n");
}

void Dog::Run()
{
        printf("Dog runs\n");
}

void Dog::Speak()
{
        printf("Dog speaks\n");
}

int main()
{
        Animal *dog1 = (Animal *) new Dog;
    dog1->Run();
    dog1->Speak();
    dog1->Eat();
        getchar();
}
```

For virtual method, you have to have the implementation for it inside the superclass; for pure virtual method, you can just declare the method signature. The Eat method is a virtual method while Speak is a pure virtual method. Both methods needed to be overridden inside the subclass.

Because the Run method is not virtual, it isn't overridden by the subclass. So the output of the main method will be

```
Animal Runs
Dog Speaks
Dog Eats
```

Multiple Inheritance

In C++, your class can inherit from many superclasses, so you can reuse more properties and methods. For example, your Teacher class can inherit from both Employee and Person class, as in Figure 9–4.

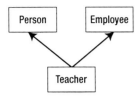

Figure 9–4. *Multiple inheritance*

You can declare your class to inherit multiple classes by using

```
class Teacher : public Person, public Employee {
}
```

There is one common problem with multiple inheritance: when two superclasses share the same method. For example, GetIncome can be declared from both Person and Employee class. So, when you call your Teacher object to get its income, you need to specify the superclass that you call it from.

If you simply write

```
int currentIncome = pTeacher→GetIncome();
```

you will get a compiler error

```
Member is ambiguous: 'Person::GetIncome' and 'Employee::GetIncome'
```

You need to resolve this ambiguity by explicitly calling the superclass's function you want to invoke.

```
int currentIncome = pTeacher→Employee::GetIncome();
```

Template

In C++, you can define classes or methods to receive a specific type of objects only. For example, you can define a method that only receives two data of the same type to compare and return results.

```
template <class T>
T GetMax (T a, T b) {
 return (a>b)? a : b;
}

int main () {
 int i=5, j=6, k;
 long l=10, m=5, n;
 k=GetMax<int>(i,j);
 n=GetMax<long>(l,m);
 return 0;
}
```

By defining a template method, you can make sure that a and b have the same class type and can be compared with each other. You can do the same with template class without any issue.

```
template <class T>
class mypair {
    T a, b;
  public:
    mypair (T first, T second)
      {a=first; b=second;}
    T getmax () {
return a>b? a : b;
    }
};

int main () {
  mypair <int> myobject (100, 75);
  cout << myobject.getmax();
  return 0;
}
```

A Practical Example

I will guide you through some examples to integrate C/C++ library inside the Objective-C code. One example is to integrate with SQLite libraries, the other is a sample application to mix C++ code to Objective-C code.

SQLite

SQLite is an underlying implementation for CoreData. In terms of performance, SQLite offers slightly better performance because it is lighter and more direct. However, CoreData supports you with a better object mapping model, undo and redo features, working in batch, and thread.

The main advantage of SQLite is that if your team is already strong with relational database and relational SQL, the learning curve is slight. SQLite is also easier to port into Android and then you can share the same data layer between iPhone and Android applications.

You can read the source code example in SQLiteSample project. I will give you only the important points here.

You need to create a SQL database by opening your terminal and typing sqlite3 students.sql. This will create a new database where you can create a table, insert, and select data inside. You can create table and insert data as normal by using SQL.

```
sqlite> CREATE TABLE students (pk INTEGER PRIMARY KEY, name VARCHAR(25));
sqlite> INSERT INTO students (name) VALUES ('khang');
sqlite> INSERT INTO students (name) VALUES ('vo');
sqlite> INSERT INTO students (name) VALUES ('duy');
sqlite> .quit
```

Figure 9–5 demonstrates more clearly what happens inside the terminal.

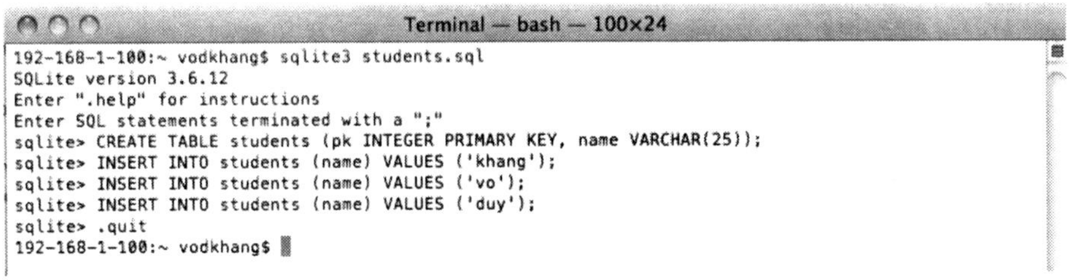

Figure 9–5. *SQLite database*

Then, you can find the `students.sql` file in your Home folder (which is the default folder if you don't change to any folder in terminal). You need to add that file into Xcode and then add the library `libsqlite3.0.dylib`.

```
- (void)viewDidAppear:(BOOL)animated {
    NSString *path = [[NSBundle mainBundle] pathForResource:@"students" ofType:@"sql"];

    if (sqlite3_open([path UTF8String], &database) == SQLITE_OK) {
        // Get the primary key for all books.
        const char *sql = "SELECT pk, name FROM students";
        sqlite3_stmt *statement;

        // Preparing a statement compiles the SQL query into a byte-code program in the
SQLite library.
        // The third parameter is either the length of the SQL string or -1 to read up to
the first null terminator.
        if (sqlite3_prepare_v2(database, sql, -1, &statement, NULL) == SQLITE_OK) {
            // We "step" through the results - once for each row.
            while (sqlite3_step(statement) == SQLITE_ROW) {
                const unsigned char *name = sqlite3_column_text(statement, 1);
                NSString *nameString = [NSString stringWithCString:(char *)name
encoding:NSASCIIStringEncoding];
            }
        }

        // "Finalize" the statement - releases the resources associated with the
statement.
        sqlite3_finalize(statement);
    } else {

        // Even though the open failed, call close to properly clean up resources.
        sqlite3_close(database);
        NSAssert1(0, @"Failed to open database with message '%s'.",
sqlite3_errmsg(database));

    }

    [self.tableView reloadData];
}
```

There are a couple of methods that you need to remember:

- `sqlite3_open([path UTF8String], &database) == SQLITE_OK` initializes and assigns the new database object to your pointer.

- `sqlite3_prepare_v2(database, sql, -1, &statement, NULL) == SQLITE_OK` executes your sql command and puts the result into the statement.

- `while (sqlite3_step(statement) == SQLITE_ROW):` Step over the results from executing the statement.

Integrate C++ into Your Application

It takes almost no effort to integrate C into your application because Objective-C is the superset of C. However, you need to be careful about some details when you integrate C++ into your application.

Firstly, you need to create your C++ class inside the normal header and implementation files as normal (`.h` and `.cpp files`). And then, you need to wrap your C++ file by an Objective-C file with the extension `.mm` (which tells iOS environment that these files are Objective-C++ files). Any file that wants to use these .mm files need to be a .mm file as well.

You can look at the sample project `TestC_CPlus`. First, you can see that there are two files, `Foo_Cpp.h` and `Foo_Cpp.cpp,` that declare the `Foo_Cpp` C++ Class. Then, you wrap this file over by Objective-C++ files called `MyObject.h` and `MyObject.m`.

The last step is to integrate these behind logic into the view controller. You can call the object MyObject anywhere in the project as normal. You only need to rename the calling files to end with `.mm`.

Summary

There are plenty of high-performance and task-specialized C/C++ libraries available in the programming world. You should not reinvent the wheel or try hard to convert all this C/C++ code into Objective-C code, which would take forever. Understanding C/C++ can help you understand the libraries better so you can integrate them into your existing applications.

Objective-C is a superset of C so there are many C features that you may already know. I discussed the main important points of C programming, including the pointer concept. You also learned about function pointers and bitwise operations, which give you the best capabilities to leverage the high performance features of C.

C++ is harder to learn and understand if you have no experience with coding. I discussed only the main points of C++ and main differences between C++ and Objective-C. It may not be enough information to write a big-scale C++ application, but it's enough for you to integrate (and modify if necessary) the existing C++ libraries into your iPhone applications.

In the last section, I used a real example with SQLite to demonstrate the usage of C in Objective-C. It's not too hard to do so, except for some differences in syntax and memory management. I don't go too deeply into a C++ library; I just demonstrated how you can have C++ code inside your iPhone application.

EXERCISES

1. 1. Write a function in C to compare two string, s1 and s2. If s1 < s2 returns negative, s1 = s2 returns 0, s1 > s2, returns positive.

2. 2. Write a function in C to append the string s2 to the end of string s1.

3. 3. Finish the linked list C-program by filling the method `delete_list`.

## Chapter 10

Comparing Android and Windows Phone Performance Problems

In this chapter, you will learn the following:

- General knowledge and differences between the three platforms and three programming languages used in Smartphone development.

- How to revise many important aspects of application performance that you learned for iOS to apply to Android and Windows Phone, such as:

  - How to benchmark applications for Android and Windows Phone.

  - How to optimize the scrolling performance.

  - The differences in caching and data storage.

  - A brief lesson in data structure and algorithms for the three platforms.

  - A brief lesson in multithreading on the three platforms. Android is different than the other two platforms.

  - Lessons about memory constraints.

  - The different ways these platforms handle multitasking.

  - How to integrate C/C++ code into your Android application.

This chapter will provide a general vision of the three main important Smartphone platforms in the near future: iPhone, Android, and Windows Phone. They are growing up and making huge innovations to keep a competitive advantage against their competitors. For some basic and trivial applications, you won't care to optimize performance for each platform because it takes so much time and effort; you can write a cross-platform application to save time.

Unsurprisingly, cross platform release has a significant delay of up to several weeks or months after the main SDK is released. It also lacks some of the detailed features compared to the main APIs. Therefore, to succeed in any of these three platform markets, you will need to use the main language and features to optimize performance and take advantage of advanced features and APIs for that platform.

I will provide an overview of the main difficulties regarding Android and Windows Phone performance. The approach is simplified by going through the chapters of this book: instruments, the emulator, list view, caching, storage, data structure and algorithms, multithreading, multitasking, memory management, and native C/C++ programming support. For reasons of space, I can't cover all details of each platform nor conjecture which platform is the best. After reading this chapter, you will be aware of the most important difficulties for each platform so that switching and learning a new platform will be easy.

General Knowledge

iPhone uses Objective-C as a main programming language for iOS development. It has no garbage collector but ARC to help with memory management. Only three devices use iOS: iPod Touch, iPhone, and iPad with two different screen resolutions.

Android uses Java as a main programming language and it provides garbage collection for easy memory management. Android has many screen sizes and device hardware specifications. There are some devices with core-duo chips and there are some really weak (much slower processor and limited memory) devices.

Windows Phone uses C# as a main programming language and Silverlight as a user interface framework. C# has garbage collection. There are many devices that support Windows Phone but all must meet the necessary hardware requirements.

Benchmarking on Emulator and Devices

In iOS, as you learned in Chapter 2, the simulator is far faster than the device so there are cases where you need to use the device to test that things work well. The architectures of the simulator and the devices of iOS, Android, and Windows Phone are quite different so there are different approaches to running benchmark tests on each of the platform.

Emulator and Devices

The Android emulator (Figure 10–1) is really slow. You can use it as the lowest benchmark for performance testing. Android also has so many different devices, so for performance, it is hard to keep all Android users happy. You may need to test on different devices to see the range of performance results.

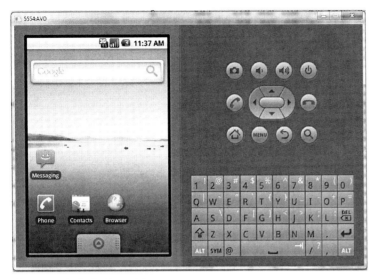

Figure 10–1. *Android emulator*

The Windows Phone emulator (Figure 10–2) runs at a normal performance, so it's is almost the same as a real device. If you want a fast simulator so you can run a quick test in the same way you develop iOS application, it's possible to improve the performance of the emulator; you can find the information easily on the Internet.

Figure 10–2. *Windows Phone emulator*

The iPhone simulator runs extremely fast compared to the real device, as mentioned in Chapter 2, so it's hard to detect any performance issues in it.

Benchmarking

It is important to know which tools are available to you when you need to run benchmarking. Android provides a limited set of tools while Windows Phone provides a wider range of tools that help you to find the performance problem. Many of these tools cover the same functionality as tools supplied by the iOS; they support benchmarking of memory, CPU usage, and user interface processing.

Android

Eclipse for Android doesn't provide a complete list of instrument tools as Xcode does for iPhone. It provides four main instrument tools that you can use to track your performance: thread, heap, object allocation, and file access. You can combine these tools with logging (using Debug.trace()) to measure the general performance of your application.

Although Android provides garbage collection, it has its disadvantages. When the garbage collection runs, it stops your application. This will make your UI cease responding for a couple of milliseconds, or at least not render enough frames (a good rendering frame rate should be around 16-30ms/frame).

Figure 10–3 and 10–4 shows the heap and allocation tracker for Android. You can use these tools to see in what classes or methods you create the most objects.

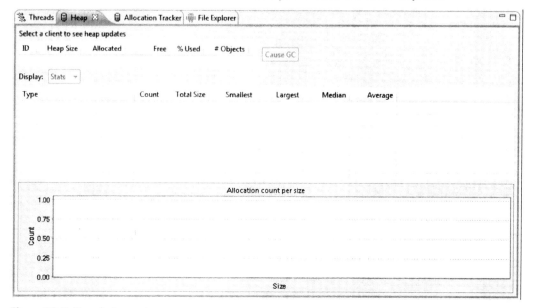

Figure 10–3. *Heap instrument*

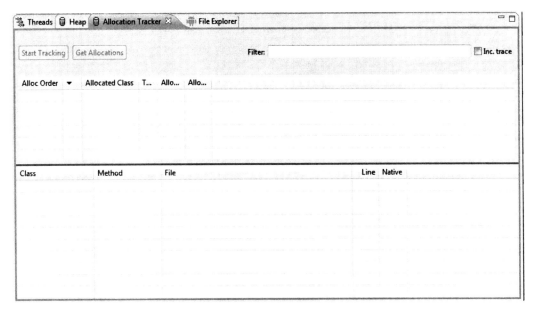

Figure 10–4. *Allocation instrument*

Windows Phone

Windows Phone offers a much better performance profiling tool. Figure 10–5 shows the result of running the Windows Phone profiling tool and getting the data back.

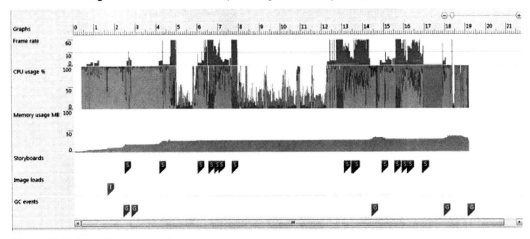

Figure 10–5. *Allocation instrument*

The performance tool supports many different metrics for performance benchmarking: frame rate, CPU usage, memory usage, image loads and garbage collection events. This helps you locate the performance bottleneck so you can solve it more easily.

ListView Performance

All ListViews (or TableViews) in iOS, Android, and Windows Phone share similar performance issues. You always need to return data back to the list as soon as possible; otherwise, user will see a lot of jerkiness when scrolling down. Loading images will need to be asynchronous so user can scroll the list smoothly and see data first. Whenever the image is loaded, it will be displayed in the list later.

There are some common issues with view rendering for all three platforms:

- You should always use opaque views whenever possible.

- You should not use a complicated, nested list view structure because it starts to display slowly.

There are specific issues for each platform when it comes to this ListView scrolling issue. To have a customized ListView, Android and Windows Phone use a different approach to displaying data into the ListView. The way Android does it is similar to iPhone where you return data and view only if necessary. Windows Phone uses an automatic binding mechanism to bind data into the view. The Windows Phone way is easier to implement for developers but it causes more performance issues than the Android way.

With Windows Phone, when you have a big array of objects, you will soon have a problem with memory and performance because the operating system can't store more objects into the memory and fetch them out to bind with the ListView. This is the main difference between ListView in iPhone, Android, and Windows Phone. In the first two platforms, you only need to decide the size of the list; while scrolling, you can get data to display. Memory should not be an issue with iOS TableView when you can discard the unused objects in the array and only store necessary objects. I will explain briefly how both platforms are implemented and how to solve the problems with both platforms.

Android

In Android, you can map your data with the default layout without any difficulty.

```
String [] cities= new String[] {"Melbourne", "Victoria", "Adealide"};
this.setListAdapter(new ArrayAdapter<String>(this, R.layout.list_item, cities);
```

However, if you need to come up with a more complex layout, you can use your own adapter to map the data with the view.

```
<?xml version="1.0" encoding="utf-8"?>
<LinearLayout xmlns:android="http://schemas.android.com/apk/res/android"
        android:layout_width="wrap_content" android:layout_height="wrap_content">
        <ImageView android:id="@+id/icon" android:layout_height="wrap_content"
                android:src="@drawable/icon" android:layout_width="22px">
        </ImageView>
        <TextView android:text="@+id/TextView01" android:layout_width="wrap_content"
                android:layout_height="wrap_content" android:id="@+id/label"
                android:textSize="30px"></TextView>
```

```
</LinearLayout>
```

My sample application includes an image view in the left and a text view in the right, as the default cell in UITableView of iOS.

```
public class MySimpleArrayAdapter extends ArrayAdapter<String> {
    @Override
        public View getView(int position, View convertView, ViewGroup parent) {
        LayoutInflater inflater = context.getLayoutInflater();
        View rowView = inflater.inflate(R.layout.rowlayout, null, true);

        TextView textView = (TextView) rowView.findViewById(R.id.label);
        ImageView imageView = (ImageView) rowView.findViewById(R.id.icon);
        textView.setText(names[position]);

        // Change the icon for Windows and iPhone
        imageView.setImageResource(R.drawable.ok);

        return rowView;
    }
}
```

Creating Java objects (especially View objects) consumes time and CPU, so Android reuses rows that are not displayed any more. For example, if a row disappears off the top or the bottom of the view, Android gives this view back to the `Adapter` method as a parameter `convertView.` To use this in your method, you have to check first if `convertView` is not null, then you can use it to display the next data item.

Another important optimization to note: since the method `findViewByID()` is an expensive operation, you should avoid using it whenever possible. Instead, you should use `setTag()` and `getTag()` method to retrieve the necessary view.

Taking into account these facts, you can rewrite the previous source code as the following:

```
@Override
public View getView(int position, View convertView, ViewGroup parent) {
    // ViewHolder will buffer the assess to the individual fields of the row
    // layout

    ViewHolder holder;
    // Recycle existing view if passed as parameter
    // This will save memory and time on Android
    // This only works if the base layout for all classes are the same
    View rowView = convertView;
    if (rowView == null) {
        LayoutInflater inflater = context.getLayoutInflater();
        rowView = inflater.inflate(R.layout.rowlayout, null, true);
        holder = new ViewHolder();

        // Only findViewByID() at the first time, then use setTag()
```

```
        holder.textView = (TextView) rowView.findViewById(R.id.label);
        holder.imageView = (ImageView) rowView.findViewById(R.id.icon);

        rowView.setTag(holder);

    } else {
        holder = (ViewHolder) rowView.getTag();
    }

    holder.textView.setText(names[position]);

    // Change the icon for Windows and iPhone
    String s = names[position];
    holder.imageView.setImageResource(R.drawable.ok);

    return rowView;
}
```

As you can see, `convertView` is reused so if it's not null, you can use it as-is. You can also see that I created a wrapper to contain the text view and the image view. You can contain as many views inside the view holder as you want and name the parameter to be anything. You can imagine the view holder as a map that has the attributes as the keys and put other views as values.

Windows Phone

Windows Phones use data binding in a different way, which creates a huge performance and memory problem. In Windows Phone, the UI is still reused, just as in Android and iOS; however, the data is bound directly. This means that if you need to display 1,000 items into the ListView (called ListBox in Windows Phone), all 1,000 items need to be created and loaded into the memory. This works fine for a Silverlight desktop application. But in Windows Phone the memory is more limited, so the phone can't afford to load all 1,000 items.

The main issue with the current Windows Phone binding is that it binds to `IEnumerables`. This can be solved using another data bind that implements `IList`, which already supports `Count` and `IndexOf` method.

```
public class MyDataSource : IList
{
  const int MAX_ITEMS = 1000;

  public int Count
  {
    get { return MAX_ITEMS; }
  }

  public int IndexOf(object value)
  {
    if (value == null)
    {
      Debug.WriteLine("IndexOf(null)");
      return -1;
    }
```

```
    DataItem item = (DataItem)value;
    return item.Index;
  }

  public object this[int index]
  {
    get
    {
      DataItem itemToReturn = new DataItem { Index = index, Text = "NEW ITEM" };
      return itemToReturn;
    }
    set
    {
      throw new NotImplementedException();
    }
  }


  // None of the other IList stuff is necessary for data virtualization
  #region Unimplemented stuff
  // Fill in non-implemented methods here
  #endregion
}

public class DataItem
{
  public int Index { get; internal set; }
  public string Text { get; set; }
  public override string ToString()
  {
    return Text + " [" + Index + "]";
  }
}
```

As an exercise, you should integrate this code with the main ListBox code that you use on the UI.

Data Caching

All algorithms and terms that you learned in Chapter 3 for iOS programming can be applied for Android and Windows Phone without any problems. What you should learn are techniques related directly to Windows Phone and Android, such as where to store your cache, how often you should cache, and in what format you should cache your data.

The memory caching part should be no different from iOS either because the hardware specifications for the three platforms are not different. You can have the same memory caching algorithms as the iOS approach. I will focus on how to utilize the file storage to get the best performance.

Android

There are many places where you can store the cache data.

- *Shared preferences*: This is exactly the same as NSUserDefaults. You can store primitive data here. It is usually used for settings storage or lightweight storage.

- *Internal storage:* You can store private data in device's storage. It's actually a file area inside the internal storage. Other applications can't access this storage.

- *External storage:* In most Android phones, users can have more storage by having a removable storage media (such as an SD card). Files saved here are public to the world and can be modified even by the user. The user can enable USB mass storage to transfer files to their computers.

- *SQLite*: This is a database, and you access it using Java and SQL as normal without any much difference. That's why if you choose to store your data in SQLite Database in iPhone, you can actually reuse it here.

Shared Preferences

The SharedPreferences class is stored into two layers of structure. The first layer allows you to store the name of the preferences that you want to store, such as "Network Preferences" or "Setting Preferences." The second layer is the key-value storage layer where you actually store your primitive data.

```
SharedPreferences settings = getSharedPreferences(PREFS_NAME, 0);
boolean silent = settings.getBoolean("silentMode", false);
```

Internal Storage

Files are stored here for longer term and are private to only your application. You can store a file in this storage area by using the following code:

```
String FILENAME = "hello_file";
String string = "hello world!";

FileOutputStream fos = openFileOutput(FILENAME, Context.MODE_PRIVATE);
fos.write(string.getBytes());
fos.close();
```

This code writes the string into the file and then saves that file.

To save data in a cache folder that can be deleted usually by the operating system without letting you know, use the path inside getCacheDir().

NOTE: To save your files into the application, similar to the way the application bundle does in iOS, you can save into the project directory `res/raw/`. You can read the file by using `openRawResource()` but you can't write into these files.

External Storage

This is removable storage so you will need to check if that storage media is attached to the current device or not.

```
String state = Environment.getExternalStorageState();
if (Environment.MEDIA_MOUNTED.equals(state)) {
  // YOU CAN READ AND WRITE DATA
} else if (Environment.MEDIA_MOUNTED_READ_ONLY.equals(state)) {
  // YOU CAN ONLY READ
} else {
  // YOU CAN NEITHER READ OR WRITE
}
```

This media has a much bigger storage capacity so you can save more data in it. However, user can mistakenly delete data, or not attach the media to the device. These files will also be deleted when your application is uninstalled. If you don't want that to happen or you want to share the data with other applications, you can save them into directories at the root by calling `getExternalStoragePublicDirectory()`. You also have a specific cache directory in the external media where you should save unimportant cache data: `getExternalCacheDir()`.

SQLite Database

Storing in a database can lead to complex problems but it can also help solve many performance issues. There are many techniques to help you improve the performance of database access, such as better indexing, partitioning database, and unique key. I won't cover database optimization in depth, as it is a very large and specialized topic. Suffice it to say that SQLite is broadly similar to any other SQL database.

Windows Phone

Microsoft released a new update to Windows Phone that includes a local database. If you start building a new application and want to use a database, you can now do so. Otherwise, if your application is using some other storage mechanism intensively, you may choose to optimize it rather than rebuilding the whole database.

In Windows Phone, there are also four main approaches to storing files.

- `IsolatedStorageSettings`: Key value storage, exactly the same as `NSUserDefaults`.

```
IsolatedStorageSettings appSettings = IsolatedStorageSettings.ApplicationSettings;
```

```
appSettings.Add("email", "myemail@gmail.com");
var myEmail = (string)appSettings["email"];
```

- IsolatedStorageFile: Used in Windows Phone to store files into the file system. It doesn't have a default directory for specific purpose like Cache or Public. You need to create your own directory to handle the storage process.

- XML storage: For the old applications, you may need to choose the XML as your main storage mechanism if you don't have database support.

- Local database: The new release with Mango will have local database support for Windows Phone. Many problems with local storage performance will be solved with this new release.

IsolatedStorageFile

File storage in Windows Phone is simple; you have the whole application directory to do whatever you want. The operating system will not take care of anything like automatically deleting or restricting the storage limit on this directory.

```
IsolatedStorageFile myStore = IsolatedStorageFile.GetUserStoreForApplication();
myStore.CreateDirectory("Cache");

// Specify the file path and options.
using (var isoFileStream = new IsolatedStorageFileStream("Text1.txt",
FileMode.OpenOrCreate, myStore))
{
  //Write the data
  using (var isoFileWriter = new StreamWriter(isoFileStream))
  {
    isoFileWriter.WriteLine(txtWrite.Text);
  }
}
```

To read the file, use this code:

```
using (var isoFileStream = new IsolatedStorageFileStream("Cache\\Text1.txt ",
FileMode.Open, myStore))
{
  // Read the data.
  using (var isoFileReader = new StreamReader(isoFileStream))
  {
    txtRead.Text = isoFileReader.ReadLine();
  }
}
```

You need to specify the read/write permission that you want to read, write, or append data in.

XML Storage

Using XML to store and then LINQ XML to read/write to the XML format is a painful process and can significantly hurt the performance of your Windows Phone application.

The main performance issue with storage using LINQ for XML is that you need to load or save the whole XML every time you need to modify or read your data. This is because LINQ uses DOM to access the data. It also causes memory issues when you store the whole big XML file into the memory to access it. If you have a small XML file, it's not any trouble.

There are two ways developers work around this XML issue.

- You have a main file containing the main structure of all of your data. Then you have several smaller files to store data about each main data item. For example, to have an RSS reader, you can store all the channel information into the main file, then have a separate file for each channel.

- You only cache the most recent data. Any data that is older than 10 days may be deleted. This will reduce the amount of data you have in your local XML file and reduce the complexity of your work. The drawback is that you need to redownload the old data if necessary.

Database Support

With the new Mango release, Windows Phone will have support for local database storage. You will soon have all the powers of indexing, partitioning, key, and random access to the database. With this new release, you should use LINQ to SQL to have good code reuse, because LINQ to SQL and LINQ to XML share many codebase items.

Data Structure and Algorithms

C#, Java, and Objective-C have similar built-in data structures to support the three main types of object collections: set, array, and map. Table 10–1 provides a summary of these types of collections, their subtype, and how you can implement one yourself.

Table 10–1. *Description Summary of Object Collections*

Collection Type	iOS	Android	Windows Phone
Set			
Normal Set	NSSet and NSMutableSet	HashSet	No implementation.
Sorted Set (the set is always sorted)	No implementation. You can have a set then sort it when you need.	TreeSet	No implementation.
List			
ArrayList	NSArray and NSMutableArray	ArrayList	List
LinkedList	No implementation. You can look back Chapter 5 to see an implementation.	LinkedList	LinkedList
Dictionary/Map			
Normal Dictionary	NSDictionary or NSMutableDictionary	HashMap	Dictionary
Sorted Dictionary (a dictionary always sorted)	No implementation. You can get the set of keys out and sort it when necessary.	TreeMap	No implementation. You may need to get the key list out and sort it.

There are some less important data structures such as stack and queue but you can always implement them yourself based on what you learned in Chapter 5.

For XML parser, Android supports both SAX and DOM XML parser by default so you won't need to add another library just to support it. For C# on Windows Phone, you will need to use LINQ over XML to handle the work in most cases because it provides much better code maintenance and is actually faster than DOM. In case of a really big XML files, consider using XmlReader.

Multithreading

C# and Java are powerful programming languages when it comes to managing multithreading. Similar to iOS multithreading, the jobs for updating the UI will need to be done on the UI thread; other long running operations need to be done in the background thread.

The thread locking mechanisms for the three platforms are similar, based on the notification mechanism. There are, though, some important differences in the way each platform implements and sets specific rules for its multithreading mechanism.

Android

Java has a multithreading mechanism but Android prefers to use its own multithreading management mechanism. In Android, there is a really strict rule for the UI thread. If the UI thread is blocked for more than a few seconds (5 seconds currently), the user is presented with the well-known pop up saying "Application not responding". After that, your application is forced to close.

In Java, you can create a thread simply by subclassing the Thread class or implementing the Runnable interface. One of the simplest ways is to use an anonymous method.

```
new Thread(new Runnable() {
  public void run() {
    // Your background code.
  }
}).start();
```

If you create new class, which extends the Thread class, you can simply call new Thread().start. If class B implements the Runnable interface, then you can have new Thread(B).start.

There are several ways that you can update the UI in the UI thread, similar to the way the following iOS method is called:

```
[obj performSelectorOnMainThread:mySelector withObject:nil waitUntilDone:YES];
```

Android offers this list of ways you can update the UI thread:

- `Activity.runOnUiThread(Runnable)`
- `View.post(Runnable)`
- `View.postDelayed(Runnable, long)`
- `Handler`

For example, you can use the following code to get the image in the background thread and then update the UI thread:

```
public void loadImage() {
  new Thread(new Runnable() {
    public void run() {
```

```
    final Bitmap bitmapImage = loadBitmapImage();
    myImageView.post(new Runnable() {
      public void run() {
        myImageView.setImageBitmap(bitmapImage);
      }
    });
  }
}).start();
}
```

The code can become more complex if inside your thread and inside the UI update code you do a lot of processing. You can also create a class that implements the Runnable interface and calls the run method of this class. Android also offers a simpler way to handle a complex thread processing logic: the AsyncTask class. It's a better thread management structure to handle your threading issues.

```
private class myAsyncTask extends AsyncTask<X, Y, Z>
  protected void onPreExecute(){
  }

  protected Z doInBackground(X...x){
  }

  protected void onProgressUpdate(Y y){
  }

  protected void onPostExecute(Z z){
  }
}
```

- onPreExecute: This method is called before your background thread is executed.

- doInBackground: The main method runs in background thread.

- onProgressUpdate: When you need to update the view in the main thread with the current progress of the background thread.

- onPostExecute: When your background thread finishes, this method is called on the UI thread, and you can update your UI with the result of the background thread.

As you can see from the class structure, you can define three generic type parameters: X, Y and Z.

- X: The parameter type that you pass into the background thread. You can pass an array of objects with type X into the background task.

- Y: The parameter type you are going to enter in the onProgressUpdate method. This method is called when you call publishProgress(Y) inside the doInBackground method. For example, you want to show the progress of the operation by a progress bar.

- Z: The parameter type of the result from the operations you have done in the background process.

The image download sample source code shown previously can be rewritten as

```
public void loadImage() {
 new DownloadImageTask().execute("http://example.com/image.png");
}

private class DownloadImageTask extends AsyncTask<String, Void, Bitmap> {
    protected void onPreExecute(){
    }

    protected Bitmap doInBackground(String... urls) {
        return loadImageFromNetwork(urls[0]);
    }

    protected void onPostExecute(Bitmap result) {
        mImageView.setImageBitmap(result);
    }
}
```

For a locking thread to avoid thread race condition and avoid deadlock, you can use a similar mechanism as iOS programming with the wait, notify and notifyAll methods. Here are similarities between these methods and NSCondition methods you learned in Chapter 6:

- wait: Similar to [condition lock], it locks the method or block of code.

- notify and notifyAll: Similar to [condition signal] and [condition unlock], it unlocks the method and tells the other threads to come in. The difference between notify and notifyAll is the first one will randomly pick a thread to let it run while notifyAll will let all threads run.

Windows Phone

You start a new thread in Windows Phone with

```
public void loadImageFromNetwork()
{
}

Thread t = new Thread (loadImageFromNetwork);
t.Start();
```

As normal, you will need to update your user interface in the UI thread. This can be done by calling

```
Dispatcher.BeginInvoke(() => UpdateUI());
```

I used a normal lambda expression. If you don't understand it, just leave it like the sample source code and put your method call in.

To avoid race condition and deadlock, you will need to use locking mechanism, the same way as in Java:

```
obj.notify() => Monitor.Pulse(obj)
obj.notifyAll() => Monitor.PulseAll(obj)
obj.wait() =>  Monitor.Wait(obj)
```

Asynchronous Download

In Windows Phone, because of the API restriction, you can only use an asynchronous request to download the data from the Internet. You will need to use WebClient or HttpWebRequest to make the request to the server. The following is code to initiate a new web request and receive back data:

```
WebClient webClient = new WebClient();
webClient.OpenReadCompleted += new OpenReadCompletedEventHandler(wc_OpenReadCompleted);
webClient.OpenReadAsync(new Uri(arbitraryImageUriThatKeepsChanging), webClient);

void wc_OpenReadCompleted(object sender, OpenReadCompletedEventArgs e)
{
  if (e.Error == null && !e.Cancelled)
  {
    try
    {
      BitmapImage image = new BitmapImage();
      image.SetSource(e.Result);
      imgContent.Source = image;
    }
    catch (Exception ex)
    {
        //Exception handle appropriately for your app
    }
  }
}
```

Memory Management

Android and Windows Phone have their own garbage collectors, so in many cases, you won't need to worry too much about memory management. Because the general approach to garbage collection of Android and Windows Phone look similar to each other, I will illustrate the general point of garbage collection and then I will go into some specific details and cases for Android.

For limited environments like Smartphones (especially the Android phones that only have 32MB of memory), it's your job to make sure that you use the least memory every time. If you don't need to cache an image in memory, release that image. You can release an image by setting the object to null, and the garbage collector will do its job.

You will only have memory leak if you set a reference to an object for the whole application lifecycle without setting it to null at the appropriate time. Unless your view has a long lifecycle and contains too many objects when it's running, you shouldn't worry.

There are specific issues related to each platform that I will discuss in detail in the following sections.

Android

Android has specific platform features that iOS and Windows Phone don't really have: multitasking and TabView. Multitasking in Android is different than multitasking in iOS. Android applications can start services, and these services run in background forever until some of them get destroyed.

Context Activity Leak

In Android, you have a context that is shared between different activities, and this context stores data and the whole view hierarchy inside. The problem is that this context is passed around objects and methods that need to have it, like when you initiated a text view.

```
TextView myTextView = new TextView(myContext);
```

So, if the myTextView leaks, the whole context activity is leaky. Now, consider a case where you need to maintain your background image when the phone changes orientation. When your application changes orientation, it destroys the activity and all the data inside that activity, including your background image. So, the best practice is to keep the image static.

```
private static Drawable sBackground;

@Override
protected void onCreate(Bundle state) {
  super.onCreate(state);

  TextView label = new TextView(myContext);
  label.setText("Leaks are bad");

  if (sBackground == null) {
    sBackground = getDrawable(R.drawable.large_bitmap);
  }
  label.setBackgroundDrawable(sBackground);

  setContentView(label);
}
```

Now you can see that the background has a reference to the label, and the label has a reference to the context myContext. And because the background image is static, it will never be released, so you will simply leak the whole context and the old view hierarchy.

Memory in Multitasking

In Android, because all applications can run in background at any time, memory becomes even more restricted. If your application uses too much memory, it will force the operating system to kill other applications to get back memory. This is why good memory management and usage can become significant for you to handle properly.

TabView

There is a similarity between Android and iPhone when it comes to TabView. If you're using a TabView, all of your views in all tabs are loaded into memory, even if they don't get displayed. This usually causes a huge memory issue for all kinds of applications when views are the most memory consuming elements. Think twice before you go for a TabView.

Windows Phone

Windows Phone doesn't have a multitasking feature so your application can utilize all possible memory and run with high performance. There are, however, some view hierarchy issues that can affect your memory if you don't use them properly.

Panorama and Pivot

There are two main important view hierarchies in Windows Phone: Pivot and Panorama. You can use other ways to create a Windows Phone application with a normal view. Pivot and Panorama are similar to each other although the UI concepts are different. Pivot is used more for applications with similar views but for different purpose, for example, weather in different places (London, Paris, New York, California); see Figure 10–6. Panorama is used more for applications that need to display a large picture of the same thing, as shown in Figure 10–7.

Figure 10–6. *Pivot application*

Figure 10–7. *Panorama application*

There is a big performance problem with panorama applications: you need to load the whole view into the memory even without displaying it. The longer the view is, the more you need to load and it will soon put your application out of memory. This is certainly a major consideration. If you use a panorama view, you should only use a short view; don't load too much data or subviews.

Multitasking

Multitasking is always an issue with all Smartphone platforms because the battery can drain quickly. As discussed in Chapter 8, iOS multitasking is not exactly multitasking. It's a combination of fast application switching and some limited background services.

Android offers multitasking via a different approach, allowing more time and freedom for applications to run and do computation in background. Windows Phone doesn't allow your applications to run in background yet; you may need to wait until the Mango release for that.

Android

In Android, to create a background process, you need to use the Service class. To clarify, using Service doesn't mean a separate thread or a separate process. When you call this service, it will tell the system that your application has something to do in the background. You can also expose some other services to other applications.

To start a new Service, you need to extend the Service class and implement the necessary methods.

```
public class MyService extends Service {
  private static final String TAG = "MyService";

  @Override
    public IBinder onBind(Intent intent) {
    return null;
```

```
  }

  @Override
  public void onCreate() {
    Log.d(TAG, "onCreate");
  }

  @Override
  public void onDestroy() {
    Log.d(TAG, "onDestroy");
  }

  @Override
  public void onStart(Intent intent, int startid) {
    Log.d(TAG, "onStart");
  }
}

public void onClick(View src) {
  switch (src.getId()) {
    case R.id.buttonStart:
      startService(new Intent(this, MyService.class));
      break;
    case R.id.buttonStop:
      stopService(new Intent(this, MyService.class));
      break;
  }
}
```

There are four main methods that you need to know, as shown in the sample source code. When the new service is started by method startService(new Intent(this, MyService.class)), the method onCreate() will be called, and then onStart() will be called. When a service is stopped by stopService(new Intent(this, MyService.class));, the method onDestroy() will be called.

You will need to put your main logic code in the onStart() method and let the background process run from here.

Support of C/C++ Programming

You can write C/C++ code inside your Android applications but that requires you to know about JNI (Java Native Interface) and how to interact with NDK (Native Development Kit). The way you interact is similar to the way you use Objective-C code to interact with C/C++ code. You may need to be careful about memory management problems and should not mess things up too much. Using Java will allow you to have garbage collection while using C/C++ requires you to manage memory manually.

Windows Phone, though, doesn't support any programming languages except C#. If you want to develop games, you will need to use XNA with C/C++. Adding and calling C/C++ code from Java using NDK is really easy; just write a little wrapper code. You need to have a wrapper method to convert between C and Java.

```
#include <jni.h>
#include <string.h>
#include <android/log.h>

void Java_com_packagename_classname_helloLog(JNIEnv * env, jobject this, jstring myLog)
{
    jboolean isCopy;
    const char * szLogThis = (*env)->GetStringUTFChars(env, logThis, &isCopy);
    (*env)->ReleaseStringUTFChars(env, logThis, szLogThis);
}
```

There is a reason for the long function name: the first word is "Java", followed by the package name, the class name, and the method name. When you need to call this method, you can call it with the following format:

```
helloLog("This will log to LogCat via the native call.");
```

You need to define the method interface inside your class so that Android can call it appropriately. This will help Android link this interface with the implementation inside the compiled native code.

```
private native void helloLog(String logThis);
```

Finally, you need to load the library. In fact, you should load the library as soon as you load the class.

```
static {
    System.loadLibrary("ndk1");
}
```

Summary

In this chapter, you learned about differences in performance optimization for three main platforms: iOS, Android, and Windows Phone. There are many similar issues between them because all three platforms are limited by the mobile devices constraint.

Having the same problem with the ListView and how to reuse the view properly, the three platforms solve the problem in a similar way—by trying to reduce loading all data and reusing the view as much as possible.

Caching and data storage in the three platforms is different because they choose different ways to implement the data storage and file structure for the application. iOS has the strongest database storage currently with CoreData while Android can utilize the strength of using external storage. The SQL database release for Windows Phone is expected by any Windows Phone developer in the next fall.

There are also big differences in the way the platforms choose to implement the same functionality, such as multitasking. Multitasking in iOS is more focused on fast app switching, Android focus on real multitasking by allowing process to run in the background, and Windows Phone doesn't support any multitasking in this version.

EXERCISE

1. 1. Implement the ListView using Virtualized Data sample code that I gave.

2. 2. Create a Windows Phone panorama with at least 20 pages, run it on your device to see if you have any memory effects. Do the same for Windows Phone Pivot.

3. 3. Implement an Android background service to download an image from the Internet and then turn off the application.

Index

A

Android
  benchmarking, 244, 245
  data caching, 250
  emulator, 242–243
  ListViews performance, 246–248
  memory management, 259–260
  multitasking, 261–262
  multithreading, 255–257
  programming language, 242
Automatic reference counting (ARC)
  coding, 180
  qualifiers
    autoreleasing, 183
    object property, 183
    strong reference, 182
    unsafe_unretained reference, 183
    variable declarations, 183
    weak reference, 182
  rules, 182
  Xcode, 181

B

Belady's algorithm, 65
Big-O notation
  computation logics, 90, 91
  CPU Sampler, 93, 94
  general performance analysis, 93
  insertion sort performance, 92
  myFirstArray and mySecondArray
      elements, 90
  myFirstCount and mySecondCount
      variables, 90
  Time Profiler, 93–95
Binary tree, 106
  insert/delete mechanism, 121

  left and right child, 121
  node and edge, 120
  O(log(n)) performance, 119
  search strategy, 117–118
  search tree, 121, 123
  sorting algorithms, 116
  uses, 119
Bottleneck
  file activity instrument, 60, 61
  file/network loading test, 60
  system usage instrument, 61

C

C programming
  advanced data types
    array, 224–225
    bitwise operators, 229–230
    function pointers, 228
    linked list, 227–228
    memory management
        mechanism, 226–227
    string, 225
    struct, 225
  benefits and costs, 220
  data types and functions, 221–222
  pointer, 222–224
C programming, 262
C++ programming, 231, 262
  .h and .cpp files, 238
  benefits and costs, 220
  class, 231–232, 238
  inheritance, 233–234
  memory management, 232
  multiple inheritance, 234–235
  MyObject.h and MyObject.m files, 238
  pointers, 232
  template, 235–236

TestC_CPlus, 238
Caching
  Belady's algorithm, 65
  cache hit, 62
  cache invalidation, 64
  cache miss, 62
  data caching. *See* Data caching
  definition, 62
  FIFO, 66–67
  image storage
    application bundle, 76
    cache directory, 73
    documents directory, 74–75
    photo album, 75–76
    temporary directory, 73
  least frequently used algorithm, 70–71
  least recently used algorithm, 68, 70
  measuring cache, 71–72
  memory caching. *See* Memory
      caching
  random replacement, 66
  replacement policy, 64–65
  retrieval cost, 63
  simple time-based algorithm, 67–68
  storage cost, 63
  UIWebView, 72
Cocoa Touch data structures
  hashing, 98
  isEqual and Hash methods, 98, 100
  NSMutableArray, 95
    access, 97
    API, 97
    array illustration, 96
    insert/delete, 96
    search, 96
    sorting, 97
  NSMutableSet
    access, 102
    API, 102–103
    hash method, 100, 101
    insert/delete, 101
    khang, 101
    NSMutableDictionary, 104–105
    search, 101
    sorting, 102
Core animation, 25–27

D, E

Data caching
  checking and deleting, 81
  CoreData storing, 78–80
  plist/xml/json storing, 77–78
  SQLite, 80–81
Data encapsulation, 83
Data structure and algorithm, 253–254
  benchmark testing, 88, 89
  Big-O notation. *See* Big-O notation
  binary tree, 106, *See also* Binary tree
  Cocoa Touch data structures. *See*
      Cocoa Touch data structures
  graph, 106
    breadth-first search algorithm,
      128, 130
    connected graph, 124
    depth-first search algorithm,
      125–128
    directed graph, 125
    path, 124
    vertex and edge, 124
    weighted graph, 125
  intersect method, 89
  linked list, 106–110
    Add Object method, 110–111
    Count method, 112
    Get Object method, 112
    Init method, 110
    ListNode, 107–108
    Node and List object, 107
    performance analysis, 113
    Remove Object method, 113
    vs. array, 106
  NSLog and NSDate, 89
  NSSet API, 88, 89
  recursion, 131–132
  SAX/DOM Parser, 132–133
  source coding, 88
  stack and queue, 106, 113–116

F, G

Facebook, 41
First In First Out (FIFO) algorithm, 66–67

H

Hashing, 98

I, J, K

iOS performance optimization
    Android and Windows Phone
        environment, 2
    Cocoa Touch Framework, 2
    Java development, 2
    Mac OS, Xcode, 3
    network data transfers, 2
    smartphone, 1
    Stack Overflow, 2
iPhone, 242

L

Legacy code
    memory garbage, 16–18
    memory leaks
        leaks instrument, 15–16
        static analyzer, 13–14

M, N

Memory caching
    Global Access *vs.* Strict Access, 82
    image preloading, 83–85
    memory allocations and usage, 82
    memory warnings, 82
Memory management
    advanced autorelease pool, 191–192
    advanced memory issues, 184–185
    ARC. *See* Automatic reference
        counting (ARC)
    autorelease method, 178–179
    autorelease pool, 179–180
    instruments
        leak instrument, 193
        memory warning levels, 195
        object allocation, 194–195
        static analyzer, 193
        Zombie, 194
    object copy, 188–190
    old object ownership policy, 178
    UIViewController. *See*
        UIViewController
Multitasking apps performance
    application life cycle events, 214

audio service, 206–207
background execution technique,
    211–213
benefits and costs, 204–205
guidelines, 213
handler methods, 202–204
iOS 3.2, 198
iOS 4.0, 199
iOS versions, 216
life cycle
    application:didEnterBackground
        method, 200, 201
    application:didFinishLaunchingWi
        thOptions method, 199
    applicationWillTerminate method,
        199
    background and suspend states,
        201
    phone interruption and home
        button, 202
location notification, 211
location service, 207
    continuous background location
        update mechanism, 210
    significant location change
        mechanism, 209–210
    standard location services,
        208–209
memory, 213–214
shared resources, 214
show splash screen, 207
system changes notification,
    215–216
user interface update, 214–215
VOIP, 211
Multithreading
    advantages, 139, 142–143, 152
    asynchronous functions, 172–173
    autorelease pool, 153
    Core Animation instrument, 140
    disadvantages, 152
    exception handler, 153
    Idle-Time Notifications, 173–174
    image loading process, 140
    instrument, iPhone, 174

liveness
    deadlock, 164–166
    NSCondition solution, 163–164
    NSLock solution, 162
    push and pop threads, 161
multi-processor system, 138
NSObject, 145
NSOperationQueue, 146
    code snippet, 147
    NSBlockOperation, 148
    NSInvocationOperation, 147
    NSOperation, 148–150
NSThread, 144
NSTimer, 171
odd/even integer code, 156
performance, 166–168
POSIX Threads, 144–145
priorities, 151
run loop, 154
safety
    application crash, 157
    lock mechanism, 159–161
    thread safety code, 157–158
single-processor system, 138
stack size, 150–151
stacks, 151
synchronization, 169–170
terminology, 139–140
thread-local storage, 151
UIImageView, 141–142
UITableViewDataSource's Method,
    141

O

Old object ownership policy, 178
OpenGL ES driver, 27–28

P, Q, R

Performance tools, 18
    battery power measurement, 31–32
    blank template, 33
    CPU measurement
        activity monitor, 23
        advantages, 22
        CPU sampler panel, 21
        disadvantages, 22–23
        Hide System Libraries, 21

running count, function call, 22
running time, function call, 22
sample and stack trace, 20
system load and user load, 21
usages, 23
file and network access
    measurement
    file activity, 29–30
    system usage, 28–29
file I/O and network access, 19
instrument applications, 19–20
instrument tools, 34–36
library list, 33
measure thread performance, 30
time measurement, 23–24
user interface response time
    measurement
    core animation, 25–26
    OpenGL ES driver, 27–28

S

Simulators and real device test
    basic tools, 9–10
    iPhone simulator environment and
        real iPhone environment, 8
    memory and runtime performance,
        8, 9
    memory tools
        automatic reference counting, 10
        convert tool, 10
        legacy code. *See* Legacy code
        memory allocation, 11–13
    performance tools. *See* Performance
        tools
SlowPerformanceTableView project, 41
Smartphone, 1
SQLite, 236–238
Stack and queue, 114–116

T

Thread-safe, 169

U

UITableView performance
    cell preparation process, 54
    CoreAnimation tool, 40–41
    custom cell drawing

custom drawing code, 51
drawInRect method, 53
drawRect method, 53
images reusing, 51
source code, 52
TableViewCell, 52
user interface, 50
editing/reordering performance, 56
Facebook, 41
graphical effects, 55–56
height caching, 54
images reusing, 48–49
initial benchmark, 43
NSLog, 40
opaque, 55
preparation time reduction, 49
ReuseIdentifier, 54
SlowPerformanceTableView project,
    41
standard benchmark, 42–43
tableView dequeues, 39
UITableViewCell reusing
    benchmarks, 47
    CPU-intensive process, 43
    custom class
        ReuseTableViewCell, 45
    custom code, 46

interface builder, 44–45
Nib file, 46
standard TableView Cell, 44
UIViewController
life cycle, 185
load view process, 185–186
unload view process, 186–187
viewDidAppear method, 188
viewDidDisappear method, 188
viewWillAppear method, 187
viewWillDisappear method, 188

■ **V**
Voice Over IP (VOIP), 211

■ **W, X, Y, Z**
Windows phone
automatic binding mechanism, 246
benchmarking, 245
C# programming language, 242
data caching, 251–253
emulator, 243
ListViews performance, 248–249
memory management, 260–261
multithreading, 257–258
user interface framework, 242

CPSIA information can be obtained at www.ICGtesting.com
Printed in the USA
LVOW121537171111

255454LV00001B/3/P